HOLT
SCIENCE &
TECHNOLOGY

Astronomy

HOLT, RINEHART AND WINSTON

A Harcourt Classroom Education Company

Austin · New York · Orlando · Atlanta · San Francisco · Boston · Dallas · Toronto · London

Acknowledgments

Chapter Writers

Kathleen Meehan Berry
Science Chairman
Canon-McMillan School
   District
Canonsburg, Pennsylvania

Robert H. Fronk, Ph.D.
*Chair of Science and
   Mathematics Education
   Department*
Florida Institute of Technology
West Melbourne, Florida

**Mary Kay Hemenway,
   Ph.D.**
*Research Associate and Senior
   Lecturer*
Department of Astronomy
The University of Texas
Austin, Texas

Kathleen Kaska
Life and Earth Science Teacher
Lake Travis Middle School
Austin, Texas

Peter E. Malin, Ph.D.
Professor of Geology
Division of Earth and Ocean
   Sciences
Duke University
Durham, North Carolina

Karen J. Meech, Ph.D.
Associate Astronomer
Institute for Astronomy
University of Hawaii
Honolulu, Hawaii

Robert J. Sager
*Chair and Professor of Earth
   Sciences*
Pierce College
Lakewood, Washington

Lab Writers

Kenneth Creese
Science Teacher
White Mountain Junior
   High School
Rock Springs, Wyoming

Linda A. Culp
Science Teacher and Dept. Chair
Thorndale High School
Thorndale, Texas

Bruce M. Jones
Science Teacher and Dept. Chair
The Blake School
Minneapolis, Minnesota

Shannon Miller
Science and Math Teacher
Llano Junior High School
Llano, Texas

Robert Stephen Ricks
Special Services Teacher
Department of Classroom
   Improvement
Alabama State Department
   of Education
Montgomery, Alabama

James J. Secosky
Science Teacher
Bloomfield Central School
Bloomfield, New York

Academic Reviewers

Mead Allison, Ph.D.
*Assistant Professor of
   Oceanography*
Texas A&M University
Galveston, Texas

Alissa Arp, Ph.D.
*Director and Professor of
   Environmental Studies*
Romberg Tiburon Center
San Francisco State University
Tiburon, California

Paul D. Asimow, Ph.D.
*Assistant Professor of Geology
   and Geochemistry*
Department of Physics and
   Planetary Sciences
California Institute of
   Technology
Pasadena, California

G. Fritz Benedict, Ph.D.
*Senior Research Scientist and
   Astronomer*
McDonald Observatory
The University of Texas
Austin, Texas

**Russell M. Brengelman,
   Ph.D.**
Professor of Physics
Morehead State University
Morehead, Kentucky

John A. Brockhaus, Ph.D.
*Director—Mapping, Charting,
   and Geodesy Program*
Department of Geography and
   Environmental Engineering
United States Military Academy
West Point, New York

Michael Brown, Ph.D.
*Assistant Professor of Planetary
   Astronomy*
Department of Physics
   and Astronomy
California Institute of
   Technology
Pasadena, California

Wesley N. Colley, Ph.D.
Postdoctoral Fellow
Harvard-Smithsonian Center
   for Astrophysics
Cambridge, Massachusetts

Andrew J. Davis, Ph.D.
*Manager—ACE Science Data
   Center*
Physics Department
California Institute of
   Technology
Pasadena, California

Peter E. Demmin, Ed.D.
*Former Science Teacher and
   Department Chair*
Amherst Central High School
Amherst, New York

James Denbow, Ph.D.
Associate Professor
Department of Anthropology
The University of Texas
Austin, Texas

Roy W. Hann, Jr., Ph.D.
Professor of Civil Engineering
Texas A&M University
College Station, Texas

Frederick R. Heck, Ph.D.
Professor of Geology
Ferris State University
Big Rapids, Michigan

Richard Hey, Ph.D.
Professor of Geophysics
Hawaii Institute of Geophysics
   and Planetology
University of Hawaii
Honolulu, Hawaii

John E. Hoover, Ph.D.
Associate Professor of Biology
Millersville University
Millersville, Pennsylvania

**Robert W. Houghton,
   Ph.D.**
Senior Staff Associate
Lamont-Doherty Earth
   Observatory
Columbia University
Palisades, New York

Steven A. Jennings, Ph.D.
Assistant Professor
Department of Geography &
   Environmental Studies
University of Colorado
Colorado Springs, Colorado

Eric L. Johnson, Ph.D.
Assistant Professor of Geology
Central Michigan University
Mount Pleasant, Michigan

John Kermond, Ph.D.
Visiting Scientist
NOAA–Office of Global
   Programs
Silver Spring, Maryland

Zavareh Kothavala, Ph.D.
Postdoctoral Associate Scientist
Department of Geology and
   Geophysics
Yale University
New Haven, Connecticut

Karen Kwitter, Ph.D.
*Ebenezer Fitch Professor of
   Astronomy*
Williams College
Williamstown, Massachusetts

Valerie Lang, Ph.D.
*Project Leader of Environmental
   Programs*
The Aerospace Corporation
Los Angeles, California

Philip LaRoe
Professor
Helena College of Technology
Helena, Montana

Julie Lutz, Ph.D.
Astronomy Program
Washington State University
Pullman, Washington

Acknowledgments (cont.)

Duane F. Marble, Ph.D.
Professor Emeritus
Department of Geography
and Natural Resources
Ohio State University
Columbus, Ohio

Joseph A. McClure, Ph.D.
Associate Professor
Department of Physics
Georgetown University
Washington, D.C.

Frank K. McKinney, Ph.D.
Professor of Geology
Appalachian State University
Boone, North Carolina

Joann Mossa, Ph.D.
Associate Professor of Geography
University of Florida
Gainesville, Florida

LaMoine L. Motz, Ph.D.
Coordinator of Science Education
Department of Learning Services
Oakland County Schools
Waterford, Michigan

Barbara Murck, Ph.D.
Assistant Professor of Earth Science
Erindale College
University of Toronto
Mississauga, Ontario, Canada

Hilary Clement Olson, Ph.D.
Research Associate
Institute for Geophysics
The University of Texas
Austin, Texas

Andre Potochnik
Geologist
Grand Canyon Field Institute
Flagstaff, Arizona

John R. Reid, Ph.D.
Professor Emeritus
Department of Geology and
Geological Engineering
University of North Dakota
Grand Forks, North Dakota

Gary Rottman, Ph.D.
Associate Director
Laboratory for Atmosphere
and Space Physics
University of Colorado
Boulder, Colorado

Dork L. Sahagian, Ph.D.
Professor
Institute for the Study of
Earth, Oceans, and Space
University of New Hampshire
Durham, New Hampshire

Peter Sheridan, Ph.D.
Professor of Chemistry
Colgate University
Hamilton, New York

David Sprayberry, Ph.D.
*Assistant Director for
Observing Support*
W.M. Keck Observatory
California Association for
Research in Astronomy
Kamuela, Hawaii

Lynne Talley, Ph.D.
Professor
Scripps Institution of
Oceanography
University of California
La Jolla, California

Glenn Thompson, Ph.D.
Scientist
Geophysical Institute
University of Alaska
Fairbanks, Alaska

Martin VanDyke, Ph.D.
Professor of Chemistry, Emeritus
Front Range Community
College
Westminister, Colorado

Thad A. Wasklewicz, Ph.D.
Assistant Professor of Geography
University of Memphis
Memphis, Tennessee

Hans Rudolf Wenk, Ph.D.
*Professor of Geology and
Geophysical Sciences*
University of California
Berkeley, California

Lisa D. White, Ph.D.
Associate Professor of Geosciences
San Francisco State University
San Francisco, California

Lorraine W. Wolf, Ph.D.
Associate Professor of Geology
Auburn University
Auburn, Alabama

Charles A. Wood, Ph.D.
*Chairman and Professor of
Space Studies*
University of North Dakota
Grand Forks, North Dakota

Safety Reviewer

Jack Gerlovich, Ph.D.
Associate Professor
School of Education
Drake University
Des Moines, Iowa

Teacher Reviewers

Barry L. Bishop
Science Teacher and Dept. Chair
San Rafael Junior High
School
Ferron, Utah

Yvonne Brannum
*Science Teacher and Dept.
Chair*
Hine Junior High School
Washington, D.C.

Daniel L. Bugenhagen
*Science Teacher and Dept.
Chair*
Yutan Junior & Senior High
School
Yutan, Nebraska

Kenneth Creese
Science Teacher
White Mountain Junior High
School
Rock Springs, Wyoming

Linda A. Culp
*Science Teacher and Dept.
Chair*
Thorndale High School
Thorndale, Texas

Alonda Droege
Science Teacher
Pioneer Middle School
Steilacom, Washington

Laura Fleet
Science Teacher
Alice B. Landrum Middle
School
Ponte Vedra Beach, Florida

Susan Gorman
Science Teacher
Northridge Middle School
North Richland Hills, Texas

C. John Graves
Science Teacher
Monforton Middle School
Bozeman, Montana

Janel Guse
*Science Teacher and Dept.
Chair*
West Central Middle School
Hartford, South Dakota

Gary Habeeb
Science Mentor
Sierra–Plumas Joint Unified
School District
Downieville, California

Dennis Hanson
*Science Teacher and Dept.
Chair*
Big Bear Middle School
Big Bear Lake, California

Norman E. Holcomb
Science Teacher
Marion Local Schools
Maria Stein, Ohio

Tracy Jahn
Science Teacher
Berkshire Junior-Senior High
School
Canaan, New York

David D. Jones
Science Teacher
Andrew Jackson Middle
School
Cross Lanes, West Virginia

Howard A. Knodle
Science Teacher
Belvidere High School
Belvidere, Illinois

Michael E. Kral
Science Teacher
West Hardin Middle School
Cecilia, Kentucky

Kathy LaRoe
Science Teacher
East Valley Middle School
East Helena, Montana

Scott Mandel, Ph.D.
*Director and Educational
Consultant*
Teachers Helping Teachers
Los Angeles, California

Kathy McKee
Science Teacher
Hoyt Middle School
Des Moines, Iowa

Michael Minium
*Vice President of Program
Development*
United States Orienteering
Federation
Forest Park, Georgia

Jan Nelson
Science Teacher
East Valley Middle School
East Helena, Montana

Dwight C. Patton
Science Teacher
Carroll T. Welch Middle
School
Horizon City, Texas

Joseph Price
*Chairman—Science
Department*
H. M. Brown Junior High
School
Washington, D.C.

Terry J. Rakes
Science Teacher
Elmwood Junior High School
Rogers, Arkansas

Steven Ramig
Science Teacher
West Point High School
West Point, Nebraska

Helen P. Schiller
Science Teacher
Northwood Middle School
Taylors, South Carolina

Bert J. Sherwood
Science Teacher
Socorro Middle School
El Paso, Texas

Larry Tackett
Science Teacher and Dept. Chair
Andrew Jackson Middle
School
Cross Lanes, West Virginia

Walter Woolbaugh
Science Teacher
Manhattan Junior High
School
Manhattan, Montana

Alexis S. Wright
*Middle School Science
Coordinator*
Rye Country Day School
Rye, New York

Gordon Zibelman
Science Teacher
Drexel Hill Middle School
Drexel Hill, Pennsylvania

J Astronomy

Skills Development

Process Skills

QuickLabs

Chapter Labs

Skills Development

Research and Critical Thinking Skills

Connections

To the Student

This book was created to make your science experience interesting, exciting, and fun!

Go for It!

Science is a process of discovery, a trek into the unknown. The skills you develop using *Holt Science & Technology*— such as observing, experimenting, and explaining observations and ideas— are the skills you will need for the future. There is a universe of exploration and discovery awaiting those who accept the challenges of science.

Science & Technology

You see the interaction between science and technology every day. Science makes technology possible. On the other hand, some of the products of technology, such as computers, are used to make further scientific discoveries. In fact, much of the scientific work that is done today has become so technically complicated and expensive that no one person can do it entirely alone. But make no mistake, the creative ideas for even the most highly technical and expensive scientific work still come from individuals.

Activities and Labs

The activities and labs in this book will allow you to make some basic but important scientific discoveries on your own. You can even do some exploring on your own at home! Here's your chance to use your imagination and curiosity as you investigate your world.

Keep a ScienceLog

In this book, you will be asked to keep a type of journal called a ScienceLog to record your thoughts, observations, experiments, and conclusions. As you develop your ScienceLog, you will see your own ideas taking shape over time. You'll have a written record of how your ideas have changed as you learn about and explore interesting topics in science.

Know "What You'll Do"

The "What You'll Do" list at the beginning of each section is your built-in guide to what you need to learn in each chapter. When you can answer the questions in the Section Review and Chapter Review, you know you are ready for a test.

Check Out the Internet

You will see this $^{SCI}_{LINKS}$ ＮＳＴＡ logo throughout the book. You'll be using *sci*LINKS as your gateway to the Internet. Once you log on to *sci*LINKS using your computer's Internet link, type in the *sci*LINKS address. When asked for the keyword code, type in the keyword for that topic. A wealth of resources is now at your disposal to help you learn more about that topic.

In addition to *sci*LINKS you can log on to some other great resources to go with your text. The addresses shown below will take you to the home page of each site.

---

internet **connect**

This textbook contains the following on-line resources to help you make the most of your science experience.

Visit **go.hrw.com** for extra help and study aids matched to your textbook. Just type in the keyword HST HOME.	Visit **www.scilinks.org** to find resources specific to topics in your textbook. Keywords appear throughout your book to take you further.	Visit **www.si.edu/hrw** for specifically chosen on-line materials from one of our nation's premier science museums.	Visit **www.cnnfyi.com** for late-breaking news and current events stories selected just for you.

CHAPTER 1

Sections

Pre-Reading Questions

1. What are constellations?
2. How do astronomers observe objects they cannot see?

Observing the Sky

EYES TO THE SKY

This may look like an ordinary building to you, but inside is something that will make you see stars, and it's painless! In this building is the Harlan J. Smith Telescope (HJST). You can find it in one of the darkest places in America. The HJST is part of the McDonald Observatory located in the Davis Mountains of West Texas. Since the late 1960s, astronomers have used this telescope to view stars. In this chapter, you will learn about the different types of stars and how they evolve.

INDOOR STARGAZING

In this activity, you will measure an object's altitude using a simple instrument called an astrolabe (AS troh LAYB).

Procedure

1. Attach one end of a 12 cm long **piece of string** to the center of the straight edge of a **protractor** with tape. Attach a **paper clip** to the other end of the string.

2. Tape a **soda straw** lengthwise along the straight edge of the protractor. Your astrolabe is complete!

3. Hold the astrolabe in front of your face so you can look along the straw with one eye. The curve of the astrolabe should be pointed toward the floor.

4. Looking along the straw, use your astrolabe to sight one corner of the ceiling.

5. Pinch the string between your thumb and the protractor. Count the number of degrees between the string and the 90° marker on the protractor. This angle is the altitude of the corner. Record this measurement in your ScienceLog.

Analysis

6. How does this activity relate to observing objects in the sky? Explain how you would find the altitude of a star.

TRY at HOME

SECTION 1

READING WARM-UP

Terms to Learn

astronomy   month
calendar   day
year   leap year

What You'll Do

◆ Identify the units of a calendar.
◆ Evaluate calendars from different ancient civilizations.
◆ Explain how our modern calendar developed.
◆ Summarize how astronomy began in ancient cultures and developed into a modern science.

Astronomy—The Original Science

Astronomy is the study of all physical objects beyond Earth. Before astronomy became a science, people in ancient cultures used the seasonal cycles of celestial objects to make calendars and organize their lives. Over time, some people began to observe the sky for less practical reasons—mainly to understand Earth's place in the universe. Today, astronomers all over the world are using new technologies to better understand the universe.

The Stars and Keeping Time

Most ancient cultures probably did not fully understand how celestial objects in our solar system move in relation to each other. However, they did learn the seasonal movements of these objects as they appeared in the Earth's sky and based their calendars on these cycles. People in ancient cultures gradually learned to depend on calendars to keep track of time. For example, by observing the yearly cycle of the sun's movement among the stars, early farmers learned the best times of year to plant and harvest various foods.

After learning the seasonal cycles of celestial objects many civilizations made calendars. One such calendar is shown in **Figure 1.** A **calendar** is a system for organizing time. Most calendars organize time within a single unit called a year. A **year** is the time required for the Earth to orbit the sun once. Within a year are smaller units of time called months. A **month** is roughly the amount of time required for the moon to orbit the Earth once. Within a month are even smaller units of time called days. A **day** is the time required for the Earth to rotate once on its axis.

Ancient Calendars Ancient cultures based their calendars on different observations of the sky. Examine **Figure 2** at the top of the next page to see how different cultures around the world used objects in the sky differently to keep track of time.

Figure 1 *This stone is a calendar used by the Aztecs in pre-colonial America.*

4   Chapter 1

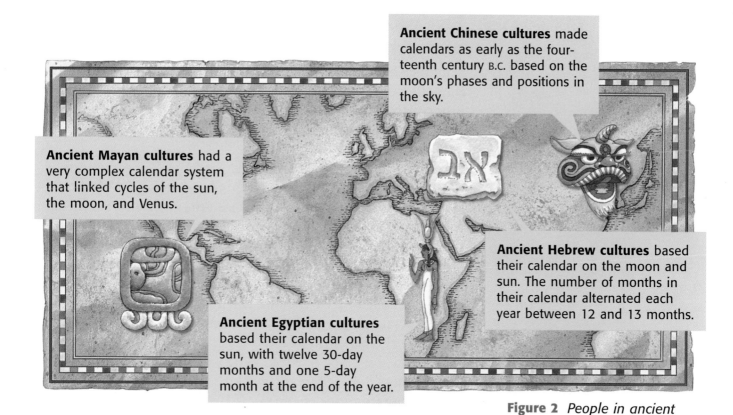

Ancient Chinese cultures made calendars as early as the fourteenth century B.C. based on the moon's phases and positions in the sky.

Ancient Mayan cultures had a very complex calendar system that linked cycles of the sun, the moon, and Venus.

Ancient Hebrew cultures based their calendar on the moon and sun. The number of months in their calendar alternated each year between 12 and 13 months.

Ancient Egyptian cultures based their calendar on the sun, with twelve 30-day months and one 5-day month at the end of the year.

Figure 2 *People in ancient cultures based their calendars on different kinds of celestial cycles.*

Toward a Modern Calendar The early Roman calendar had exactly 365 days in a year and 7 days in a week. The calendar worked well at first, but gradually the seasons shifted away from their original positions in the year.

It was then determined that there are actually about 365.25 days in a year. To correct this, Julius Caesar created the *Julian calendar.* He began by adding 90 days to the year 46 B.C., which put the seasons back to their original positions. He then added an extra day every 4 years to keep them from shifting again. A year in which an extra day is added to the calendar is called a **leap year.**

In the mid-1500s, people noticed that the Julian calendar was incorrect. Pope Gregory XIII presented this problem to a group of astronomers who determined that there are actually 365.242 days in a year. To solve the problem, a new calendar—the *Gregorian calendar*—was created. The Pope dropped 10 days from the year 1582 and restricted leap years to years that are divisible by 4 but not by 100 (except for years that are divisible by 400). This lowered the number of leap years that occur and made the average length of 1 year closer to 365.242 days. Today most countries use the Gregorian calendar, which scientists calculate will be accurate for another 3,000 years.

Early Observers—The Beginnings of Astronomy

Scientists have found evidence for ancient astronomic. ities all over the world. Some records are more complet. .nan others. However, they all show that early humans recognized the cycles of celestial objects in the sky.

Nabta   The earliest record of astronomical observations is a 6,000 to 7,000-year-old group of stones near Nabta, in southern Egypt. Some of the stones are positioned such that they would have lined up with the sun during the summer solstice 6,000 years ago. The *summer solstice* occurs on the longest day of the year. Artifacts found at the site near Nabta suggest that it was created by African cattle herders. These people probably used the site for many purposes, including trade, social bonding, and ritual. **Figure 3** shows some of the stones at the site near Nabta.

Figure 3 *Some stones are still standing at the site near Nabta, in the Sahara Desert.*

Stonehenge   Another ancient site that was probably used to make observations of the sky is Stonehenge, near Salisbury, England. Stonehenge, shown in **Figure 4,** is a group of stones arranged primarily in circles. Some of the stones are aligned with the sunrise during the summer and winter solstices. People have offered many explanations for the purpose of Stonehenge as well as for who built and used it. Careful studies of the site reveal that it was built over a period of about 1,500 years, from about 3000 B.C. to about 1500 B.C. Most likely, Stonehenge was used as a place for ceremony and ritual. But the complete truth about Stonehenge is still a mystery.

Figure 4 *Although its creators have long since gone, Stonehenge continues to indicate the summer and winter solstices each year.*

The Babylonians   The ancient civilization of Babylon was the heart of a major empire located in present-day Iraq. From about 700 B.C. to about A.D. 50, the Babylonians precisely tracked the positions of planets and the moon. They became skilled at forecasting the movements of these celestial bodies, which enabled them to make an accurate calendar.

Ancient Chinese Cultures As early as 1000 B.C., ancient Chinese cultures could predict eclipses. *Eclipses* occur when the sun, the moon, and the Earth line up in space. The Chinese had also named 800 stars by 350 B.C. The Chinese skillfully tracked and predicted the same motions in the sky as the civilizations that influenced Western astronomy. The Chinese continued to improve their knowledge of the sky at the same time as many other civilizations, as shown in **Figure 5.**

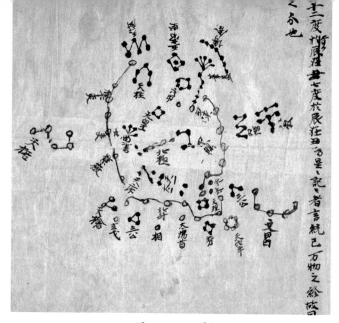

Figure 5 *This ancient Chinese manuscript is the world's oldest existing portable star map. It is more than 1,000 years old.*

The Ancient Greeks Like many other civilizations, the ancient Greeks learned to observe the sky to keep track of time. But the Greeks also took a giant leap forward in making astronomy a science. Greek philosophers tried to understand the place of Earth and humans in the universe. Their tools were logic and mathematics, especially geometry. One of the most famous Greek philosophers, Aristotle (ER is TAHT'L), successfully explained the phases of the moon and eclipses. He also correctly argued that the Earth is a sphere—an idea that was not very popular in his time.

Native Americans Archaeological records show that many of the pre-colonial civilizations in the Americas were skilled in observing the sky. Perhaps the most highly-skilled observers were the Maya, who flourished in the present-day Yucatan about 1,000 years ago. The Maya had complex systems of mathematics and astronomy. Many Mayan buildings, such as the one in **Figure 6,** are aligned with celestial bodies during certain astronomical events.

The Ancient Arabs After Greek, Roman, and early Christian civilizations weakened, the ancient Arabs inherited much of the Greeks' knowledge of astronomy. The Arabs continued to develop astronomy as a science while Europe fell into the Dark Ages. Today many stars have Arabic names. The Arabs also invented the astrolabe, algebra, and the number system that we use today.

Figure 6 *This Mayan building is the Caracol at Chichén Itzá, in the Yucatán. Many parts of the building align with Venus and the sun on certain days.*

The Who's Who of Early Astronomy

The science of astronomy has come a long way since the early days. The earliest astronomers had no history to learn from—almost everything they knew about the universe came from what they could discover with their own eyes and minds. Not surprisingly, most early astronomers thought that the universe consisted of the sun, moon, and planets, with all the stars occupying the edge of the universe. While they could not have known that our solar system is a very small part of a much larger universe, they had to start somewhere.

Ptolemy In A.D. 140, a Greek astronomer named Claudius Ptolemy (KLAW dee uhs TAHL uh mee) wrote a book that combined all the ancient knowledge of astronomy that he could find. Ptolemy expanded Aristotle's theories with careful mathematical calculations in what was called the *Ptolemaic theory.* As shown in **Figure 7,** Ptolemy thought that the Earth is at the center of the universe—with the sun and the other planets revolving around the Earth.

Even though it was incorrect, the Ptolemaic theory predicted the motions of the planets better than any known method at that time. For more than 1,500 years in Europe, the Ptolemaic theory was the most popular theory for the structure of the universe.

Figure 7 *According to the Ptolemaic theory, the Earth is at the center of the universe.*

Copernicus In 1543, a Polish astronomer named Nicolaus Copernicus (NIK uh LAY uhs koh PUHR ni kuhs) published a new theory that would eventually revolutionize astronomy. According to his theory, which is shown in **Figure 8,** the sun is at the center of the universe and the planets—including the Earth—orbit the sun. While Copernicus was correct about all the planets orbiting the sun, his theory did not immediately replace Ptolemy's theory.

Figure 8 *According to Copernicus's theory, the sun is at the center of the universe.*

Tycho Brahe Danish astronomer Tycho Brahe (TIE koh BRAW uh) used several large tools, such as the one shown in **Figure 9,** to observe the sky. Tycho favored an Earth-centered theory that was different from Ptolemy's. Tycho believed that the other planets revolve around the sun but that the sun and the moon revolve around the Earth. While Tycho's theory was not correct, he did record very precise observations of the planets and stars for several years.

Johannes Kepler After Tycho died, his assistant, Johannes Kepler, continued Tycho's work. Kepler did not agree with Tycho's theory, but he recognized how precise and valuable Tycho's data were. In 1609, after analyzing the data, Kepler announced some new laws of planetary motion. Kepler stated that all the planets revolve around the sun in elliptical orbits and that the sun is not in the exact center of the orbits.

Figure 9 *Tycho used the mural quadrant, which is a large quarter-circle on a wall, to measure the positions of stars and planets.*

Galileo Galilei In 1609, Galileo became the first person to use a telescope to observe celestial bodies. His telescope is shown in **Figure 10.** Galileo discovered four moons orbiting Jupiter, craters and mountains on the moon, sunspots on the sun, and phases of Venus. These discoveries showed that the planets are not just dots of light—they are physical bodies like the Earth. Galileo favored Copernicus's theory over Ptolemy's.

Figure 10 *Galileo's telescope is much simpler than those used by astronomers today.*

Isaac Newton Finally, in 1687 a scientist named Sir Isaac Newton explained *why* planets orbit the sun and why moons orbit planets. Newton explained that the force that keeps all of these objects in their orbit is the same one that holds us on the Earth—gravity. Newton's laws of motion and gravitation completed the work of Copernicus, Tycho, Kepler, and Galileo.

✔ Self-Check

Name two astronomers who favored an Earth-centered universe and two astronomers who favored a sun-centered universe. *(See page 200 to check your answer.)*

Modern Astronomy

With Galileo's successful use of the telescope and Newton's discoveries about planetary motion, astronomy began to become the modern science that it is today. Gradually, people began to think of stars as more than dots of light at the edge of the universe.

From Fuzzy Patches to an Expanding Universe William Herschel, who discovered Uranus in 1781, used a telescope to study the stars in our galaxy. As he studied these stars, he found small, fuzzy patches in the sky. Herschel did not know what these patches were, but he did record their positions in a catalog.

The invention of photography in the 1800s allowed astronomers to make even better observations of the sky. In 1923, Edwin Hubble used photography to discover that some of the patches Herschel had found are actually other galaxies beyond our own. Before this discovery, scientists thought that the Milky Way galaxy was the entire universe! Hubble also discovered that the universe is expanding. In other words, distant objects in space are moving farther and farther away from each other.

Larger and Better Telescopes Today astronomers still gaze at the sky, trying to assign order to the universe. Larger and better telescopes on Earth and in space, supercomputers, spacecraft, and new models of the universe allow us to study objects both near and far. Many questions about the universe have been answered, but our studies continue to bring new questions to investigate.

Figure 11 *Today computers and telescopes are linked together. Computers not only control telescopes, but they also process the information gathered by the telescopes so that astronomers may better analyze it.*

internet connect

SC*I*LINKS.
NSTA

TOPIC: The Stars and Keeping Time, Early Theories in Astronomy
GO TO: www.scilinks.org
*sci*LINKS NUMBER: HSTE430, HSTE435

SECTION REVIEW

1. Which ancient civilization's calendar gave rise to our modern calendar?

2. What advantage did Galileo have over the astronomers that went before him, and how did it help him?

3. **Analyzing Relationships** Is Copernicus's theory completely correct? Why or why not? How does his theory relate to what we know today about the sun's position in our solar system and in the universe?

Mapping the Stars

Terms to Learn

constellation   celestial equator
altitude   ecliptic
right ascension light-year
declination

What You'll Do

◆ Describe constellations and explain how astronomers use them.
◆ Explain how to measure altitude.
◆ Explain right ascension and declination.
◆ Evaluate the scale of the universe.

Ancient cultures organized the sky by linking stars together in patterns. These patterns reflected the culture's beliefs and legends. Different civilizations often gave the stars names that indicated the stars' positions in their pattern. Today we can see the same star patterns that people in ancient cultures saw. Modern astronomers still use many of the names given to stars centuries ago.

Astronomers can now describe a star's location with precise numbers. These advances have led to a better understanding of just how far away stars are and how big the universe is.

Constellations

When people in ancient cultures linked stars in a section of the sky into a pattern, they named that section of the sky according to the pattern. **Constellations** are sections of the sky that contain recognizable star patterns. Many cultures organized the sky into constellations that honored their gods or reflected objects in their daily lives. Constellations helped people organize the sky and track the apparent motions of planets and stars.

In the Eye of the Beholder . . . Different civilizations had different names for the same constellations. For example, where the Greeks saw a hunter (Orion) in the northern sky, the Japanese saw a drum (*tsuzumi*), as shown in **Figure 12.** Today different cultures still interpret the sky differently.

Figure 12 *The drawing at left shows that the ancient Greeks saw Orion as a hunter. The drawing at right shows that the Japanese saw the same set of stars as a drum.*

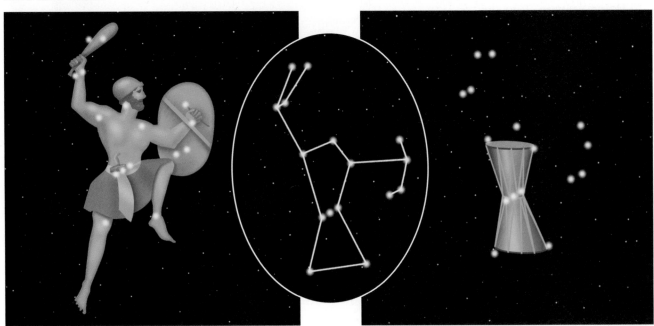

Self-Check

If a celestial object is said to be "in the constellation of Ursa Minor," does it have to be a part of the stick figure that makes up that constellation? Explain. (See page 200 to check your answer.)

Regions of the Sky When you think of constellations, you probably think of the stick figures made by connecting bright stars with imaginary lines. To an astronomer, however, a constellation is something more. As you can see in **Figure 13** below, a constellation is an entire region of the sky. Each constellation shares a border with its neighboring constellations. For example, in the same way that the state of Texas is a region of the United States, Ursa Major is a region of the sky. Every star or galaxy in the sky is located within a constellation. Modern astronomers divide the sky into 88 constellations. Around the world, astronomers use the same names for these constellations to make communication easier.

Figure 13 *This sky map shows some of the constellations in the Northern Hemisphere. Ursa Major is a region of the sky that includes all the stars that make up that constellation.*

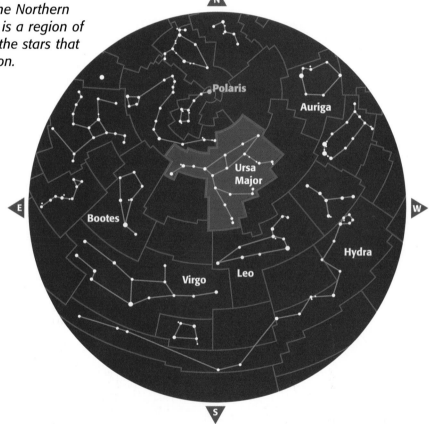

QuickLab

Using a Sky Map

1. Hold your **textbook** over your head with the cover facing upward. Turn the book so that the direction at the bottom of the sky map is the same as the direction you are facing.

2. Notice the location of the constellations in relation to one another.

3. If you look up at the **sky** at night in the spring, you should see the stars positioned as they are on your map.

4. Why are *E* and *W* on sky maps the reverse of how they appear on land maps?

Seasonal Changes As we go around the sun each year, the constellations change from season to season. This is one reason that people in ancient cultures were able to keep track of the right time of year to plant and harvest their crops. Notice that the sky map in Figure 13 shows the night sky as seen from the Northern Hemisphere in the spring. This map would not be accurate for the other three seasons. Sky maps for summer, fall, and winter are in the Appendix of this book.

Finding Stars in the Night Sky

You can use what you learned in the Investigate to make your own observations of the sky. Have you ever tried to show another person a star or planet by pointing to it—only to have them miss what you were seeing? With just a few new references, as shown in **Figure 14,** you can tell them exactly where it is.

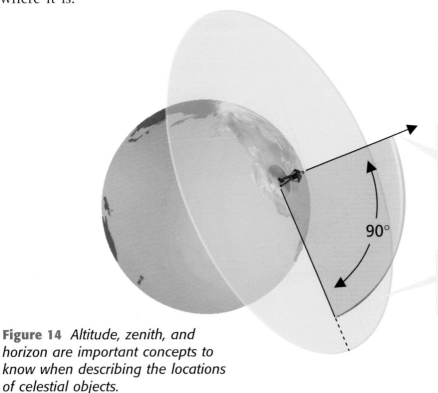

In astronomy, **altitude** is the angle between the object and the horizon.

The **zenith** is an imaginary point in the sky directly above an observer on Earth. The zenith always has an altitude of 90°.

The **horizon** is the line where the sky and the Earth appear to meet.

Figure 14 *Altitude, zenith, and horizon are important concepts to know when describing the locations of celestial objects.*

Figure 15 *With an astrolabe, you can measure the altitude of a star by measuring the angle between your horizon and the star. The altitude of any celestial object depends on where you are and when you look.*

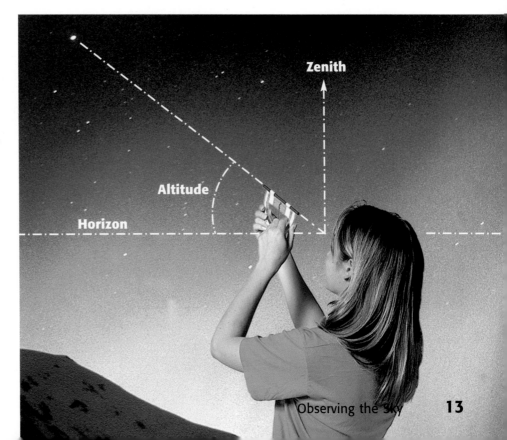

Describing a Star's Position

Finding a star's altitude is one thing, but describing its position in a way that doesn't depend on where you are is another. To do this, astronomers have invented a reference system known as the *celestial sphere*. The celestial sphere surrounds the Earth and is what we look through when we observe the sky. Similar to the way we use latitude and longitude to plot positions on Earth, astronomers use right ascension (RA) and declination (dec) to plot positions in the sky. **Right ascension** is a measure of how far east an object is from the point at which the sun appears on the first day of spring. This point is called the *vernal equinox*. **Declination** is a measure of how far north or south an object is from the celestial equator.

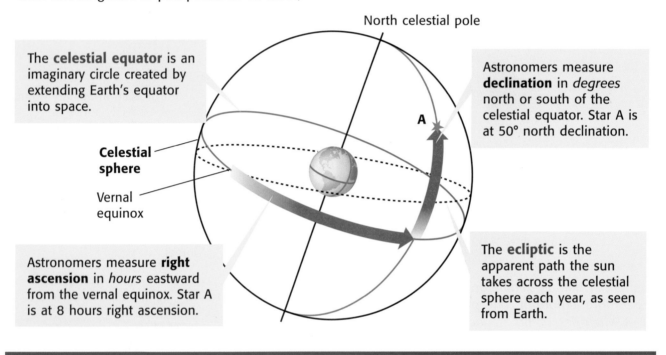

North celestial pole

The **celestial equator** is an imaginary circle created by extending Earth's equator into space.

Celestial sphere

Vernal equinox

Astronomers measure **right ascension** in *hours* eastward from the vernal equinox. Star A is at 8 hours right ascension.

Astronomers measure **declination** in *degrees* north or south of the celestial equator. Star A is at 50° north declination.

A

The **ecliptic** is the apparent path the sun takes across the celestial sphere each year, as seen from Earth.

Figure 16 *Time-lapse photography traces northern circumpolar stars, which never set below the horizon.*

Circumpolar Stars You see different stars in the sky depending on your location, the time of year, and the time of night. Why is this so? As **Figure 16** dramatically illustrates, the Earth rotates once on its axis each day. Because of this, most observers see some stars rise above and set below the horizon much like the sun does each day. Also, the combination of the Earth's motion around the sun and the tilt of Earth's axis causes different stars to be visible during different times of the year. Near the poles, however, stars are circumpolar. *Circumpolar stars* are stars that can be seen at all times of year and all times of night.

The Size and Scale of the Universe

Copernicus noticed that stars never shifted their relative position. If the stars were nearby, he reasoned, their position would appear to shift like the planets' positions do as the Earth travels around the sun. Based on this observation, Copernicus thought that the stars must be very far away from the planets.

Measuring Distance in Space Today we know that Copernicus was correct—the stars are very far away from Earth. In fact, stars are so distant that a new unit of length—the light-year—was created to measure their distance. A **light-year** is a unit of length equal to the distance that light travels through space in 1 year. One light-year is equal to about 9.46 trillion kilometers! **Figure 17** below illustrates how far away some stars that we see really are.

Even after astronomers figured out that stars were very distant, the nature of the universe was hard to understand. Some astronomers thought that our galaxy, the Milky Way, included every object in space. The other galaxies that astronomers found were thought by some to be fuzzy clouds within the Milky Way. In 1935, Edwin Hubble discovered that the Andromeda Galaxy, which is the closest major galaxy to our own, was past the edge of the Milky Way. This discovery confirmed the belief of many astronomers that the universe is much larger than was previously thought.

Physics CONNECTION

Have you ever noticed that when a driver in a passing car blows the horn, the horn's sound gets lower? This is called the *Doppler effect.* It works with both sound and light. As a light source moves away quickly, its light looks redder. This particular Doppler effect is called *red shift.* The farther apart two galaxies are moving, the faster the galaxies are moving apart. From the perspective of each galaxy, the other galaxy looks redder. Because all galaxies except our close neighbors are moving apart, the universe must be expanding.

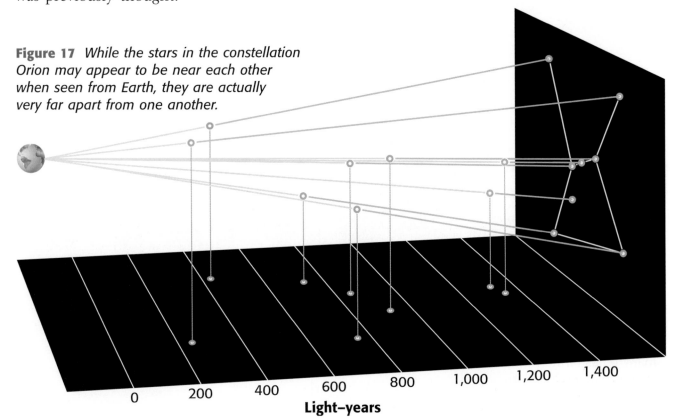

Figure 17 *While the stars in the constellation Orion may appear to be near each other when seen from Earth, they are actually very far apart from one another.*

0   200   400   600   800   1,000   1,200   1,400

Light–years

1 Let's start with something familiar, a baseball diamond. You are looking down on home plate from a distance of about 10 m.

Considering Scale in the Universe Today astronomers are studying the most distant objects yet detected in the universe. Every few months, newspapers announce new discoveries as astronomers probe deeper into space. Astronomers still argue about the size of the universe. The farthest objects we can observe are at least 10 billion light-years away.

When thinking about the universe and all the objects in it, it is important to think about scale. For example, stars appear to be very small in the night sky. But we know that most stars are a lot larger than the Earth. Examine the diagram on these two pages to better understand the scale of objects in the universe.

2 At 1,000 m away, home plate is hard to see, but now you can see the baseball stadium and the neighborhood it is located in.

3 Moving another 100 times farther away (100 km), you now see the city as a whole in relation to the countryside around it.

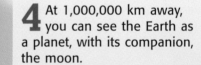

4 At 1,000,000 km away, you can see the Earth as a planet, with its companion, the moon.

$\div\ 5\ \div\ \ ^\Omega\ _\leq\ ^\infty\ +_\Omega\ ^\surd\ 9\ _\infty\ ^\leq\ \Sigma\ 2$
$+$

MATH **BREAK**

Understanding Scale

From steps 1 to 2 and from steps 2 to 3 in the diagram at right, you increased your distance by a factor of 100. How many times farther away are you in step 4 than you were in step 3? How many times farther away in step 5 than you were in step 4?

7 By the time we reach 10 light-years, the sun simply resembles any other star in space.

8 At 1 million light-years, our galaxy would look like the Andromeda galaxy shown here—an island of stars set in the blackness of space.

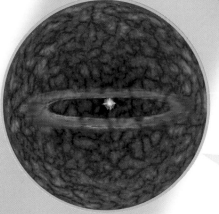

6 At 150 light-days, the solar system can be seen surrounded by a cloud of comets and other icy debris.

5 Moving 1,500,000,000 km away (83 light-minutes), we can look back at the sun and the inner planets.

9 When we reach 10 million light-years, our view shows us that the universe is crowded with galaxies, many like our own, and many strangely different.

SECTION REVIEW

1. How do constellations relate to patterns of stars? How are constellations like states?

2. How do astronomers plot a star's exact position?

3. **Analyzing Relationships** As shown in the diagram above, there are faraway objects that we can see only with telescopes. There are also objects in the universe that are too small for our unaided eyes to see. How do we detect these small objects?

internetconnect

SCiLINKS
NSTA

TOPIC: Constellations
GO TO: www.scilinks.org
sciLINKS NUMBER: HSTE440

Terms to Learn

telescope
refracting telescope
reflecting telescope
electromagnetic spectrum

What You'll Do

◆ Compare and contrast refracting telescopes with reflecting telescopes.
◆ Explain why the atmosphere is an obstacle to astronomers and how they overcome the obstacle.
◆ List the types of electromagnetic radiation, other than visible light, that astronomers use to study space.

Telescopes—Then and Now

For professional astronomers and amateur stargazers, the telescope is the standard tool for observing the sky. A **telescope** is an instrument that collects *electromagnetic radiation* from the sky and concentrates it for better observation. You will learn more about electromagnetic radiation later in this section.

Optical Astronomy

An optical telescope collects visible light for closer observation. The simplest optical telescope is made with two lenses. One lens, called the *objective lens,* collects light and forms an image at the back of the telescope. The bigger the objective lens, the more light the telescope can gather. The second lens is located in the eyepiece of the telescope. This lens magnifies the image produced by the objective lens. Different eyepieces can be selected depending on the magnification desired.

Without a telescope, you can see about 6,000 stars in the night sky. With an optical telescope, you can see millions of stars and other objects. **Figure 18** shows how much more you can see with an optical telescope.

Figure 18 *The image at left shows a section of the sky as seen with the unaided eye. The image at right shows what the small clusters of stars in the left image look like when seen through a telescope.*

Refracting Telescopes Telescopes that use a set of lenses to gather and focus light are called **refracting telescopes.** The curved objective lens in a refracting telescope bends light that passes through it and focuses the light to be magnified by the eyepiece. **Figure 19** shows how refracting telescopes work. A refracting telescope's size is limited by the objective lens. If the curved lens is too large, the glass sags under its own weight, distorting images. This is why most professional astronomers use *reflecting telescopes.*

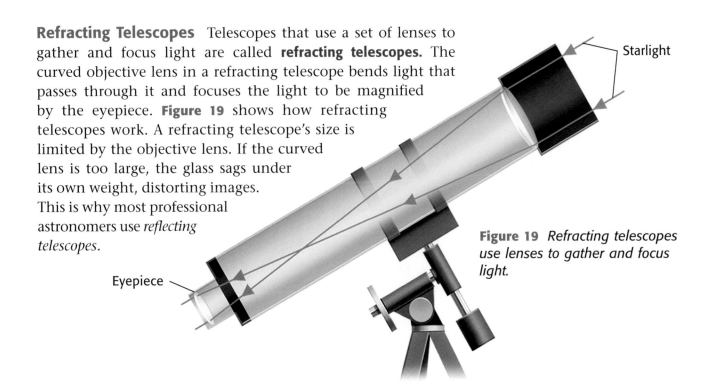

Starlight

Eyepiece

Figure 19 *Refracting telescopes use lenses to gather and focus light.*

Reflecting Telescopes Telescopes that use curved mirrors to gather and focus light are called **reflecting telescopes.** Light enters the telescope and is reflected from a large, curved mirror to a focal point above the mirror. As shown in **Figure 20,** reflecting telescopes use a second mirror in front of the focal point to reflect the light, in this case, through a hole in the side of the telescope. Here the light is collected for observation.

One advantage of reflecting telescopes over refracting telescopes is that mirrors can be made very large, which allows them to gather more light than lenses gather. Also, mirrors are polished on their curved side, preventing light from entering the glass. Therefore, any flaws in the glass do not affect the light. A third advantage is that mirrors reflect all colors of light to the same place, while lenses focus different colors of light at slightly different distances. Reflecting telescopes thus allow all colors of light from an object to be seen in focus at the same time.

Want to make your own telescope? Turn to page 162 in the LabBook to find out how to build and use a telescope.

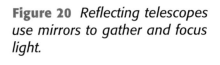

Eyepiece

Starlight

Figure 20 *Reflecting telescopes use mirrors to gather and focus light.*

Very Large Reflecting Telescopes

In some very large reflecting telescopes, several mirrors work together to collect light and deliver it to the same focus. The Keck Telescopes, in Hawaii, shown in **Figure 21,** are twin telescopes that each have 36 hexagonal mirrors working together. Linking several mirrors allows more light to be collected and focused in one spot.

Figure 21 *The 36 hexagonal mirrors in each of the Keck Telescopes combine to form a light-reflecting surface that is 10 m across.*

Optical Telescopes and the Atmosphere The light gathered by telescopes on Earth is affected by the atmosphere. Earth's atmosphere causes starlight to shimmer and blur. Also, light pollution from large cities can make the sky look bright, which limits an observer's ability to view faint objects. Astronomers often place telescopes in dry areas to avoid water vapor in the air. Mountaintops are also good places to use a telescope because the air is thinner at higher elevations. The fact that air pollution and light pollution are generally lower on mountaintops also increases the visibility of stars.

Optical Telescopes in Space! To avoid interference by the atmosphere altogether, scientists have put telescopes in space. Although the mirror in the Hubble Space Telescope, shown below in **Figure 22,** is only 2.4 m across, the optical telescope produces images that are as good or better than any images produced by optical telescopes on Earth.

Figure 22 *The Hubble Space Telescope has provided clearer images of objects in deep space than any ground-based optical telescope.*

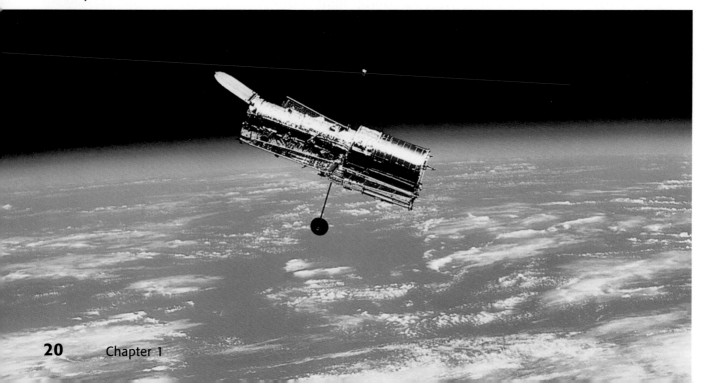

Non-Optical Astronomy

For thousands of years, humans have observed the universe with their eyes. But scientists eventually discovered that there are more forms of radiation than the kind we can see—*visible light*. In 1800, William Herschel discovered an invisible form of radiation called *infrared radiation*. We sense infrared radiation as heat.

In 1852, James Clerk Maxwell showed that visible light is a form of *electromagnetic radiation*. Each color of visible light represents a different wavelength of electromagnetic radiation. Visible light is just a small part of the electromagnetic spectrum, as shown in **Figure 23**. The **electromagnetic spectrum** is made of all of the wavelengths of electromagnetic radiation. Humans can see radiation only from blue light, which has a short wavelength, to red light, which has a longer wavelength. The rest of the electromagnetic spectrum is invisible to us!

Most electromagnetic radiation is blocked by the Earth's atmosphere. Think of the atmosphere as a screen that lets only certain wavelengths of radiation in. These wavelengths include infrared, visible light, some ultraviolet, and radio. All other wavelengths are blocked.

Activity

Artificial light at night is often needed for safety and security. But it also causes light pollution that interferes with stargazing. Do some research on this problem, and list some possible solutions. What compromises can be made so that people feel safe and stargazers can see objects in the night sky?

TRY at HOME

Figure 23 *Radio waves have the longest wavelengths and gamma rays have the shortest. Visible light is only a small band of the electromagnetic spectrum.*

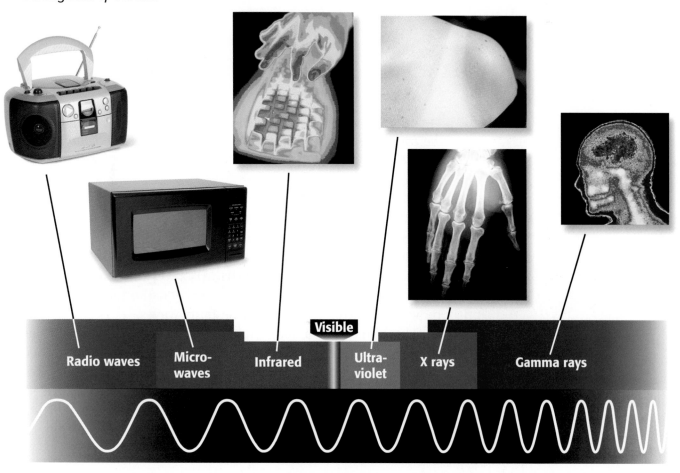

Radio waves | Micro-waves | Infrared | Visible | Ultra-violet | X rays | Gamma rays

The Night Sky Through Different Eyes Astronomers are interested in all forms of electromagnetic radiation because different objects radiate at different wavelengths. For each type of radiation, a different type of telescope or detector is needed. For example, infrared telescopes have polished mirrors similar to those of reflecting telescopes, but the detectors are more sensitive to infrared waves than to visible light waves. As you can see in **Figure 24,** the universe looks much different when observed at other wavelengths.

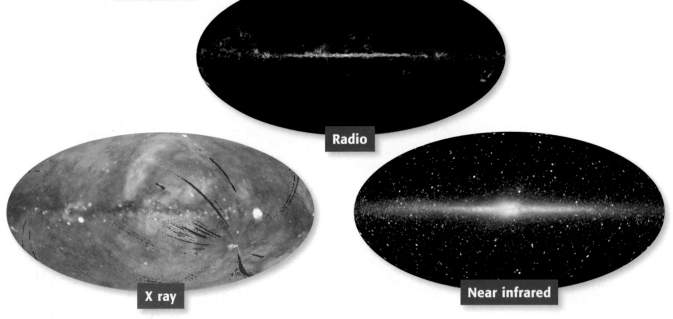

Gamma ray

Radio

X ray

Near infrared

Figure 24 *Each image shows the night sky as it would appear if we could see other wavelengths of electromagnetic radiation. The "cloud" that goes across each picture is the Milky Way galaxy.*

Figure 25 *The Arecibo radio telescope is 305 m across. That is about the length of three football fields arranged end to end!*

Radio Telescopes Radio telescopes receive and focus radio waves. Radio telescopes have to be much larger than optical telescopes because radio wavelengths are about 1 million times longer than optical wavelengths. Also, very little radio radiation reaches Earth from objects in space. Radio telescopes must be very sensitive to detect these faint waves.

The surface of a radio telescope does not have to be as flawless as the lens of an optical telescope. In fact, the surface of a radio telescope does not even have to be completely solid. When it was first built, the Arecibo radio telescope, shown in **Figure 25,** was covered with chicken wire! To a radio wave, a surface made of chicken wire is solid because the wavelength is so much longer than the diameter of the holes.

Linking Radio Telescopes Together Astronomers can get clearer images of radio waves by using two or more radio telescopes at the same time. When radio telescopes are linked together, they work like a single giant telescope. For example, the Very Large Array (VLA), shown in **Figure 26,** consists of 27 separate telescopes that can be spread out 30 km. When the dishes are spread out to the maximum distance, they work as a single telescope that is 30 km across! The larger the area that linked telescopes cover, the more detailed the collected data are.

Figure 26 *The radio telescopes of the Very Large Array near Socorro, New Mexico, work together as one giant telescope.*

X-ray Vision Most electromagnetic waves are blocked by the Earth's atmosphere. To detect these blocked waves, scientists have put special telescopes in space. These telescopes include ultraviolet telescopes, infrared telescopes, gamma-ray telescopes, and X-ray telescopes. Each type of telescope is made to receive one type of radiation. For example, **Figure 27** shows a telescope that is designed to detect X rays.

Figure 27 *Launched in 1999, the Chandra X-ray Observatory is the most powerful X-ray telescope ever built.*

SECTION REVIEW

1. Name one way in which refracting telescopes and reflecting telescopes are similar and one way they are different.

2. Name two ways the atmosphere limits what astronomers can detect. What single method do astronomers use to solve both problems?

3. **Summarizing Data** Make two lists—one for electromagnetic wavelengths that commonly penetrate Earth's atmosphere and one for other wavelengths. Which wavelengths can astronomers detect from Earth? How do they detect each wavelength?

internet**connect**

*sci*LINKS.
NSTA

TOPIC: Telescopes
GO TO: www.scilinks.org
*sci*LINKS **NUMBER:** HSTE445

Design Your Own Lab

Create a Calendar

Imagine that you live in the first colony on Mars. You have been trying to follow the Earth calendar, but it just isn't working anymore. Mars takes almost two Earth years to revolve around the sun—almost 687 Earth days to be exact! That means that there are only two Martian seasons for every Earth calendar year. One year, you get winter and spring, but the next year, you get only summer and fall! And Martian days are longer than Earth days. Mars takes 24.6 Earth hours to rotate on its axis. Even though they are similar, Earth days and Martian days just don't match. This won't do!

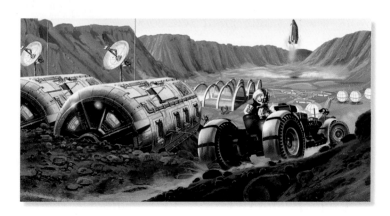

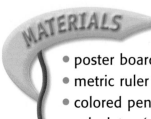

MATERIALS

- poster board
- metric ruler
- colored pencils
- calculator (optional)
- marker

Ask a Question

1 How can I create a calendar based on the Martian cycles of rotation and revolution that includes months, weeks, and days?

Form a Hypothesis

2 In your ScienceLog, write a few sentences that answer the question above.

Test the Hypothesis

3 Use the following formulas to determine the number of Martian days in a Martian year:

$$\frac{687 \text{ Earth days}}{1 \text{ Martian year}} \times \frac{24 \text{ Earth hours}}{1 \text{ Earth day}} = \text{Earth hours per Martian year}$$

$$\text{Earth hours per Martian year} \times \frac{1 \text{ Martian day}}{24.6 \text{ Earth hours}} = \text{Martian days per Martian year}$$

4 Decide how to divide your calendar into a system of Martian months, weeks, and days. Will you have a leap day, a leap week, a leap month, or a leap year? How often will it occur?

5 Choose names for the months and days of your calendar. In your ScienceLog, explain why you chose each name. If you have time, explain how you would number the Martian years. For instance, would the first year correspond to a certain Earth year?

6 Follow your design to create your own calendar for Mars. Draw the calendar on your piece of poster board. Make sure it is brightly colored and easy to follow.

7 Present your calendar to the class. Explain how you chose your months, weeks, and days.

Analyze the Results

8 What advantages does your calendar design have? Are there any disadvantages to your design?

9 Which student or group created the most original calendar? Which design was the most useful? Explain.

10 What might you do to improve your calendar?

Draw Conclusions

11 Take a class vote to decide which design should be chosen as the new calendar for Mars. Why was this calendar chosen? How did it differ from other designs?

12 Why is it useful to have a calendar that matches the cycles of the planet on which you live?

Chapter Highlights

SECTION 1

Vocabulary

astronomy *(p. 4)*

calendar *(p. 4)*

year *(p. 4)*

month *(p. 4)*

day *(p. 4)*

leap year *(p. 5)*

Section Notes

- Calendars are based on movements of objects in the sky.

- Many ancient civilizations developed calendars.

- Our modern calendar developed from the Roman calendar.

- There is evidence all around the world for ancient astronomical observations.

- The Ptolemaic theory states that Earth is at the center of the universe, while Copernicus's theory states that the sun is at the center of the universe.

- Isaac Newton was the first scientist to explain why celestial objects move as they do.

- Galileo's use of the telescope brought the technology of astronomy to a new level.

SECTION 2

Vocabulary

constellation *(p. 11)*

altitude *(p. 13)*

right ascension *(p. 14)*

declination *(p. 14)*

celestial equator *(p. 14)*

ecliptic *(p. 14)*

light-year *(p. 15)*

Section Notes

- Astronomers divide the sky into 88 sections called *constellations.*

- Different constellations are visible from different locations, at different times of the year, and at different times of night.

- Star patterns appear as they do because of Earth's position in space. Most stars that appear close together are actually very far apart.

☑ Skills Check

Math Concepts

KEEPING IT SIMPLE Scientific notation is a way that scientists and others can use large numbers more easily. By using exponents, many place-holding zeros can be eliminated.

> For example:
> 1,000 can be written as 1×10^3, and
> 1,000,000 can be written as 1×10^6.

Notice that the exponent represents the number of zeros in each number. For more practice with scientific notation, turn to page 183 in the Appendix.

Visual Understanding

OPTICAL ILLUSION Constellations look like they do only because we see them from our location on Earth in patterns we recognize. Look back at Figure 17 on page 15. The constellation Orion would be unrecognizable if seen from the side.

- The north celestial pole, the celestial equator, the zenith, and the horizon are imaginary markers used to locate objects in the sky.

- Right ascension and declination, which are similar to latitude and longitude, give coordinates of objects in the sky.

- Astronomers measure the distance to most objects in the universe in light-years.

- The size and distance of celestial objects detected in the universe can be difficult to determine. Scale must always be considered.

Labs

The Sun's Yearly Trip Through the Zodiac *(p. 160)*

Vocabulary

telescope *(p. 18)*
refracting telescope *(p. 19)*
reflecting telescope *(p. 19)*
electromagnetic spectrum *(p. 21)*

Section Notes

- Telescopes collect and focus electromagnetic radiation.

- Humans can see only visible light. To detect other wavelengths of radiation, astronomers use special telescopes or detectors.

- Types of telescopes include optical, radio, ultraviolet, infrared, X-ray, and gamma-ray.

- Some telescopes are launched into space to avoid the blurring effects of Earth's atmosphere or to collect radiation that can't penetrate Earth's atmosphere.

- Telescopes are often linked together to function as one giant telescope.

Labs

Through the Looking Glass *(p. 162)*

internet connect

GO TO: go.hrw.com

Visit the **HRW** web site for a variety of learning tools related to this chapter. Just type in the keyword:

KEYWORD: HSTOBS

*SCiLINKS*sm

N S T A

GO TO: www.scilinks.org

Visit the **National Science Teachers Association** on-line Web site for Internet resources related to this chapter. Just type in the *sci*LINKS number for more information about the topic:

TOPIC: Images from Space	*sci*LINKS NUMBER: HSTE425
TOPIC: The Stars and Keeping Time	*sci*LINKS NUMBER: HSTE430
TOPIC: Early Theories in Astronomy	*sci*LINKS NUMBER: HSTE435
TOPIC: Constellations	*sci*LINKS NUMBER: HSTE440
TOPIC: Telescopes	*sci*LINKS NUMBER: HSTE445

Chapter Review

For each set of terms, explain the similarities and differences in their meanings.

1. reflecting telescope/refracting telescope

2. celestial equator/horizon

3. X rays/microwaves

4. right ascension/declination

5. leap year/light-year

UNDERSTANDING CONCEPTS

Multiple Choice

6. The length of a day is based on
   a. the Earth orbiting the sun.
   b. the rotation of the Earth on its axis.
   c. the moon orbiting the Earth.
   d. the rotation of the moon on its axis.

7. Which of the following civilizations directly affected the development of our modern calendar?
   a. The Chinese
   b. The Maya
   c. The Romans
   d. The Polynesians

8. According to __?__, the Earth is at the center of the universe.
   a. the Ptolemaic theory
   b. Copernicus's theory
   c. Galileo's theory
   d. none of the above

9. The first scientist to successfully use a telescope to observe the night sky was
   a. Tycho.   c. Herschel.
   b. Galileo.   d. Kepler.

10. Astronomers divide the sky into
    a. galaxies.   c. zeniths.
    b. constellations.   d. phases.

11. The stars that you see in the sky depend on
    a. your latitude.
    b. the time of year.
    c. the time of night.
    d. All of the above

12. The altitude of an object in the sky is its angular distance
    a. above the horizon.
    b. from the north celestial pole.
    c. from the zenith.
    d. from the prime meridian.

13. Right ascension is a measure of how far east an object in the sky is from
    a. the observer.
    b. the vernal equinox.
    c. the moon.
    d. Venus.

14. Telescopes that work grounded on the Earth include all of the following except
    a. radio telescopes.
    b. refracting telescopes.
    c. X-ray telescopes.
    d. reflecting telescopes.

15. Which of the following is true about X-ray and radio radiation from objects in space?

  a. Both types of radiation can be observed with the same telescope.

  b. Separate telescopes are needed to observe each type of radiation, and both telescopes can be on Earth.

  c. Separate telescopes are needed to observe each type of radiation, and both telescopes must be in space.

  d. Separate telescopes are needed to observe each type of radiation, but only one of the telescopes must be in space.

Short Answer

Write one or two sentences to answer the following questions:

16. Explain how right ascension and declination are similar to latitude and longitude.

17. How does a reflecting telescope work?

Concept Mapping

18. Use the following terms to create a concept map: right ascension, declination, celestial sphere, degrees, hours, celestial equator, vernal equinox.

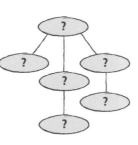

19. Why was it easier for people in ancient cultures to see celestial objects in the sky than it is for most people today?

20. Many forms of radiation do not penetrate Earth's atmosphere. While this limits astronomer's activities, how does it benefit humans in general?

MATH IN SCIENCE

21. How many kilometers away is an object whose distance is 8 light-years?

INTERPRETING GRAPHICS

Examine the sky map below, and answer the questions that follow. (Hint: The star Aldebaran is located at about 4 hours, 30 minutes right ascension, 16 degrees declination.)

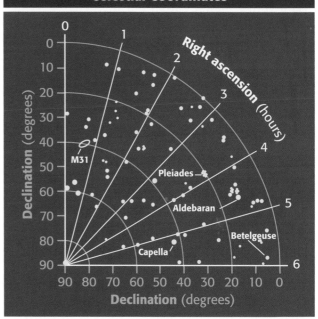

Celestial Coordinates

22. What object is located at 5 hr, 55 min right ascension and 7 degrees declination?

23. What are the celestial coordinates for the Andromeda galaxy (M31)? (Round off right ascension to the nearest half-hour.)

Reading Check-up

Take a minute to review your answers to the Pre-Reading Questions found at the bottom of page 2. Have your answers changed? If necessary, revise your answers based on what you have learned since you began this chapter.

Science, Technology, and Society

Planet or Star?

Humans have long wondered if there are inhabited planets in our galaxy or in far-off galaxies. For the first time, NASA's powerful Hubble Space Telescope has photographed what some astronomers believe is a young planet within our own galaxy. This gaseous object, called TMR-1C, is nearly 450 light-years from Earth. Is it really a planet, or is it a star?

Discovering Planets

Scientists have had trouble finding planets beyond our solar system because distant planets are often masked by the light of brighter stars. *Protoplanets,* planets in the process of forming, may be difficult to see because they are often surrounded by clouds of cosmic dust. As a planet revolves around a star, its gravity tugs on the star. This causes the star to move back and forth slightly. If the planet is massive enough, astronomers can see this movement as a "wobble" in the star's motion. Scientists use state-of-the-art technology to detect these minute changes in the star's velocity relative to Earth.

The picture of TMR-1C could be the first photographic evidence that planets exist outside our solar system. Astronomers discovered TMR-1C racing through space at 32,000 km/h in the constellation of Taurus. Scientists believe that TMR-1C was hurled into space by two stars that acted like a giant slingshot. The Hubble Space Telescope's camera used sensitive infrared light to penetrate through the cosmic clouds surrounding TMR-1C. Because TMR-1C is still hot from forming, it emits light, which is picked up by the telescope's camera.

The Birth of a Planet

Scientists believe that it takes millions of years for planets to form. Photographs of TMR-1C, however, have led some researchers to speculate that this process may be much quicker than was previously thought. The stars that ejected TMR-1C are only a few hundred thousand years old. Researchers have not determined for certain whether TMR-1C is a planet. If TMR-1C turns out to be older than these stars, it could not have been ejected from them. If that is the case, TMR-1C may prove to be a *brown dwarf* rather than a planet. Meanwhile, the research continues until scientists know for certain.

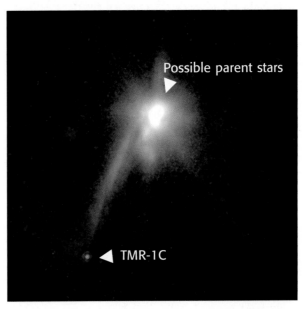

Possible parent stars

TMR-1C

▲ *TMR-1C is 209 billion km from possible parent stars.*

Think About It!

▶ So far, only a few of the many recently discovered planets may be habitable. One such planet, near the star 70 Virginis, is just the right distance from its star for the planet's water to be liquid rather than solid or gaseous. What other features would be necessary for this planet to sustain life as we know it on Earth?

EYE ON THE ENVIRONMENT

Eyes in the Sky

Have you ever gazed up at the sky on a crystal-clear night? What did you see? You probably noticed the moon and countless twinkling stars. It may surprise you to learn that some of those points of light are not stars at all. A few of them may be phonies.

Phony Stars Exposed

Some of the objects that we think are stars are really satellites circling Earth in low Earth orbit (LEO). The satellites in LEO specialize in observation. You might say that when we watch the sky, satellites are watching us as well. LEO is ideal for observation because of its proximity to Earth's surface.

In order to stay in orbit, satellites in LEO must travel very fast. Traveling at approximately 27,358 km/h, one of these satellites can circle the Earth in only 90 minutes! During these revolutions, some satellites gather weather information, while others might transmit phone calls or observe remote terrain. These "eyes in the sky" can even observe you taking a walk.

Space Junk Explosion

Like many things, satellites do not last forever. They eventually break down and may even explode into hundreds of pieces. Most of the time, these pieces continue to travel in LEO for many years. Some of these pieces are large enough to be catalogued by the United States Space Command. As of January 1, 2000, about 2,647 human-made satellites were recorded orbiting, along with 6,022 pieces of debris, or space junk. This debris poses no immediate threat to astronauts or space shuttles that travel through LEO, but there is the potential that one little piece of space junk could smash into an unwary space traveler with explosive results!

The Satellites Just Keep on Coming

We are dependent on satellites for many everyday tasks. Our ever-increasing quest for knowledge drives us to launch more satellites every year. In the booming satellite industry, there is fierce competition for a position in LEO. Many companies are willing to pay top dollar to ensure their position in space. With LEO quickly becoming a satellite highway, it may soon face a traffic jam.

Satellite Search

▶ Unlike stars, satellites in LEO move noticeably across the sky. Research different types of satellites that orbit Earth. Look at the night sky, and try to spot some satellites. What kinds of satellites did you find? Present your observations to the class.

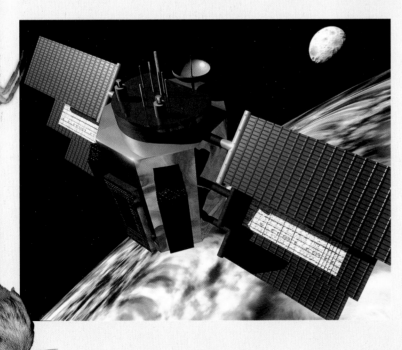

CHAPTER 2

Formation of the Solar System

Sections

Pre-Reading
Questions

1. What keeps the planets in
   their orbits?
2. Why does the sun shine?
3. Why is the Earth round?

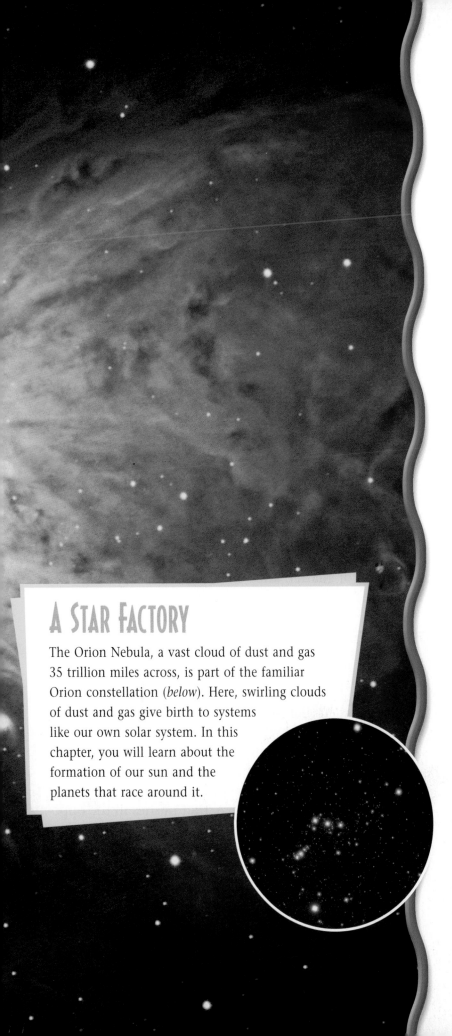

A Star Factory

The Orion Nebula, a vast cloud of dust and gas 35 trillion miles across, is part of the familiar Orion constellation (*below*). Here, swirling clouds of dust and gas give birth to systems like our own solar system. In this chapter, you will learn about the formation of our sun and the planets that race around it.

Activity

STRANGE GRAVITY

If you drop a heavy object, will it fall faster than a lighter one? According to the law of gravity, the answer is no. In 1971, *Apollo 15* astronaut David Scott stood on the moon and dropped a feather and a hammer. Television audiences were amazed to see both objects strike the moon's surface at the same time. Now you can perform a version of this classic experiment in the classroom.

Procedure

1. Select **two pieces of identical notebook paper.** Crumple one piece of paper into a ball.

2. Place the flat piece of paper on top of a **book** and the paper ball on top of the flat piece of paper.

3. Hold the book waist high, and then drop it to the floor.

Analysis

4. Which piece of paper reached the bottom first? Did either piece of paper fall slower than the book? Explain your observations in your ScienceLog.

5. Now hold the crumpled paper in one hand and the flat piece of paper in the other. Drop both pieces of paper at the same time. What else affected the speed of the falling paper besides gravity? Record your observations in your ScienceLog, and share your ideas with your classmates.

Try at Home

Terms to Learn

solar system   orbit
nebula   revolution
solar nebula   period of revolution
planetesimal   ellipse
rotation   astronomical unit

What You'll Do

◆ Explain the basic process of planet formation.
◆ Compare the inner planets with the outer planets.
◆ Describe the difference between rotation and revolution.
◆ Describe the shape of the orbits of the planets, and explain what keeps them in their orbits.

A Solar System Is Born

You probably know that Earth is not the only planet orbiting the sun. In fact, it has eight fellow travelers in its cosmic neighborhood. Together these nine planets and the sun are part of the solar system. The **solar system** is composed of the sun (a star) and the planets and other bodies that travel around the sun. But how did our solar system come to be?

The Solar Nebula

All the ingredients for building planets are found in the vast, seemingly empty regions between the stars. But these regions are not really empty—they contain a mixture of gas and dust. The gas is mostly hydrogen and helium, while the dust is made up of tiny grains of elements such as carbon and iron. The dust and gas clump together in huge interstellar clouds called **nebulas** (or *nebulae*), which are so big that light takes many years to cross them! Nebulas, like the one shown in **Figure 1,** are cold and dark. Over time, light from nearby stars interacts with the dust and gas, forming many new chemicals. Eventually, complex molecules similar to those necessary for life form deep within the nebulas. These clouds are the first ingredients of a new planetary system.

Gravity Pulls Matter Together   Because these clouds of dust and gas consist of matter, they have mass. *Mass,* which is a measure of the amount of matter in an object, is affected by the force of gravity. But because the matter in a nebula is so spread out, the attraction between the dust and gas particles is very small. If a nebula's density were great enough, then the attraction between the particles might be strong enough to pull everything together into the center of the cloud. But even large clouds don't necessarily collapse toward the center because there is another effect, or force, that pushes in the opposite direction of gravity. You'll soon find out what that force is.

Figure 1 *The Horsehead nebula is a cold, dark cloud of gas and dust as well as a possible site for future star formation.*

Pressure Pushes Matter Apart *Temperature* is a measure of how fast the particles in an object move around. If the gas molecules in a nebula move very slowly, the temperature is very low and the cloud is cold. If they move fast, the temperature is high and the cloud is warm. Because the cloud has a temperature that is above absolute zero, the gas molecules are moving. There is no particular structure in the cloud, and individual gas molecules can move in any direction. Sometimes they crash into each other. As shown in **Figure 2,** these collisions create a push, or *pressure,* away from the other gas particles. This pressure is what finally balances the gravity and keeps the cloud from collapsing.

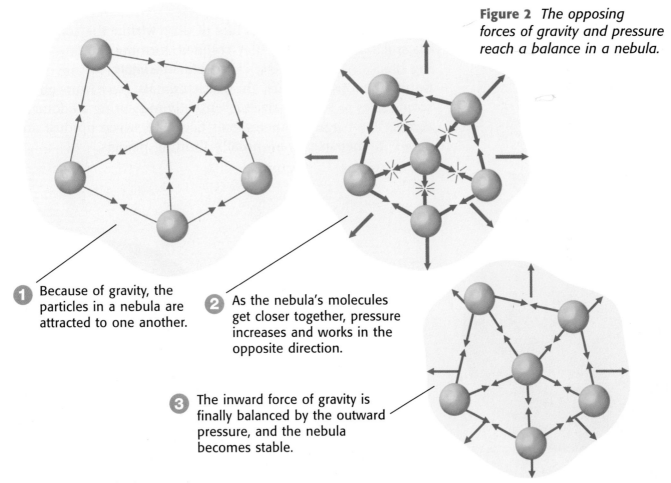

Figure 2 *The opposing forces of gravity and pressure reach a balance in a nebula.*

1 Because of gravity, the particles in a nebula are attracted to one another.

2 As the nebula's molecules get closer together, pressure increases and works in the opposite direction.

3 The inward force of gravity is finally balanced by the outward pressure, and the nebula becomes stable.

The Solar Nebula Forms Sometimes something happens to upset this balance. Two nebulas can crash into each other, for example, or a nearby star can explode, causing material from the star to crash into the cloud. These events compress small regions of the cloud so that gravity overcomes the pressure. Gravity then causes the cloud to collapse inward. At this point, the stage is set for the formation of a star and, as in the case of our sun, its planets. The **solar nebula** is the name of the nebula that formed into our own solar system.

> ✓ **Self-Check**
>
> What keeps a nebula from collapsing? *(See page 200 to check your answer.)*

From Planetesimals to Planets

Once the solar nebula started to collapse, things happened quickly, at least on a cosmic time scale. As the dark cloud collapsed, matter in the cloud got closer and closer together. This made the attraction between particles even stronger. The stronger attraction pulled the cloud together, and the gas and dust particles moved at a faster rate, increasing the temperature at the center of the cloud.

As things began to get crowded near the center of the solar nebula, particles of dust and gas in the cloud began to bump into other particles more often. Eventually much of the dust and gas began slowly rotating about the center of the cloud. The rotating solar nebula eventually flattened into a disk.

Planetesimals Sometimes bits of dust within the solar nebula stuck together when they collided, forming the tiny building blocks of the planets, called **planetesimals.** Within a few hundred thousand years, the planetesimals grew from microscopic sizes to boulder-sized, eventually measuring a kilometer across. The biggest planetesimals began to sweep up dust and debris in their paths, eventually forming planets.

Figure 3 The Process of Solar System Formation

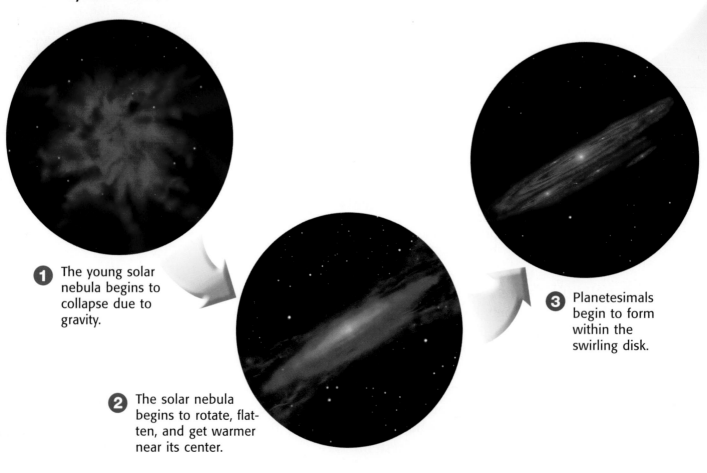

❶ The young solar nebula begins to collapse due to gravity.

❷ The solar nebula begins to rotate, flatten, and get warmer near its center.

❸ Planetesimals begin to form within the swirling disk.

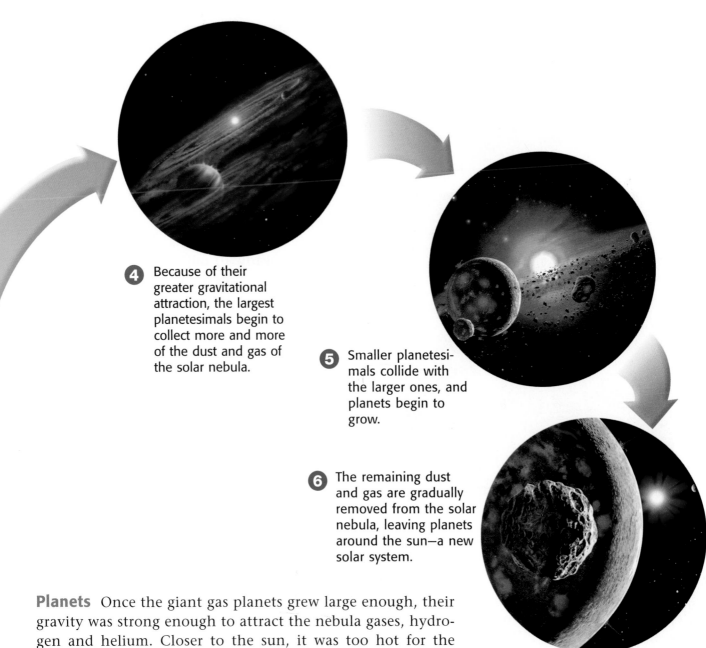

④ Because of their greater gravitational attraction, the largest planetesimals begin to collect more and more of the dust and gas of the solar nebula.

⑤ Smaller planetesimals collide with the larger ones, and planets begin to grow.

⑥ The remaining dust and gas are gradually removed from the solar nebula, leaving planets around the sun—a new solar system.

Planets Once the giant gas planets grew large enough, their gravity was strong enough to attract the nebula gases, hydrogen and helium. Closer to the sun, it was too hot for the gases to remain, so the inner planets are made mostly of rocky material.

Craters and Comets Collisions with smaller planetesimals became more violent as pieces of debris became larger, leaving many craters on the surface of the rocky planets. We see evidence of this today particularly on Mercury, Mars, and our moon.

In the final steps of planet formation, the remaining planetesimals crashed down on the planets or got thrown to the outer edge of the solar nebula by the gravity of the larger planets. Occasionally something, perhaps a passing star, sends them journeying toward the sun. If the planetesimal is icy, we see this visitor as a *comet*.

 Self-Check

Why are the giant gas planets so large? *(See page 200 to check your answer.)*

Birth of a Star   But what was happening at the middle of the solar nebula? The central part of the solar nebula contained so much mass and had become so hot that hydrogen fusion began. This created so much pressure at the center of the solar nebula that outward pressure balanced the inward force of gravity. At this point, the gas stopped collapsing. As the sun was born, the remaining gas and dust of the nebula were blown into deep space by a strong solar wind, and the new solar system was complete.

From the time the nebula first started to collapse, it took nearly 10 million years for the solar system to form. So how do we know that our ideas of star and planet formation are correct when nobody was around to watch it? Powerful telescopes, such as the Hubble Space Telescope, are now able to show us some of the fine details inside distant nebulas. One such nebula is shown in **Figure 4.** For the first time, scientists can see disks of dust around stars that are in the process of forming.

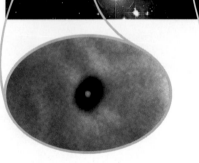

Figure 4 *The Orion nebula contains several "star nurseries"—disks of gas and dust where new stars form. The insets show newly-formed stars within some of these disks.*

internetconnect

SC*i*LINKS.
NSTA

TOPIC: The Planets
GO TO: www.scilinks.org
*sci*LINKS NUMBER: HSTE455

SECTION REVIEW

1. What two forces balance each other to keep a nebula of dust and gas from collapsing or flying apart?

2. Why does the composition of the giant gas planets differ from that of the rocky inner planets?

3. Explain why there is only one planet in each orbit around the sun.

4. **Making Inferences**   Why do all the planets go around the sun in the same direction, and why do the planets all lie in a flat plane?

Planetary Motion

The solar system, which is now 4.6 billion years old, is not simply a collection of stationary planets and other bodies around the sun. Each one moves according to strict physical laws. The ways in which the Earth moves, for example, cause seasons and even day and night.

Rotation and Revolution How does the motion of the Earth cause day and night? The answer has to do with the Earth's spinning on its axis, or **rotation.** As the Earth rotates, only one-half of the Earth faces the sun at any given time. The half facing the sun is light (day), and the half facing away from the sun is dark (night).

In addition to rotating on its axis, the Earth also travels around the sun in a path called an **orbit.** This motion around the sun along its orbit is called **revolution.** The other planets in our solar system also revolve around the sun. The amount of time it takes for a single trip around the sun is called a **period of revolution.** The period for the Earth to revolve around the sun is 365 days. Mercury orbits the sun in 88 days.

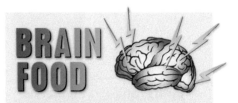

BRAIN FOOD

All planets *revolve* around the sun in the same direction. If you could look down on the solar system from above the sun's north pole, you would see all the planets revolving in a counterclockwise direction. Not all planets *rotate* in the same direction, however. Venus, Uranus, and Pluto rotate backward compared with the rest of the planets.

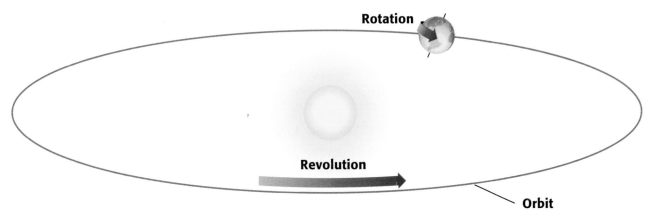

Rotation

Revolution

Orbit

Figure 5 *A planet rotates on its own axis and revolves around the sun in a path called an orbit.*

Planetary Orbits But why do the planets continue to revolve around the sun? Does something hold them in their orbit? Why doesn't gravity pull the planets toward the sun? Or why don't they fly off into space? To answer these questions, we need to go back in time to look at the discoveries made by the scientists of the 1500s and 1600s.

Danish astronomer Tycho Brahe (TIE koh BRAW uh) carefully observed the positions of the planets for over a quarter of a century. When he died in 1601, his young assistant, Johannes Kepler, inherited all of his records. Kepler set out to understand the motions of the planets and to make a simple description of the solar system.

Quick Lab

Staying in Focus

1. Take a short piece of **string,** and pin both ends to a **piece of paper** with two **thumbtacks.**

2. Keeping the string stretched tight at all times, use a **pencil** to trace out the path of an ellipse.

3. Change the distance between the thumbtacks to change the shape of the ellipse.

4. How does the position of the thumbtacks (foci) affect the ellipse?

TRY at HOME

MATH BREAK

Kepler's Formula

Kepler's third law can be expressed with the formula

$$P^2 = a^3$$

where P is the period of revolution and a is the semimajor axis of an orbiting body. For example, Mars's period is 1.88 years, and its semimajor axis is 1.523 AU. Therefore, $1.88^2 = 1.523^3 = 3.53$. If astronomers know either the period or the distance, they can figure the other one out.

Kepler's First Law of Motion Kepler's first discovery, or *first law of motion,* came from his careful study of the movement of the planet Mars. He discovered that the planet did not move in a circle around the sun, but in an elongated circle called an *ellipse.* An **ellipse** is a closed curve in which the sum of the distances from the edge of the curve to two points (called *foci*) inside the ellipse is always the same, as shown in **Figure 6.**

Figure 6 Parts of an Ellipse

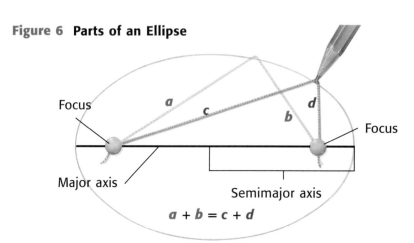

The maximum length of an ellipse is called its *major axis,* and half of this distance is the *semimajor axis,* which is usually used to give the size of an ellipse. The semimajor axis of Earth's orbit, for example, is 150 million kilometers. It represents the average distance between the Earth and the sun and is called one **astronomical unit,** or one AU.

Kepler's Second Law Kepler also discovered that the planets seem to move faster when they are close to the sun and slower when they are farther away. To illustrate this, imagine that a planet is attached to the sun by a string. The string will sweep out the same area in equal amounts of time. To keep the area of *A,* for example, equal to the area of *B,* the planet must move farther around its orbit in the same amount of time. This is Kepler's *second law of motion.*

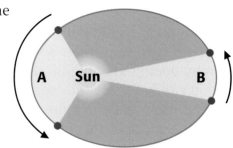

Kepler's Third Law Kepler's *third law of motion* compares the period of a planet's revolution with its semimajor axis. By doing some mathematical calculations, Kepler was able to demonstrate that by knowing a planet's period of revolution, the planet's distance from the sun can be calculated.

Newton's Law of Universal Gravitation

Kepler wondered what caused the planets closest to the sun to move faster than the planets farther away, but he never got an answer. It was Sir Isaac Newton who finally put the puzzle together. He did this with his ideas about *gravity*. Newton didn't understand *why* gravity worked or what caused it. Even today, modern scientists do not fully understand gravity. But Newton was able to combine the work of earlier scientists to explain *how* the force of attraction between matter works.

An Apple One Day Newton reasoned that small objects fall toward the Earth because the Earth and the objects are attracted to each other by the force of gravity. But because the Earth has so much more mass than a small object, say an apple, only the object appears to move.

Newton thus developed his *law of universal gravitation*, which states that the force of gravity depends on the product of the masses of the objects divided by the square of the distance between them. In other words, if two objects are moved twice as far apart, the gravitational attraction between them will decrease by a factor of $2 \times 2 = 4$, as shown in **Figure 7.** If the objects are moved 10 times as far apart, the gravitational attraction will decrease by a factor of $10 \times 10 = 100$.

Figure 7 *If two objects are moved twice as far apart, the gravitational attraction between them will be four times less.*

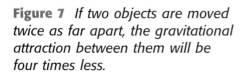

APPLY

Newton's Law and Satellites

Space engineers that plan the paths of orbiting satellites must be able to calculate the height of the most appropriate orbit and the location of the satellite at each moment. To do this, they must take into account both Kepler's laws of motion and Newton's law of universal gravitation. Try this exercise: If the mass of the Earth were twice its actual mass, by how much would the gravity increase on a satellite in orbit around Earth? If the satellite were suddenly moved three times farther away, would Earth's gravitational pull on the satellite increase or decrease? By how much?

Falling Down and Around How did Newton explain the orbit of the moon around the Earth? After all, according to gravity, the moon should come crashing into the Earth. And this is what the moon would do if it were not moving at a high velocity. In fact, if it were not for gravity, the moon would simply shoot off away from the Earth.

To understand this better, imagine twirling a ball on the end of a string. As long as you hold the string, the ball will orbit your hand. As soon as you let go of the string, the ball will fly off in a straight path. This same principle applies to the moon. But instead of a hand holding a string, gravity is keeping the moon from flying off in a straight path. **Figure 8** shows how this works. This same principle holds true for all bodies in orbit, including the Earth and other planets in our solar system.

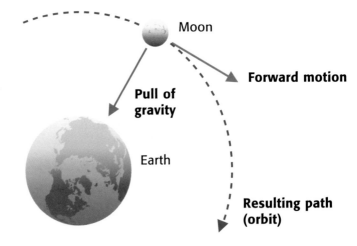

Figure 8 *Gravity is actually causing the moon to fall toward the Earth, changing what would be a straight-line path. The resulting path is a curved orbit.*

SECTION REVIEW

1. On what properties does the force of gravity between two objects depend?

2. Will a planet or comet be moving faster in its orbit when it is farther from or closer to the sun? Explain.

3. How does gravity keep a planet moving in an orbit around the sun?

4. **Applying Concepts** Suppose a certain planet had two moons, one of which was twice as far from the planet as the other. Which moon would complete one revolution of the planet first? Explain.

The Sun: Our Very Own Star

Terms to Learn

corona	radiative zone
chromosphere	core
photosphere	nuclear fusion
convective zone	sunspot

What You'll Do

- ◆ Describe the basic structure and composition of the sun.
- ◆ Explain how the sun produces energy.
- ◆ Describe the surface activity of the sun, and name some of its effects on Earth.

There is nothing special about our sun, other than the fact that it is close enough to the Earth to give us light and warmth. Otherwise, the sun is similar to most of the other stars in our galaxy. It is basically a large ball of gas made mostly of hydrogen and helium held together by gravity. But let's take a closer look.

The Structure of the Sun

Although it may look like the sun has a solid surface, it does not. When we see a picture of the sun, we are really seeing through the sun's outer atmosphere, down to the point where the gas becomes so thick we cannot see through it anymore. As shown in **Figure 9,** the sun is composed of several layers.

Figure 9 Structure of the Sun and Its Atmosphere

a
The **corona** forms the sun's outer atmosphere and can extend outward a distance equal to 10–12 times the diameter of the sun. The gases in the corona are so thin that it is visible only during a total solar eclipse.

b
The **chromosphere** is a thin region below the corona, only 3,000 km thick. Like the corona, the deep, red chromosphere is too faint to see unless there is a total solar eclipse.

c
The **photosphere** is where the gases get thick enough to see. The photosphere is what we know as the visible surface of the sun. It is only about 600 km thick.

d
The **convective zone** is a region about 200,000 km thick where gases circulate in convection currents. Hot gases rise from the interior while cooler gases sink toward the interior.

e
The **radiative zone** is a very dense region about 300,000 km thick. The atoms in this zone are so closely packed that light can take millions of years to pass through.

f
The **core** is at the center of the sun. This is where the sun's energy is produced. The core has a radius of about 200,000 km and a temperature near 15,000,000°C.

Energy Production in the Sun

The sun has been shining on the Earth for about 4.6 billion years. How can it stay hot for so long? And what makes it shine? Over the years, several theories have been proposed to answer these questions. Because the sun is so bright and hot, many people thought that it was burning fuel to create the energy. But the amount of energy that is released during burning would not be enough to power the sun. If the sun were simply burning, it would last for only 10,000 years.

Burning or Shrinking? It eventually became clear that burning wouldn't last long enough to keep the sun shining. Scientists began to think that the sun was slowly shrinking due to gravity and that perhaps this would release enough energy to heat the sun. While the release of gravitational energy is more powerful than burning, it is still not enough to power the sun. If all of the sun's gravitational energy were released, the sun would last for only 45 million years. We know that dinosaurs roamed the Earth more than 65 million years ago, so this couldn't be the explanation. Something even more powerful was needed.

Figure 10 *Ideas about the source of the sun's energy have changed over time.*

Some type of burning fuel was first thought to be the source of the sun's energy.

A shrinking sun was another explanation for solar energy.

Nuclear Fusion At the beginning of the twentieth century, Albert Einstein demonstrated that matter and energy are interchangeable. Matter can be converted to energy according to his famous formula: $E = mc^2$, where E is energy, m is mass, and c is the speed of light. Because the speed of light is so large, even a small amount of matter can produce a large amount of energy. This idea paved the way for an understanding of a very powerful source of energy. **Nuclear fusion** is the process by which two or more nuclei with small masses (such as hydrogen) join together, or fuse, to form a larger, more massive nucleus (such as helium). During the process, energy is produced—a lot of it!

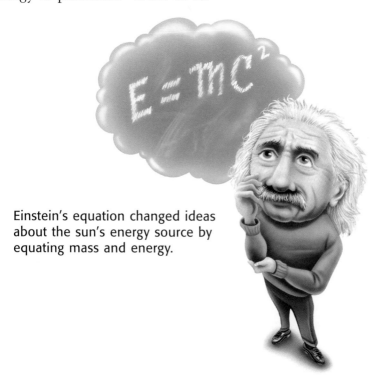

Einstein's equation changed ideas about the sun's energy source by equating mass and energy.

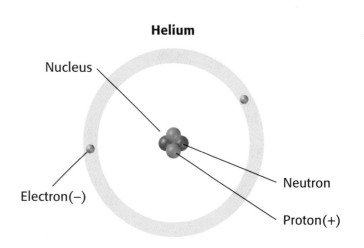
Atomic Review

Let's do a little review. *Atoms* are the smallest particles of matter that keep their chemical identity. An atom consists of a *nucleus* surrounded by one or more *electrons,* which have a negative charge. A nucleus is made up of two types of particles—*protons,* with a positive charge, and *neutrons,* with no charge. The positively charged protons in the nucleus are balanced by an equal number of negatively charged electrons. The number of protons and electrons gives the atom its chemical identity. A helium atom, for example, has two protons and two electrons.

Helium

Nucleus

Electron(−)

Neutron

Proton(+)

Figure 11 *Like charges repel, just like similar poles on a pair of magnets.*

Fusion in the Sun Under normal conditions, the nuclei of hydrogen atoms never get close enough to combine. This is because they are positively charged, and like charges repel each other, as shown in **Figure 11.** In the center of the sun, however, the temperature and pressure are very high because of the huge amount of matter within the core. This gives the hydrogen nuclei enough energy to overcome the repulsive force, allowing the conversion of hydrogen to helium, as shown in **Figure 12.**

Figure 12 Fusion of Hydrogen in the Sun

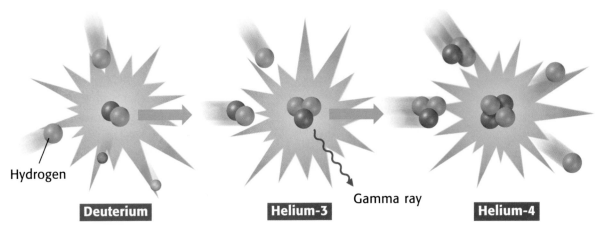

1 Two hydrogen nuclei (protons) collide. One proton emits particles and energy, then becomes a neutron. The proton and neutron combine to produce a heavy form of hydrogen called *deuterium.*

2 Deuterium combines with another hydrogen nucleus to form a variety of helium called helium-3. More energy is released, as well as gamma rays.

3 Two helium-3 atoms then combine to form ordinary helium-4, releasing more energy and a pair of hydrogen nuclei.

The energy produced in the core of the sun takes millions of years to reach the sun's surface. In the radiative zone, the matter is so crowded that the light and energy keep getting blocked and sent off in different directions. Eventually the energy reaches the convective zone, where hot gases carry it up to the photosphere relatively quickly. From there the energy leaves the sun as light, taking only 8.3 minutes to reach Earth.

Activity on the Sun's Surface

The photosphere, or the visible surface of the sun, is a very dynamic place. As energy from the sun's interior reaches the surface, it causes the gas to boil and churn, a result of the rising and sinking of gases in the convective zone below.

The energy released during the nuclear fusion of 1 g of hydrogen is equal to about 100 tons of TNT! Each second, the sun converts about 5 million tons of matter into pure energy.

Sunspots The circulation of the gases within the sun, in addition to the sun's own rotation, produces magnetic fields that reach out into space. But these magnetic fields also tend to slow down the activity in the convective zone. This causes areas on the photosphere above to be slightly cooler than surrounding areas. These areas show up as sunspots. **Sunspots** are cooler, dark spots on the sun, as shown in **Figure 13.**

The number of sunspots and their location on the sun change in a regular cycle. Records of the number of sunspots have been kept ever since the invention of the telescope. In **Figure 14,** the sunspot cycle is shown, with the exception of the years 1645–1715, when sunspots were not observed.

Solar Flares The magnetic fields that cause sunspots also cause disturbances in the solar atmosphere. Giant storms on the surface of the sun, called *solar flares,* have temperatures of up to 5 million degrees Celsius. Solar flares send out huge streams of particles from the sun. These particles interact with the Earth's upper atmosphere, causing spectacular light shows called *auroras.* Solar flares can interrupt radio communications on Earth. They can also affect satellites in orbit. Scientists are trying to find ways to predict solar activity and give advanced warning of such events.

Figure 13 *Sunspots mark cooler areas on the sun's surface. They are related to changes in the magnetic properties of the sun.*

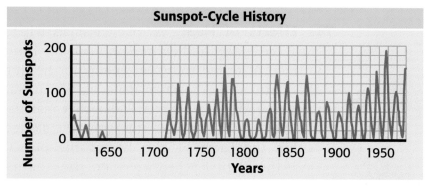

Figure 14 *This graph shows the number of sunspots that have occurred each year since Galileo's first observations, in 1610.*

SECTION REVIEW

1. According to modern understanding, what is the source of the sun's energy?

2. If nuclear fusion in the sun's core suddenly stopped today, would the sky be dark in the daytime tomorrow? Why?

3. **Interpreting Illustrations** In Figure 12, the nuclear fusion process ends up with one helium-4 nucleus and two free protons. What might happen to the two protons next?

internetconnect

SC*i*LINKS
NSTA

TOPIC: The Sun
GO TO: www.scilinks.org
*sci*LINKS NUMBER: HSTE465

What You'll Do

- ◆ Describe the shape and structure of the Earth.
- ◆ Explain how the Earth got its layered structure and how this process affects the appearance of Earth's surface.
- ◆ Explain the development of Earth's atmosphere and the influence of early life on the atmosphere.
- ◆ Describe how the Earth's oceans and continents were formed.

The Earth Takes Shape

Investigating the early history of the Earth is not easy because no one was there to study it directly. Scientists develop ideas about what happened based on their knowledge of chemistry, biology, physics, geology, and other sciences. Astronomers are also gathering evidence from other stars where planets are forming to better understand how our own solar system formed.

The Solid Earth Takes Form

As scientists now understand it, the Earth formed from the accumulation of planetesimals. This would have taken place within the first 10 million years of the collapse of the solar nebula—the blink of an eye on the cosmic time scale!

The Effects of Gravity When a young planet is still small, it can have an irregular shape, like a potato. As more matter builds up on the young planet, the force of gravity increases and the material pushing toward the center of the planet gets heavier. When a rocky planet, such as Earth, reaches a diameter of about 350 km, pressure from all this material becomes greater than the strength of the rock. At this point, the planet starts to become spherical in shape as the rock in the center is crushed by gravity.

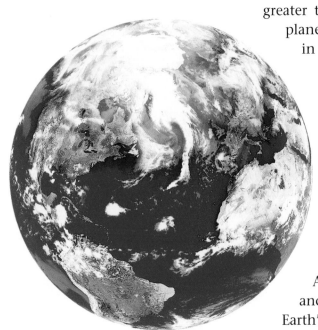

Figure 15 *The Earth has not always looked as inviting as it does today.*

The Effects of Heat As planetesimals fell to Earth, the energy of their motion made the Earth warmer. A second source of energy for heating the Earth was radioactive material, which was present in the solar nebula. Radioactive material radiates energy, and as this energy collected within the Earth, it also heated the planet. Once the Earth reached a certain size, the interior could not cool off as fast as its temperature rose, and the rocky material inside began to melt. As you will see on the next page, the effects of heat and gravity contributed to the formation of the Earth's layers.

> ## ✓ Self-Check
>
> Why is the Earth spherical in shape, while most asteroids and comets are not? *(See page 200 to check your answer.)*

The Earth and Its Layers Have you ever dropped pebbles into water or tried mixing oil and vinegar together for a salad? What happens? The heavier material (either solid or liquid) sinks, and the lighter material floats to the top. This is because of gravity. The material with a higher density is more strongly attracted and falls to the bottom. The same thing happened in the young Earth. As its rocks melted, the heavy elements, such as nickel and iron, sank to the center of the Earth, forming what we call the *core.* Lighter materials floated to the surface. This process is illustrated in **Figure 16.**

Figure 16 Earth's Materials Separate into Layers

Rocks melt, and dense materials separate and sink.

All materials in the early Earth are randomly mixed.

Less-dense materials rise, and layers are formed.

The Earth's Interior The Earth is divided into three distinct layers according to the composition of its materials. These layers are shown in **Figure 17.** Geologists map the interior of the Earth by measuring how sound waves pass through the planet during earthquakes and underground explosions.

Figure 17 *The interior of the Earth consists of three layers.*

❶ The **crust** is the outermost layer of the Earth. It forms a thin skin over the entire planet, ranging from 5 km to 100 km thick.

❷ The **mantle** lies below the crust, extending from about 100 km to about 2,900 km below the surface. The mantle contains denser rocks than the crust.

❸ The **core,** at the center, contains the heaviest material (nickel and iron) and extends from the base of the mantle to the center of the Earth—almost 6,400 km below the surface.

The Cassini Mission to Saturn (launched in October 1997) will study the chemistry of Saturn's moon Titan. Titan's atmosphere, like Earth's, is composed mostly of nitrogen, but it also contains many hydrogen-rich compounds. Scientists want to study how molecules essential to life may form in this atmosphere.

The Atmosphere Evolves

Other than the presence of life, one of the biggest differences between the Earth of today and the Earth of 4.6 billion years ago is the character of its atmosphere. Earth's atmosphere today is composed of 21 percent oxygen, 78 percent nitrogen, and about 1 percent argon (with tiny amounts of many other gases). But it has not always been this way. Read on to discover how the Earth's atmosphere has changed through time.

Earth's First Atmosphere Earth's early atmosphere was very different from the atmosphere of today. In the 1950s, laboratory experiments on the origins of life were based on the hypothesis that Earth's early atmosphere was largely made up of methane, ammonia, and water. And because the solar nebula was rich in hydrogen, many scientists thought that Earth's first atmosphere also contained a lot of hydrogen compounds.

New Evidence New evidence is changing the way we think about Earth's first atmosphere. For one thing, 85 percent of the Earth's matter probably came from material similar to *meteoroids*—planetesimals made of rock. The other 15 percent probably came from the outer solar system in the form of *comets*—planetesimals made of ice.

Volcanic Gases During the final stages of formation, the Earth was hit many times by planetesimals, and the surface was very hot, even molten in places, as illustrated in **Figure 18.** The ground would have been venting large amounts of gas released from the heated minerals. The composition of meteorites tells us that much of that gas would have been water vapor and carbon dioxide. These two gases are also commonly released during volcanic eruptions. Earth's first atmosphere was probably a steamy atmosphere made of water vapor and carbon dioxide.

Figure 18 *This is an artist's view of what Earth's surface may have looked like shortly after Earth's formation.*

The Role of Impacts Planetesimal impacts may have helped release gases from the Earth. In addition, they may have also helped to knock some of those gases back into space. Because planetesimals travel very fast, their impacts can speed up gas molecules in the atmosphere enough for them to overcome gravity and escape into space.

Heavier elements, such as iron, that were on the surface of the Earth also reacted chemically with water, giving off hydrogen—the lightest element. And because the early Earth was very warm, this hydrogen also had enough energy to escape.

Comets brought in a range of elements, such as carbon, hydrogen, oxygen, and nitrogen. They may also have brought water that eventually helped form the oceans, as shown in **Figure 19.**

Figure 19 *Comets may have brought some of the water that formed Earth's early oceans.*

Earth's Second Atmosphere After the Earth cooled off and the core formed, it became possible for the Earth's second atmosphere to take shape. This atmosphere formed from gases contributed by both volcanoes and comets. Volcanoes, like the one in **Figure 20,** produced large amounts of water vapor, along with chlorine, nitrogen, sulfur, and large amounts of carbon dioxide. This carbon dioxide kept the planet much warmer than it is today.

Figure 20 *As this volcano in Hawaii shows, a large amount of gas is released during an eruption.*

Environment
C O N N E C T I O N

Because carbon dioxide is a very good *greenhouse gas*—one that traps thermal energy—scientists have tried to estimate how much carbon dioxide the Earth must have had in its second atmosphere in order to keep it as warm as it was. For example, if all of the carbon dioxide that is now tied up in the rocks and minerals of the ocean floor were released, it would make an atmosphere of carbon dioxide 60 times as thick as our present atmosphere.

Earth's Current Atmosphere How did this early atmosphere change to become the atmosphere we know today? It happened with the help of solar ultraviolet (UV) radiation, the very thing that we worry about now for its cancer-causing ability. Solar UV light is dangerous because it has a lot of energy and can break molecules apart in the air or in your skin. Today we are shielded from most of the sun's ultraviolet rays by Earth's protective ozone layer. But Earth's early atmosphere had no ozone, and many molecules were broken apart in the atmosphere. The pieces were later washed out into shallow seas and tide pools by rain. Eventually a rich supply of these pieces of molecules collected in protected areas, forming a rich organic solution that is sometimes called a "primordial soup."

The Source of Oxygen Although there was no ozone, water offered protection from the effects of ultraviolet radiation. In these sheltered pools of water, complex molecules may have been able to form. Then, sometime between 4.6 and 3.9 billion years ago, life began on Earth. By 3.7 to 3.4 billion years ago, living organisms had evolved that were able to photosynthesize energy from sunlight and produce oxygen as a byproduct. These early life-forms are still around today, as shown in **Figure 21.**

Figure 21 *Fossilized algae (left) are among the earliest signs of life discovered. Today's stromatolites (right) are mats of microorganisms thought to be similar to the first life on Earth.*

Eventually, between 2.5 and 2.0 billion years ago, the amount of oxygen started to increase rapidly—reaching about 20 percent of the amount we have in the atmosphere today. As plants began to cover the land, oxygen levels increased because plants produce oxygen during photosynthesis. Therefore, it was the emergence of life that completely changed our atmosphere into the one we have today.

Oceans and Continents

It is hard to say exactly when the first oceans appeared on Earth, but they probably formed early, as soon as the Earth was cool enough for rain to fall and remain on the surface. We know that Earth's second atmosphere had plenty of water vapor. After millions of years of rainfall, water began to cover the Earth, and by 4 billion years ago, a giant global ocean covered the planet. For the first few hundred million years of the Earth's history, there were no continents.

So how and when did the continents appear? Continental crust material is very light compared with material in the mantle. The composition of the granite and other rocks making up the continents tells geologists that the rocks of the crust have melted and cooled many times in the past. Each time the rocks melted, the heavier elements sank, leaving the lighter ones to rise to the surface. This process is illustrated in **Figure 22.**

The Growth of Continents After a while, some of the rocks were light enough that they no longer sank, and they began to pile up on the surface. This was the beginning of the earliest continents. After gradually thickening, the continents slowly rose above the surface of the ocean. These scattered young continents didn't stay in the same place, however, because the slow convection in the mantle pushed them around. By around 2.5 billion years ago, continents really started to grow. By 1.5 billion years ago, the upper mantle had cooled and become denser and heavier, so it was easier for the colder parts of it to sink. Then the real continental action, or *plate tectonics,* began.

internet**connect**

SCiLINKS
NSTA

TOPIC: The Layers of the Earth,
        The Oceans
GO TO: www.scilinks.org
*sci*LINKS NUMBER: HSTE470, HSTE475

Figure 22 *The slow convective motion in the Earth's mantle was the engine that caused mantle rock to rise and sink, forming the continents.*

Hot rocks, which are less dense, rose to the surface and melted, erupting through volcanoes.

Cooler materials, which are denser, sank because of gravity and became reheated. This started the process over again.

SECTION REVIEW

1. Why did the Earth separate into distinct layers?

2. How did the Earth's atmosphere change composition to become today's nitrogen and oxygen atmosphere?

3. Which are older, oceans or continents? Explain.

4. **Drawing Conclusions** If the Earth were not hot inside, would we have moving continents (plate tectonics)? Explain.

Discovery Lab

USING SCIENTIFIC
METHODS

How Far Is the Sun?

It doesn't slice, it doesn't dice, but it can give you an idea of how big our universe is! You can build your very own stellar-distance measuring device from household items. Amaze your friends by figuring out how many metersticks can be placed between Earth and the sun.

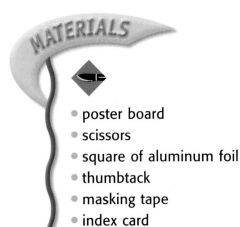

MATERIALS

- poster board
- scissors
- square of aluminum foil
- thumbtack
- masking tape
- index card
- meterstick
- metric ruler

Ask a Question

1 How many metersticks could I place between the Earth and the sun?

Conduct an Experiment

2 Measure and cut a 4x4 cm square from the middle of the poster board. Tape the foil square over the hole in the center of the poster board.

3 Carefully prick the foil with a thumbtack to form a tiny hole in the center. Congratulations—you have just constructed your very own stellar-distance measuring device!

4 Tape the device to a window facing the sun so that sunlight shines directly through the pinhole. **Caution:** Do not look directly into the sun.

5 Place one end of the meterstick against the window and beneath the foil square. Steady the meterstick with one hand.

6 With the other hand, hold the index card close to the pinhole. You should be able to see a circular image on the card. This image is the sun.

7 Move the card back until the image is large enough to measure. Be sure to keep the image on the card sharply focused. Reposition the meterstick so that it touches the bottom of the card.

8 Ask your partner to measure the diameter of the image on the card with the metric ruler. Record the diameter of the image in your ScienceLog.

9 Record the distance between the window and the index card by reading the point at which the card rests on the meterstick.

10 Calculate the distance between Earth and the sun using the following formula:

Distance between the sun and Earth = Sun's diameter $\times \dfrac{\text{Distance to the image}}{\text{Image's diameter}}$

Hint: The sun's diameter is 1,392,000,000 m.

1 cm	= 10 mm
1 m	= 100 cm
1 km	= 1,000 m

Analyze the Results

11 According to your calculations, how far is the sun from the Earth? Don't forget to convert your measurements to meters.

Draw Conclusions

12 You could put 150 billion metersticks between Earth and the sun. Compare this information with your result in step 11. Do you think that this activity was a good way to measure the Earth's distance from the sun? Support your answer.

Chapter Highlights

Vocabulary

solar system (*p. 34*)

nebula (*p. 34*)

solar nebula (*p. 35*)

planetesimal (*p. 36*)

rotation (*p. 39*)

orbit (*p. 39*)

revolution (*p. 39*)

period of revolution (*p. 39*)

ellipse (*p. 40*)

astronomical unit (*p. 40*)

Section Notes

- The solar system formed out of a vast cloud of cold gas and dust called a nebula.

- Gravity and pressure were balanced, keeping the cloud unchanging until something upset the balance. Then the nebula began to collapse.

- Collapse of the solar nebula caused heating in the center. As material crowded closer together, planetesimals began to form.

- The central mass of the nebula became the sun. Planets formed from the surrounding disk of material.

- It took about 10 million years for the solar system to form, and it is now 4.6 billion years old.

- The orbit of one body around another has the shape of an ellipse.

- Planets move faster in their orbits when they are closer to the sun.

- The square of the period of revolution of the planet is equal to the cube of its semimajor axis.

- Gravity depends on the masses of the interacting objects and the square of the distance between them.

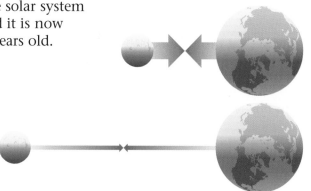

☑ Skills Check

Math Concepts

SQUARES AND CUBES Let's take another look at Kepler's third law of motion. Expanding the formula $P^2 = a^3$ to $P \times P = a \times a \times a$ may be an easier way to consider the calculation. The period of Venus, for example, is 0.61 years, and its semimajor axis is 0.72 AU. Thus,

$$P^2 = a^3$$
$$P \times P = a \times a \times a$$
$$0.61 \times 0.61 = 0.72 \times 0.72 \times 0.72$$
$$0.37 = 0.37$$

Visual Understanding

LIKE AN ONION The sun is formed of six different layers of gas. From the inside out, the layers are the core, radiative zone, convective zone, photosphere, chromosphere, and corona. Look back at Figure 9 on page 43 to review the characteristics of each layer.

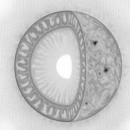

SECTION 2

Vocabulary

corona *(p. 43)*

chromosphere *(p. 43)*

photosphere *(p. 43)*

convective zone *(p. 43)*

radiative zone *(p. 43)*

core *(p. 43)*

nuclear fusion *(p. 45)*

sunspot *(p. 47)*

Section Notes

- The sun is a gaseous sphere made primarily of hydrogen and helium.

- The sun produces energy in its core by a process called nuclear fusion.

- Magnetic changes within the sun cause sunspots and solar flares.

SECTION 3

Vocabulary

crust *(p. 49)*

mantle *(p. 49)*

core *(p. 49)*

Section Notes

- The Earth is divided into three main layers—crust, mantle, and core.

- Materials with different densities separated because of melting inside Earth. Heavy elements sank to the center because of Earth's gravity.

- Earth's original atmosphere formed from the release of gases brought to Earth by meteorites and comets.

- Earth's second atmosphere arose from volcanic eruptions and impacts by comets. The composition was largely water and carbon dioxide.

- The presence of life dramatically changed Earth's atmosphere, adding free oxygen.

- Earth's oceans formed shortly after the Earth did, when it had cooled off enough for rain to fall.

- Continents formed when lighter materials gathered on the surface and rose above sea level.

internetconnect

GO TO: go.hrw.com

Visit the **HRW** Web site for a variety of learning tools related to this chapter. Just type in the keyword:

KEYWORD: HSTSOL

SCiLINKS **N S T A**

GO TO: www.scilinks.org

Visit the **National Science Teachers Association** on-line Web site for Internet resources related to this chapter. Just type in the *sci*LINKS number for more information about the topic:

TOPIC: The Planets	*sci*LINKS NUMBER: HSTE455
TOPIC: Kepler's Laws	*sci*LINKS NUMBER: HSTE460
TOPIC: The Sun	*sci*LINKS NUMBER: HSTE465
TOPIC: The Layers of the Earth	*sci*LINKS NUMBER: HSTE470
TOPIC: The Oceans	*sci*LINKS NUMBER: HSTE475

Chapter Review

USING VOCABULARY

For each pair of terms, explain the difference in their meanings.

1. rotation/revolution

2. ellipse/circle

3. solar system/solar nebula

4. planetesimal/planet

5. temperature/pressure

6. photosphere/corona

To complete the following sentences, choose the correct term from each pair of terms below.

7. It takes millions of years for light energy to travel through the sun's ___?___. (*radiative zone* or *convective zone*)

8. ___?___ of the Earth causes night and day. (*Rotation* or *Revolution*)

9. Convection in Earth's mantle causes ___?___. (*plate tectonics* or *nuclear fusion*)

UNDERSTANDING CONCEPTS

Multiple Choice

10. Impacts in the early solar system
    a. brought new materials to the planets.
    b. released energy.
    c. dug craters.
    d. All of the above

11. Which type of planet will have a higher overall density?
    a. one that forms close to the sun
    b. one that forms far from the sun

12. Which process releases the most energy?
    a. nuclear fusion
    b. burning
    c. shrinking due to gravity

13. Which of the following planets has the shortest period of revolution?
    a. Pluto   c. Mercury
    b. Earth   d. Jupiter

14. Which gas in Earth's atmosphere tells us that there is life on Earth?
    a. hydrogen   c. carbon dioxide
    b. oxygen   d. nitrogen

15. Which layer of the Earth has the lowest density?
    a. the core
    b. the mantle
    c. the crust

16. What is the term for the speed of gas molecules?
    a. temperature   c. gravity
    b. pressure   d. force

17. Which of the following objects is least likely to have a spherical shape?
    a. a comet   c. the sun
    b. Venus   d. Jupiter

Short Answer

18. Why did the solar nebula begin to collapse to form the sun and planets if the forces of pressure and gravity were balanced?

19. How is the period of revolution related to the semimajor axis of an orbit? Draw an ellipse and label the semimajor axis.

20. How did our understanding of the sun's energy change over time?

Concept Mapping

21. Use the following terms to create a concept map: solar nebula, solar system, planetesimals, sun, photosphere, core, nuclear fusion, planets, Earth.

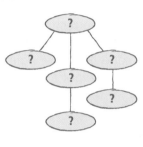

CRITICAL THINKING AND PROBLEM SOLVING

Write one or two sentences to answer the following questions:

22. Explain why nuclear fusion works inside the sun but not inside Jupiter, which is also made mostly of hydrogen and helium.

23. Why is it less expensive to launch an interplanetary spacecraft from the international space station in Earth's orbit than from Earth itself?

24. Soon after the formation of the universe, there was only hydrogen and helium. Heavier elements, such as carbon, oxygen, silicon, and all the matter that makes up the heavier minerals and rocks in the solar system, were made inside an earlier generation of stars. Do you think the first generation of stars had any planets like Earth, Venus, Mercury, and Mars? Explain.

MATH IN SCIENCE

25. Suppose astronomers discover a new planet orbiting our sun. The orbit has a semimajor axis of 2.52 AU. What is the planet's period of revolution?

26. If the planet in the previous question is twice as massive as the Earth but is the same size, how much would a person who weighs 100 lb on Earth weigh on this planet?

INTERPRETING GRAPHICS

Examine the illustration below, and answer the questions that follow.

27. Do you think this is a rocky, inner planet or a gas giant?

28. Did this planet form close to the sun or far from the sun? Explain.

29. Does this planet have an atmosphere? Why or why not?

Reading Check-up

Take a minute to review your answers to the Pre-Reading Questions found at the bottom of page 32. Have your answers changed? If necessary, revise your answers based on what you have learned since you began this chapter.

Science, Technology, and Society

Don't Look at the Sun!

You know you are not supposed to look at the sun, right? But how can we learn anything about the sun if we can't look at it? By using a solar telescope, of course! Where would you find one of these, you ask? Well, if you travel about 70 km southwest of Tucson, Arizona, you will arrive at Kitt Peak National Observatory, where you will find three of them. One telescope in particular has gone to great lengths to give astronomers extraordinary views of the sun!

Top Selection

In 1958, Kitt Peak was chosen from more than 150 mountain ranges to be the site for a national observatory. Located in the Sonoran Desert, Kitt Peak is a part of lands belonging to the Tohono O'odham nation. The McMath-Pierce Facility houses the three largest solar telescopes in the world. Astronomers come from around the globe to use these telescopes. The largest of the three, called the McMath-Pierce telescope, creates an image of the sun that is almost 1 m wide!

Too Hot to Handle

Have you ever caught a piece of paper on fire using only a magnifying glass and the rays from the sun? Sunlight that has been focused can produce a great amount of thermal energy— enough to start a fire. Now imagine a magnifying glass 1.6 m in diameter focusing the sun's rays. The resulting heat could melt metal. This is what would happen to a conventional telescope if it were pointed directly at the sun.

To avoid a meltdown, the McMath-Pierce solar telescope uses a mirror that produces a large image of the sun. This mirror directs the sun's rays down a diagonal shaft to another mirror 50 m underground. This mirror is adjustable to focus the sunlight. The sunlight is then directed to a third mirror, which directs the light to an observing room and instrument shaft.

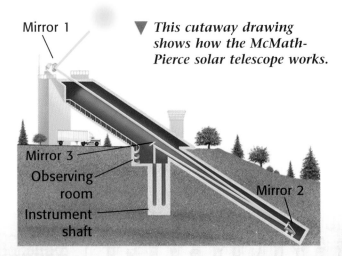

Mirror 1

▼ *This cutaway drawing shows how the McMath-Pierce solar telescope works.*

Mirror 3
Observing room
Instrument shaft
Mirror 2

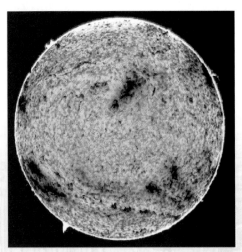

▲ *This is an image of the sun as viewed through the McMath-Pierce solar telescope.*

Scope It Out

▶ Kitt Peak Observatory also has optical telescopes, which differ from solar telescopes. Do some research to find out how optical telescopes work and what the ones at Kitt Peak are used for.

Mirrors in Space

People who live in areas that do not get much sunshine are more prone to health problems such as depression and alcoholism. The people of Siberia, Russia, experience a shortage of sunshine during the winter, when the sun shines only 6 hours on certain days. Could there be a solution to this problem?

A Mirror From *Mir*

In February 1999, the crew of the space station *Mir* was scheduled to insert a large, umbrellalike mirror into orbit. The mirror was designed to reflect sunlight to Siberia. Once placed into orbit, however, problems arose and the crew was unable to unfold the mirror. Had things gone as planned, the beam of reflected sunlight was expected to be 5 to 10 times brighter than the light from the moon. If the first mirror had worked, this would have opened the door for Russia to build many more mirrors that are larger in diameter. These larger mirrors would have been launched into space to lengthen winter days, provide additional heat, and even reduce the amount of electricity used for lighting. The idea of placing mirrors in space, however, caused some serious concerns about the effects it could have.

Overcrowding

The first mirror was about 30 m in diameter. Because it was put in Low Earth Orbit (LEO), the light beam would have been obstructed by the Earth's horizon as the mirror made its orbit. As a result, it would have reflected light on a single area for only about 30 seconds. In order to shine light on Siberia on a large scale, hundreds of larger mirrors would have to be used. But using this many mirrors could result in collisions with satellites that share LEO.

Damage to Ecosystems

It is very difficult to determine what effects extra daylight would have on Siberian ecosystems. Many plants and animals have cycles for various biological functions, such as feeding, sleeping, moving, and reproducing. Extra light and increased temperatures could adversely affect these cycles. Birds might migrate so late that they wouldn't survive the trip across the colder climates because food would be scarce. Plants might sprout too soon and freeze. Arctic ice might melt and cause flooding.

Light Pollution

Astronomers may also be affected by orbiting mirrors. Already astronomers must plan their viewing times to avoid the passing of bright planets and satellites. More sunlight directed toward the Earth would increase light pollution and could make seeing into space more difficult. A string of several hundred mirrors shining light toward the Earth would likely cause additional light pollution in certain locations as the mirrors passed overhead.

What's the Current Status?

▶ Find out more about the Russian project and where it stands now. If you had to decide whether to pursue this project, what would you decide? Why?

▲ *The end of a winter day in Siberia*

A Family of Planets

Pre-Reading
Questions

1. What are the differences
   between planets, moons,
   asteroids, comets, and
   meteoroids?

2. How can surface features
   tell us about a planet's
   history?

CLOSE NEIGHBORS IN SPACE

Can you identify the objects in this illustration? The planets
and other objects of the solar system appear almost close
enough to run into each other. From this perspective, you
can easily observe the mysterious and beautiful differences
between the planets—in terms of their visible properties.
In this chapter, you will study the properties of planets,
moons, comets, asteroids, and meteoroids—and learn
about eclipses, the moon's phases, and measuring interplanetary distances.

MEASURING SPACE

Earth's distance from the sun is about 150 million kilometers, or 1 AU. *AU* stands for astronomical unit, which is the average distance between Earth and the sun. Do the following exercise to get a better idea of your solar neighborhood.

Procedure

1. Plant a **stake with a flag attached** at the goal line of a **football field**. This stake represents the sun. Then use the table to plant **9 more stakes with flags** representing the position of each planet.

Analysis

2. After you have positioned all the "planets," what do you notice about how the planets are spaced?

Interplanetary Distances		
Planet	**Distance from sun in AU**	**Scaled distance in yards**
Mercury	0.39	1.0
Venus	0.72	1.8
Earth	1.00	2.5
Mars	1.52	3.9
Jupiter	5.20	13.3
Saturn	9.58	24.4
Uranus	19.20	48.9
Neptune	30.05	76.6
Pluto	39.24	100

Terms to Learn

astronomical unit (AU)
terrestrial planets
prograde rotation
retrograde rotation
gas giants

What You'll Do

◆ List the names of the planets in the order they orbit the sun.
◆ Describe three ways in which the inner and outer planets are different from each other.

Galileo Galilei

Figure 2 *One astronomical unit equals about 8.3 light-minutes.*

The Nine Planets

Ancient people knew about the existence of planets and could predict their motions. But it wasn't until the seventeenth century, when Galileo used the telescope to study planets and stars, that we began our first exploration of these alien worlds. Since the former Soviet Union launched *Sputnik 1*—the first artificial satellite—in 1957, over 150 successful missions have been launched to moons, planets, comets, and asteroids. **Figure 1** shows how far we have come since Galileo's time.

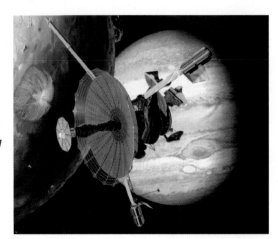

Figure 1 *Galileo Galilei (left) discovered Jupiter's four largest moons using the newly invented telescope in 1610. The Galileo spacecraft (right) arrived at Jupiter on December 7, 1995.*

Measuring Interplanetary Distances

As you have seen, one way scientists measure distances in space is by using the astronomical unit. The **astronomical unit (AU)** is the average distance between the Earth and the sun. Another way to measure distances in space is by the distance light travels in a given amount of time. Light travels at about 300,000 km per second in space. This means that in 1 second, light travels a distance of 300,000 km—or about the distance you would cover if you traveled around Earth 7.5 times.

In 1 minute, light travels nearly 18,000,000 km! This distance is also called 1 *light-minute*. For example, it takes light from the sun 8.3 minutes to reach Earth, so the distance from the Earth to the sun is 8.3 light-minutes. Distances within the solar system can be measured in light-minutes and light-hours, but the distances between stars are measured in light-years!

Sun

1 Light-minute

Earth

1 Astronomical unit

The Inner Planets

The solar system is divided into two groups of planets—the inner planets and the outer planets. As you learned from the Investigate, the inner planets are more closely spaced than the outer planets. Other differences between the inner and outer planets are their sizes and the materials of which they are made. The inner planets are called **terrestrial planets** because they are like Earth—small, dense, and rocky. The outer planets, except for icy Pluto, are much larger and are made mostly of gases.

Mercury—Closest to the Sun If you were to visit the planet Mercury, you would find a very strange world. For one thing, on Mercury you would weigh only 38 percent of what you weigh on Earth. The weight you experience on Earth is due to *surface gravity*, which is less on less massive planets. Also, a day on Mercury is almost 59 Earth days long! This is because Mercury spins on its axis much more slowly than Earth does. The spin of an object in space is called *rotation*. The amount of time it takes for an object to rotate once is called its *period of rotation*.

Another curious thing about Mercury is that its year is only 88 Earth days long. As you know, a year is the time it takes for a planet to go around the sun once. The motion of a body as it *orbits* another body in space is called *revolution*. The time it takes for an object to revolve around the sun once is called its *period of revolution*. Every 88 Earth days, or 1.5 Mercurian days, Mercury completes one revolution around the sun.

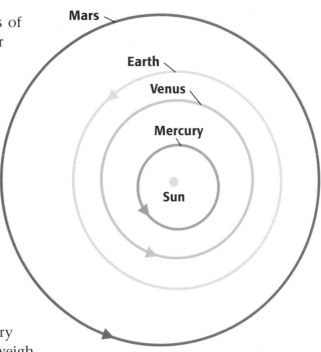

Figure 3 *The lines show orbits of the inner planets. The arrows indicate the direction of motion and the location of each planet on January 1, 2005.*

Figure 4 *This image of Mercury was taken by the* Mariner 10 *spacecraft on March 24, 1974, from a distance of 5,380,000 km.*

Mercury Statistics	
Distance from sun	**3.2** light-minutes
Period of rotation	**58** days, **16** hours
Period of revolution	**88** days
Diameter	**4,879** km
Density	**5.43** g/cm^3
Surface temperature	**−173** to **427°**C
Surface gravity	**38%** of Earth's

Figure 5 *This image of Venus was taken by* Mariner 10 *on February 5, 1974. The uppermost layer of clouds consists of sulfuric acid.*

Venus Statistics	
Distance from sun	**6.0** light-minutes
Period of rotation	**243** days, (R)*
Period of revolution	**224** days, **17** hours
Diameter	**12,104** km
Density	**5.24** g/cm³
Surface temperature	**464°C**
Surface gravity	**91%** of Earth's

*R = retrograde rotation

Venus—Earth's Twin? In many ways Venus is more similar to Earth than is any other planet—they have about the same size, mass, and density. But in other ways Venus is very different from Earth. Unlike on Earth, on Venus the sun rises in the west and sets in the east. This is because Venus rotates in the opposite direction that Earth rotates. Earth is said to have **prograde rotation,** because when viewed from above its north pole, Earth appears to spin in a *counterclockwise* direction. If a planet spins in a *clockwise* direction, it is said to have **retrograde rotation.**

The Atmosphere of Venus At 90 times the pressure of Earth's atmosphere, the atmosphere of Venus is the densest of the terrestrial planets. It consists mostly of carbon dioxide, but it also contains some of the most corrosive acids known. The carbon dioxide in the atmosphere traps thermal energy from sunlight in a process known as the *greenhouse effect.* This is why the surface temperature is so high. With an average temperature of 464°C, Venus has the hottest surface of any planet in the solar system.

Mapping Venus's Surface Between 1990 and 1992, the *Magellan* spacecraft mapped the surface of Venus by using radar waves. The radar waves traveled through the clouds and bounced off the planet's surface. The radar image in **Figure 6** shows that, like Earth, Venus has an active surface.

Figure 6 *This false-color image of a volcano on the surface of Venus was made with radar data gathered by the* Magellan *spacecraft. Bright areas indicate massive lava flows.*

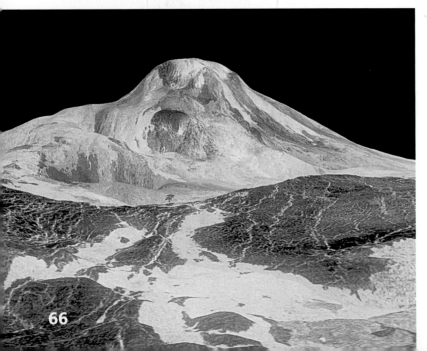

Earth—An Oasis in Space As viewed from space, Earth is like a sparkling blue oasis suspended in a black sea. Constantly changing weather patterns create the swirls of clouds that blanket the blue and brown sphere we call home. Why did Earth have such good fortune while its two nearest neighbors, Venus and Mars, are unsuitable for life as we know it?

Water on Earth Earth is fortunate enough to have formed at just the right distance from the sun. The temperatures are warm enough to prevent most of its water from freezing but cool enough to keep it from boiling away. Liquid water was the key to the development of life on Earth. Water provides a means for much of the chemistry that living things depend on for survival.

The Earth from Space You might think the only goal of space exploration is to make discoveries beyond Earth. But NASA has a program to study Earth using satellites—just as we study other planets. The goal of this project, called the Earth Science Enterprise, is to study the Earth as a system and to determine the effects humans have in changing the global environment. By studying Earth from space, we hope to understand how different parts of the global system—such as weather, climate, and pollution—interact.

Figure 7 *Earth is the only planet we know of that supports life.*

Figure 8 *This image of Earth was taken on December 7, 1972, by the crew of the* Apollo 17 *spacecraft while on their way to the moon.*

Earth Statistics	
Distance from sun	**8.3** light-minutes
Period of rotation	**23** hours, **56** minutes
Period of revolution	**365** days, **6** hours
Diameter	**12,756** km
Density	**5.52** g/cm^3
Surface temperature	**−13** to **37°C**
Surface gravity	**100%** of Earth's

Mars Statistics	
Distance from sun	**12.7** light-minutes
Period of rotation	**24** hours, **37** minutes
Period of revolution	**1** year, **322** days
Diameter	**6,794** km
Density	**3.93** g/cm³
Surface temperature	**−123** to **37°C**
Surface gravity	**38%** of Earth's

Mars—The Red Planet Other than Earth, Mars is perhaps the most studied planet in the solar system. Much of our knowledge of Mars has come from information gathered by the *Viking 1* and *Viking 2* spacecraft that landed on Mars in 1976 and from the *Pathfinder* spacecraft that landed on Mars in 1997.

Figure 9 *This* Viking *orbiter image shows the eastern hemisphere of Mars. The large circular feature in the center is the impact crater Schiaparelli, with a diameter of 450 km.*

The Atmosphere of Mars Because of its thin atmosphere and its great distance from the sun, Mars is a cold planet. Mid-summer temperatures recorded by the *Pathfinder* lander ranged from −13°C to −77°C. The atmosphere of Mars is so thin that the air pressure at the planet's surface is roughly equal to the pressure 30 km above Earth's surface—about three times higher than most planes fly. The pressure is so low that any liquid water would quickly boil away. The only water you'll find on Mars is in the form of ice.

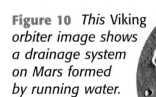

Figure 10 *This* Viking *orbiter image shows a drainage system on Mars formed by running water.*

Water on Mars Even though liquid water cannot exist on Mars's surface today, there is strong evidence that it did exist there in the past! **Figure 10** shows a region on Mars with features that look like dry river beds on Earth. This means that in the past Mars might have been a warmer place with a thicker atmosphere. Where is the water now?

Mars has two polar icecaps that contain both frozen water and frozen carbon dioxide, but this cannot account for all the water. Looking closely at the walls of some Martian craters, scientists have found that the debris surrounding the craters looks as if it were made by a mud flow rather than by the movement of dry material. Where does this suggest some of the "lost" Martian water went? Many scientists think it is frozen beneath the Martian soil.

Martian Volcanoes Mars has a rich volcanic history. Unlike on Earth, where volcanoes occur in many places, Mars has only two large volcanic systems. The largest, the Tharsis region, stretches 8,000 km across the planet. The largest mountain in the solar system, Olympus Mons, is an extinct shield volcano similar to Mauna Kea, on the island of Hawaii. Mars is not only smaller and cooler than Earth, but it also has a slightly different chemical composition. Those factors may have prevented the Martian crust from moving around as Earth's crust has, so the volcanoes kept building up in the same spots. Images and data sent back by probes like the *Sojourner* rover, shown in **Figure 11,** are helping to explain Mars's mysterious past.

Physics
C O N N E C T I O N

At sea level on Earth's surface, water boils at 100°C, but if you try to boil water on top of a high mountain, you will find that the boiling point is lower than 100°C. This is because the atmospheric pressure is less at high altitude. The atmospheric pressure on the surface of Mars is so low that liquid water can't exist at all!

Figure 11 *The* Sojourner *rover, part of the Mars Pathfinder mission, is shown here creeping up to a rock named Yogi to measure its composition. The dark panel on top of the rover collected the solar energy used to power its motor.*

SECTION REVIEW

1. What three characteristics do the inner planets have in common?

2. List three differences and three similarities between Venus and Earth.

3. **Analyzing Relationships** Mercury is closest to the sun, yet Venus has a higher surface temperature. Explain why this is so.

The Outer Planets

The outer planets differ significantly in composition and size from the inner planets. All of the outer planets, except for Pluto, are gas giants. **Gas giants** are very large planets that don't have any known solid surfaces—their atmospheres blend smoothly into the denser layers of their interiors, very deep beneath the outer layers.

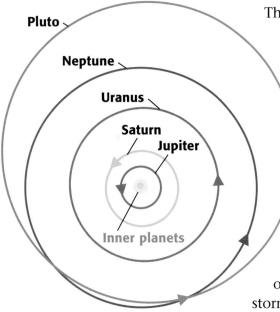

Figure 12 *This view of the solar system shows the orbits and positions of the outer planets on January 1, 2005.*

Jupiter—A Giant Among Giants Like the sun, Jupiter is made primarily of hydrogen and helium. The outer part of Jupiter's atmosphere is made of layered clouds of water, methane, and ammonia. The beautiful colors in **Figure 13** are probably due to trace amounts of organic compounds. Another striking feature of Jupiter is the Great Red Spot, which is a long-lasting storm system that has a diameter of about one and a half times that of Earth! At a depth of about 10,000 km, the pressure is high enough to change hydrogen gas into a liquid. Deeper still, the pressure changes the liquid hydrogen into a metallic liquid state. Unlike most planets, Jupiter radiates much more energy into space than it receives from the sun. This is because energy is continuously transported from Jupiter's interior to its outer atmospheric layers, where it is radiated into space.

NASA Missions to Jupiter There have been five NASA missions to Jupiter—two Pioneer missions, two Voyager missions, and the recent Galileo mission. The *Voyager 1* and *Voyager 2* spacecraft sent back images that revealed a thin faint ring around the planet, as well as the first detailed images of its moons. The *Galileo* spacecraft reached Jupiter in 1995 and released a probe that plunged into Jupiter's atmosphere. The probe sent back data on the atmosphere's composition, temperature, and pressure.

Figure 13 *This* Voyager 2 *image of Jupiter was taken at a distance of 28.4 million kilometers. Io, one of Jupiter's 28 known moons, can also be seen in this image.*

Jupiter Statistics	
Distance from sun	**43.3** light-minutes
Period of rotation	**9** hours, **56** minutes
Period of revolution	**11** years, **313** days
Diameter	**142,984** km
Density	**1.33** g/cm^3
Temperature	**–153°C**
Gravity	**236%** of Earth's

Saturn Statistics	
Distance from sun	**1.3** light-hours
Period of rotation	**10** hours, **39** minutes
Period of revolution	**29** years, **155** days
Diameter	**120,536** km
Density	**0.69** g/cm³
Temperature	**−185°C**
Gravity	**92%** of Earth's

Saturn—Still Forming Saturn, the second largest planet in the solar system, has roughly 764 times the volume of Earth and is 95 times more massive. Its overall composition, like Jupiter's, is mostly hydrogen and helium, with methane, ammonia, and ethane in the upper atmosphere. Saturn's interior is probably very similar to that of Jupiter. Like Jupiter, Saturn gives off a lot more energy than it receives from the sun. Scientists believe that, in Saturn's case, the extra energy is caused by helium raining out of the atmosphere and sinking to the core. In essence, Saturn is still forming!

Figure 14 *This* Voyager 2 *image of Saturn was taken from 21 million kilometers away. The dot you see below the rings is the shadow of Tethys, one of Saturn's moons.*

The Rings of Saturn Although all of the gas giants have rings, Saturn's rings are the largest. Saturn's rings start near the top of Saturn's atmosphere and extend out 136,000 km, yet they are only a few hundred meters thick. The rings consist of icy particles that range in size from a few centimeters to several meters across. **Figure 15** shows a close-up view of Saturn's rings.

NASA Goes to Saturn Launched in 1997, the *Cassini* spacecraft is designed to study Saturn's rings, its moons, and its atmosphere. It will return more than 300,000 color images, beginning in 2004.

Figure 15 *The different colors in this* Voyager 2 *image of Saturn's rings show differences in the chemical composition.*

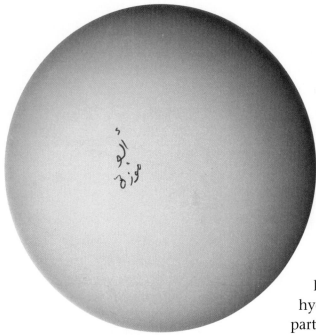

Figure 16 *This image of Uranus was taken by* Voyager 2 *at a distance of 9.1 million kilometers.*

Uranus Statistics	
Distance from sun	**2.7** light-hours
Period of rotation	**17** hours, **14** minutes (R)*
Period of revolution	**83** years, **274** days
Diameter	**51,118** km
Density	**1.27** g/cm^3
Temperature	**−214°C**
Gravity	**89%** of Earth's

*R = retrograde rotation

Uranus—A Small Giant Uranus (YOOR uh nuhs) was discovered by the English amateur astronomer William Herschel in 1781. Viewed through a telescope, Uranus looks like a feature-less blue-green disk. The atmosphere is mainly hydrogen and methane gas, which absorbs the red part of sunlight very strongly. Uranus and Neptune are much smaller than Jupiter and Saturn, and yet they have similar densities. This suggests that they have lower percentages of light elements and more water in their interiors.

A Tilted Planet Uranus has about 63 times the volume of Earth and is nearly 15 times as massive. One especially unusual quality of Uranus is that it is tipped over on its side—the axis of rotation is tilted by almost 90° and lies almost in the plane of its orbit. **Figure 17** shows how far Uranus's axis is inclined. For part of a Uranus year, one pole points toward the sun while the other pole is in darkness. At the other end of Uranus's orbit the poles are reversed. Scientists suggest that early in its history, Uranus got hit by a massive object that tipped the planet over.

Figure 17 *Uranus's axis of rotation is tilted so that it is nearly parallel to the plane of Uranus's orbit. In contrast, the axes of most other planets are closer to being perpendicular to the plane of their orbits.*

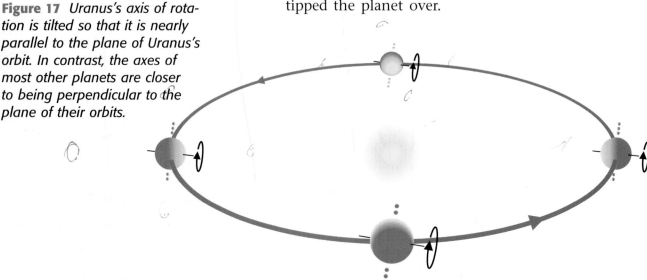

Surviving Space

Imagine that it is the year 2120 and you are the pilot of an interplanetary space-craft on your way to explore Pluto. In the middle of your journey, your navigation system malfunctions, giving you only one chance to land safely. You will not be able to make it to your original destination or back to Earth, so you must choose one of the other planets to land on. Your equipment includes two years' supply of food, water, and air. You will be stranded on the planet you choose until a rescue mission can be launched from Earth. Which planet will you choose to land on? How would your choice of this planet increase your chances of survival? Explain why you did not choose each of the other planets.

Neptune—The Blue World Irregularities in the orbit of Uranus suggested to early astronomers that there must be another planet beyond Uranus whose gravitational force causes Uranus to move off its predicted path. By using the predictions of the new planet's orbit, astronomers discovered the planet Neptune in 1846.

The Atmosphere of Neptune The *Voyager 2* spacecraft sent back images that gave us much new information about the nature of Neptune's atmosphere. Although the composition of Neptune's atmosphere is nearly the same as that of Uranus's atmosphere, Neptune's atmosphere contains belts of clouds that are much more visible. At the time of *Voyager 2*'s visit, Neptune had a Great Dark Spot, similar to the Great Red Spot on Jupiter. And like the interiors of Jupiter and Saturn, Neptune's interior releases energy to its outer layers. This helps the warm gases rise and the cool gases sink, setting up the wind patterns in the atmosphere that create the belts of clouds. *Voyager 2* images also revealed that Neptune has a set of very narrow rings.

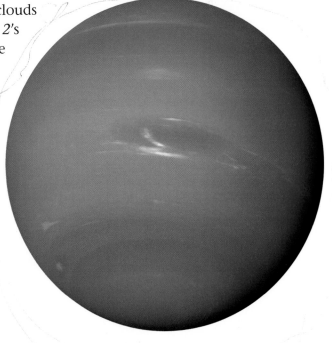

Figure 18 *This* Voyager 2 *image of Neptune, taken at a distance of more than 7 million kilometers, shows the Great Dark Spot as well as some bright cloud bands.*

Neptune Statistics	
Distance from sun	**4.2** light-hours
Period of rotation	**16** hours, **7** minutes
Period of revolution	**163** years, **265** days
Diameter	**49,528** km
Density	**1.64** g/cm³
Temperature	**−225°**C
Gravity	**112%** of Earth's

Figure 19 *This Hubble Space Telescope image is one of the clearest ever taken of Pluto (left) and its moon, Charon.*

Pluto Statistics	
Distance from sun	**5.5** light-hours
Period of rotation	**6** days, **9** hours (R)*
Period of revolution	**248** years
Diameter	**2,390** km
Density	**2.05** g/cm^3
Surface temperature	**−236°C**
Surface gravity	**6%** of Earth's

*R = retrograde rotation

Figure 20 *An artist's view of the sun and Charon from Pluto shows just how little light and heat Pluto receives from the sun.*

Pluto—A Double Planet? Pluto is the farthest planet from the sun. It is also the smallest planet—less than half the size of Mercury. Another reason Pluto is unusual is that its moon, Charon (KER uhn), is more than half its size! In fact, Charon is the largest satellite relative to its planet in the solar system. **Figure 19** shows Pluto and Charon together.

From Earth, it is hard to separate the images of Pluto and Charon because they are so far away. **Figure 20** shows just how far away from the sun Pluto and Charon really are—from the surface of Pluto the sun appears to be only a very distant, bright star.

From calculations of Pluto's density, we know that it must be made of rock and ice. A very thin atmosphere of methane has been detected. While Pluto is covered by nitrogen ice, Charon is covered by water ice. Pluto is the only planet that has not been visited by a NASA mission, but plans are underway to finally visit this world and its moon in 2010.

internet connect

sci LINKS
NSTA

TOPIC: The Nine Planets
GO TO: www.scilinks.org
sciLINKS NUMBER: HSTE480

SECTION REVIEW

1. How are the gas giants different from the terrestrial planets?

2. What is so unusual about Uranus's axis of rotation?

3. What conclusion can you draw about a planet's properties just by knowing how far it is from the sun?

4. **Applying Concepts** Why is the word *surface* not included in the statistics for the gas giants?

Terms to Learn

satellite
phases
eclipse

What You'll Do

◆ Describe the current theory for the origin of Earth's moon.
◆ Describe what causes the phases of Earth's moon.
◆ Explain the difference between a solar eclipse and a lunar eclipse.

Moons

Satellites are natural or artificial bodies that revolve around larger bodies like planets. Except for Mercury and Venus, all of the planets have natural satellites called *moons*.

Luna: The Moon of Earth

We know that Earth's moon—also called *Luna*—has a different overall composition from the Earth because its density is much less than Earth's. This tells us that the moon has a lower percentage of heavy elements than the Earth has. The composition of lunar rocks brought back by Apollo astronauts suggests that the composition of the moon is similar to that of the Earth's mantle.

The Surface of the Moon The explorations of the moon's surface by the Apollo astronauts have given us insights about other planets and moons of the solar system. For example, the lunar rocks brought back during the Apollo missions were found to be about 4.6 billion years old. Because these rocks have hardly changed since they formed, we know the solar system itself is about 4.6 billion years old.

In addition, we know that the surfaces of bodies that have no atmospheres preserve a record of almost all the impacts they have had with other objects. As shown in **Figure 22**, the moon's history is written on its face! Because we now know the age of the moon, we can count the number of impact craters on the moon and use that number to calculate the rate of cratering that has occurred since the birth of our solar system. By knowing the rate of cratering, scientists are able to use the number of craters on the surface of any body to estimate how old its surface is—without having to bring back rock samples!

Figure 21 Apollo 17 *astronaut Harrison Schmidt—the first geologist to walk on the moon—samples the lunar soil.*

Figure 22 *This image of the moon was taken by the Galileo spacecraft while on its way to Jupiter. The large dark areas are lava plains called maria.*

Moon Statistics	
Period of rotation	**27** days, **8** hours
Period of revolution	**27** days, **8** hours
Diameter	**3,476** km
Density	**3.34** g/cm^3
Surface temperature	**−170** to **134**°C
Surface gravity	**17%** of Earth's

Lunar Origins Before rock samples from the Apollo missions confirmed the composition of the moon, there were three popular explanations for the formation of the moon: (1) it was a separate body captured by Earth's gravity, (2) it formed at the same time and from the same materials as the Earth, and (3) the newly formed Earth was spinning so fast that a piece flew off and became the moon. Each idea had problems. If the moon were captured by Earth's gravity, it would have a completely different composition from that of Earth, which is not the case. On the other hand, if the moon formed at the same time as the Earth or as a spin off of the Earth, the moon would have exactly the same composition as Earth, which it doesn't.

The current theory is that a large, Mars-sized object collided with Earth while the Earth was still forming. The collision was so violent that part of the Earth's mantle was blasted into orbit around Earth to form the moon. This theory is consistent with the composition of the lunar rocks brought back by the Apollo missions.

Formation of the Moon

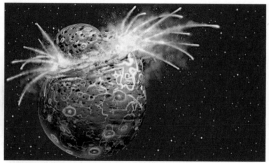

1 Impact
About 4.6 billion years ago, when Earth was still mostly molten, a large body collided with Earth. Scientists reason that the object must have been large enough to blast part of Earth's mantle into space, because the composition of the moon is similar to Earth's mantle.

2 Ejection
The resulting debris began to revolve around the Earth within a few hours of the impact. This debris consisted of mantle material from Earth and the impacting body as well as part of the iron core of the impacting body.

3 Formation
Soon after the giant impact, the clumps of material ejected into orbit around Earth began to join together to form the moon. Much later, as the moon cooled, additional impacts created deep basins and fractured the moon's surface. Lunar lava flowed from those cracks and flooded the basins to form the lunar maria we see today.

Phases of the Moon   From Earth, one of the most noticeable aspects of the moon is its continually changing appearance. Within a month, its Earthward face changes from a fully lit circle to a thin crescent and then back to a circle. These different appearances of the moon result from its changing position with respect to the Earth and the sun. As the moon revolves around the Earth, the amount of sunlight on the side of the moon that faces the Earth changes. The different appearances of the moon due to its changing position are called **phases.** The phases of the moon are shown in **Figure 23.**

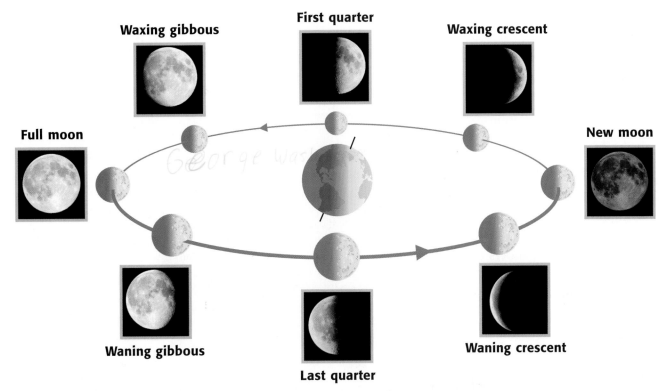

Waxing gibbous   **First quarter**   **Waxing crescent**

Full moon   **New moon**

Waning gibbous   **Waning crescent**

Last quarter

Figure 23 *The relative positions of the moon, sun, and Earth determine which phase the moon is in. The photo insets show how the moon looks from Earth at each phase.*

Waxing and Waning   When the moon is *waxing*, it means that the sunlit fraction we can see from Earth is getting larger. When it is *waning*, the sunlit fraction is getting smaller. Notice in Figure 23 that even as the phases of the moon change, the total amount of sunlight the moon gets remains the same. Half the moon is always in sunlight, just as half the Earth is always in sunlight. But because the period of rotation for the moon is the same as its period of revolution, on Earth we always see the same side of the moon. If you lived on the far side of the moon, you would see the sun for half of each lunar day, but you would never see the Earth!

Quick Lab

Clever Insight

Pythagoras (540–510 B.C.) and Aristotle (384–322 B.C.) used observations of lunar eclipses and a little logic to figure out that Earth is a sphere. Can you?

1. Cut out a circle of **heavy white paper.** This will represent Earth.

2. Find **two spherical objects** and several other **objects** with different shapes.

3. Hold each object up in front of a **lamp** (representing the sun) so that its shadow falls on the white paper circle.

4. Rotate your objects in all directions, and record the shapes of the shadows they make.

5. Which objects always cast a curved shadow?

Eclipses An **eclipse** occurs when the shadow of one celestial body falls on another. A *lunar eclipse* happens when the Earth comes between the sun and the moon, and the shadow of the Earth falls on the moon. A *solar eclipse* happens when the moon comes between the Earth and the sun, and the shadow of the moon falls on part of Earth.

Solar Eclipses By a remarkable coincidence, the moon in the sky appears to be nearly the same size as the sun. So during a solar eclipse, the disk of the moon almost always covers the disk of the sun. However, because the moon's orbit is not completely circular, sometimes the moon is farther away from the Earth, and a thin ring of sunlight shows around the outer edge of the moon. This type of solar eclipse is called an *annular eclipse.* **Figure 24** illustrates the position of the Earth and the moon during a solar eclipse.

Solar eclipse

Figure 24 *Because the shadow of the moon on Earth is small, a solar eclipse can be viewed from only a few locations.*

NEVER look directly at the sun! You can permanently damage your eyes.

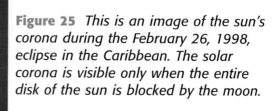

Figure 25 *This is an image of the sun's corona during the February 26, 1998, eclipse in the Caribbean. The solar corona is visible only when the entire disk of the sun is blocked by the moon.*

Lunar Eclipses As you can see in **Figure 26,** the view during a lunar eclipse is also spectacular. Earth's atmosphere acts like a lens and bends some of the sunlight into the Earth's shadow, and the interaction of the sunlight with the molecules in the atmosphere filters out the blue light. With the blue part of the light removed, most of the remaining light that illuminates the moon is red.

Figure 26 *Because of atmospheric effects on Earth, the moon can have a reddish color during a lunar eclipse.*

Lunar eclipse

Figure 27 *During a lunar eclipse, the moon passes within the Earth's shadow.*

The Moon's Orbit Is Tilted! From our discussion of the moon's phases, you might now be asking the question, "Why don't we see solar and lunar eclipses every month?" The answer is that the moon's orbit around the Earth is tilted—by about 5°—with respect to the orbit of the Earth around the sun. This tilt is enough to place the moon out of Earth's shadow for most full moons and the Earth out of the moon's shadow for most new moons.

SECTION REVIEW

1. What evidence suggests that Earth's moon formed from a giant impact?

2. Why do we always see the same side of the moon?

3. How are lunar eclipses different from solar eclipses?

4. **Analyzing Methods** How does knowing the age of a lunar rock help astronomers estimate the age of the surface of a planet with no atmosphere?

MATH BREAK

Orbits Within Orbits

The average distance between the Earth and the moon is about 384,400 km. As you have read, the average distance between the Earth and the sun is 1 AU, or about 150,000,000 km. Assume that the orbit of the Earth around the sun and the orbit of the moon around the Earth are perfectly circular. Using the distances given above, calculate the maximum and minimum distances between the moon and the sun.

The Moons of Other Planets

The moons of the other planets range in size from very small to as large as terrestrial planets. All of the gas giants have multiple moons, and scientists are still discovering new moons. Some moons have very elongated, or elliptical, orbits, and some even revolve around their planet backward! Many of the very small moons may be captured asteroids. As we are learning from recent space missions, moons can be some of the most bizarre and interesting places in the solar system!

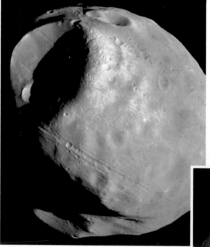

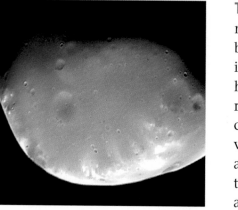

Figure 28 *Above is Mars's largest moon, Phobos, which is 28 km long. At right is the smaller moon, Deimos, which is 16 km long.*

The Moons of Mars Mars's two moons, Phobos and Deimos, are both small satellites that have irregular shapes. The two moons have very dark surfaces that reflect even less light than asphalt does. The surface materials are very similar to those found in asteroids, and scientists speculate that these two moons are probably captured asteroids.

The Moons of Jupiter Jupiter has a total of 28 known moons. The four largest—Ganymede, Callisto, Io, and Europa—were discovered in 1610 by Galileo and are known as the Galilean satellites. The largest moon, Ganymede, is even larger than the planet Mercury! Many of the smaller satellites are probably captured asteroids.

Moving outward from Jupiter, the first Galilean satellite is Io (IE oh), a truly bizarre world. Io is caught in a gravitational tug-of-war between Jupiter and Io's nearest neighbor, the moon Europa. This constant tugging stretches Io a little, causing it to heat up. Because of this, Io is the most volcanically active body in the solar system!

Recent pictures of the moon Europa support the idea that liquid water may lie beneath the moon's icy surface. This has many scientists wondering if life could have evolved in the subterranean oceans of Europa.

Figure 29 *At left is a Galileo image of Jupiter's innermost moon, Io. At right is a Galileo image of Jupiter's fourth largest moon, Europa.*

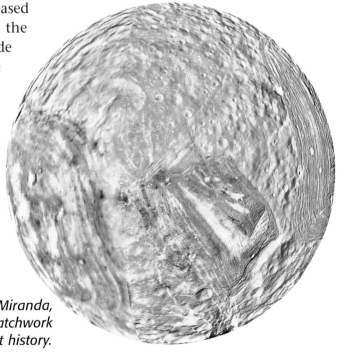

The Moons of Saturn Saturn has a total of 30 known moons. Most of these moons are small bodies made mostly of water ice with some rocky material. The largest satellite, Titan, was discovered in 1655 by Christiaan Huygens. In 1980, the *Voyager 1* spacecraft flew past Titan and discovered a hazy orange atmosphere, as shown in **Figure 30.** Titan's atmosphere is similar to what Earth's atmosphere may have been like before life began to evolve. In 1997, NASA launched the *Cassini* spacecraft to study Saturn and its moons, including Titan. By studying Titan, scientists hope to answer some of the questions about how life began on Earth.

Self-Check

What is one major difference between Titan and the early Earth that would suggest that there probably isn't life on Titan? *(See page 200 to check your answer.)*

Figure 30 *Titan is one of only two moons that have a thick atmosphere. Titan's hazy orange atmosphere is made of nitrogen plus several other gases, such as methane.*

The Moons of Uranus Uranus has 21 moons, three of which were just discovered by ground-based telescopes during the summer of 1999. Like the moons of Saturn, the four largest moons are made of ice and rock and are heavily cratered. The little moon Miranda, shown in **Figure 31,** has some of the most unusual features in the solar system. Miranda's surface includes smooth, cratered plains as well as regions with grooves and cliffs up to 20 km high. Current ideas suggest that Miranda may have been hit and broken apart in the past but was able to come together again, leaving a patchwork surface.

Figure 31 *This* Voyager 2 *image shows Miranda, the most unusual moon of Uranus. Its patchwork terrain indicates that it has had a violent history.*

The Moons of Neptune Neptune has eight moons, only one of which is large. This moon, Triton, revolves around the planet in a *retrograde,* or "backward," orbit, suggesting that it may have been captured by Neptune's gravity. Triton has a very thin atmosphere made mostly of nitrogen gas. The surface of Triton consists mainly of frozen nitrogen and methane. *Voyager 2* images revealed that it is geologically active. "Ice volcanoes," or geysers, were seen ejecting nitrogen gas high into the atmosphere. The other seven moons of Neptune are small, rocky worlds much like the smaller moons of Saturn and Jupiter.

Figure 32 *This* Voyager 2 *image shows Neptune's largest moon, Triton. The polar icecap currently facing the sun may have a slowly evaporating layer of nitrogen ice, adding to Triton's thin atmosphere.*

The Moon of Pluto Pluto's only moon, Charon, was discovered in 1978. Charon's period of revolution is the same as Pluto's period of rotation—about 6.4 days. This means that one side of Pluto always faces Charon. In other words, if you stood on the surface of Pluto, Charon would always occupy the same place in the sky. Imagine Earth's moon staying in the same place every night! Because Charon's orbit around Pluto is tilted with respect to Pluto's orbit around the sun, as seen from Earth, Pluto is sometimes eclipsed by Charon. But don't hold your breath; this happens only once every 120 years!

SECTION REVIEW

1. What makes Io the most volcanically active body in the solar system?

2. Why is Saturn's moon Titan of so much interest to scientists studying the origins of life on Earth?

3. What two properties of Neptune's moon Triton make it unusual?

4. **Identifying Relationships** Charon always stays in the same place in Pluto's sky, but the moon always moves across Earth's sky. What causes this difference?

internetconnect

*SCi*LINKS
NSTA

TOPIC: The Moons of Other Planets
GO TO: www.scilinks.org
*sci***LINKS NUMBER:** HSTE495

Terms to Learn

comet   meteoroid
asteroid   meteorite
asteroid belt   meteor

What You'll Do

◆ Explain why comets, asteroids, and meteoroids are important to the study of the formation of the solar system.
◆ Compare the different types of asteroids with the different types of meteoroids.
◆ Describe the risks to life on Earth from cosmic impacts.

Small Bodies in the Solar System

In addition to planets and moons, the solar system contains many other types of objects, including comets, asteroids, and meteoroids. As you will see, these objects play an important role in the study of the origins of the solar system.

Comets

A **comet** is a small body of ice, rock, and cosmic dust loosely packed together. Because of their composition, some scientists refer to comets as "dirty snowballs." Comets originate from the cold, outer solar system. Nothing much has happened to them since the birth of the solar system some 4.6 billion years ago. Because comets are probably the leftovers from the process of planet formation, each comet is a sample of the early solar system. Scientists want to learn more about comets in order to piece together the chemical and physical history of the solar system.

Comet Tails When a comet passes close enough to the sun, solar radiation heats the water ice so that the comet gives off gas and dust in the form of a long tail, as shown in **Figure 33**. Sometimes a comet has two tails—an *ion tail* and a *dust tail*. The ion tail consists of electrically charged particles called *ions*. The solid center of a comet is called its *nucleus*. Comet nuclei can range in size from less than half a kilometer to more than 100 km in diameter. **Figure 34** shows the different features of a comet when it passes close to the sun.

Figure 33 *Comet Hale-Bopp appeared in North American skies in the spring of 1997.*

Figure 34 *This image shows the physical features of a comet when it is close to the sun. The nucleus of a comet is hidden by brightly lit gases and dust.*

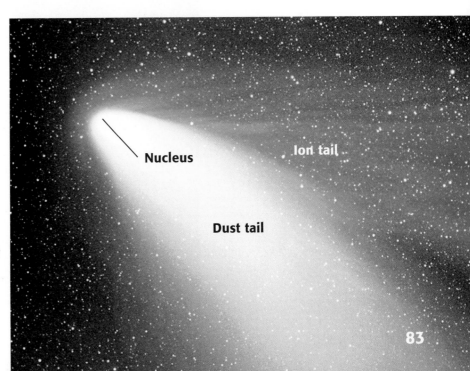

Nucleus

Ion tail

Dust tail

83

Figure 35 *When a comet's highly elliptical orbit carries it close to the sun, it can develop one or two tails. As shown here, the ion tail is blue and the dust tail is yellow.*

Comet Orbits All orbits are *ellipses*—circles that are somewhat stretched out of shape. Whereas the orbits of most planets are nearly circular, comet orbits are highly elliptical—they are very elongated.

Notice in **Figure 35** that a comet's ion tail always points directly away from the sun. This is because the ion tail is blown away from the sun by the solar wind, which also consists of ions. The dust tail tends to follow the comet's orbit around the sun and does not always point away from the sun. When a comet is close to the sun its tail can extend millions of kilometers through space!

Comet Origins Where do comets come from? Many scientists think they may come from a spherical region, called the *Oort* (ohrt) *cloud,* that surrounds the solar system. When the gravity of a passing planet or star disturbs part of this cloud, comets can be pulled in toward the sun. Another recently discovered region where comets exist is called the *Kuiper* (KIE per) *belt,* which is the region outside the orbit of Neptune. These two regions where comets orbit are shown in **Figure 36.**

Figure 36 *The Kuiper belt is a disk-shaped region that extends outward from the orbit of Neptune. The Oort cloud is a spherical region far beyond the orbit of Pluto.*

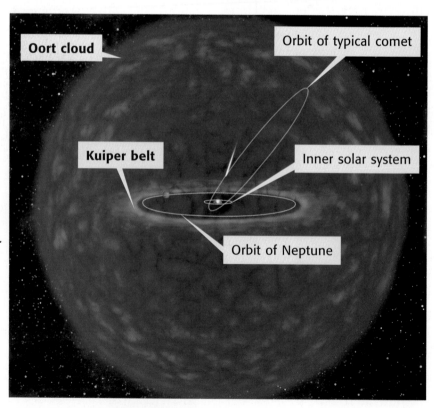

Oort cloud

Orbit of typical comet

Kuiper belt

Inner solar system

Orbit of Neptune

Asteroids

Asteroids are small, rocky bodies in orbit around the sun. They range in size from a few meters to more than 900 km in diameter. Asteroids have irregular shapes, although some of the larger ones are spherical. Most asteroids orbit the sun in a wide region between the orbits of Mars and Jupiter, called the **asteroid belt.** Like comets, asteroids are thought to be material left over from the formation of the solar system.

Types of Asteroids Asteroids can have a variety of compositions, depending on where they are located within the asteroid belt. In the outermost region of the asteroid belt, asteroids have dark reddish brown to black surfaces, which may indicate that they are rich in organic material. A little closer to the sun, asteroids have dark gray surfaces, indicating that they are rich in carbon. In the innermost part of the asteroid belt are light gray asteroids that have either a stony or metallic composition. **Figure 38** shows some examples of what some of the asteroids may look like.

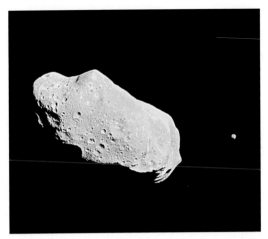

Figure 37 *The asteroid Ida has a small companion asteroid that orbits it called Dactyl. Ida is about 52 km long.*

Figure 38 *The asteroid belt is a disk-shaped region located between the orbits of Mars and Jupiter.*

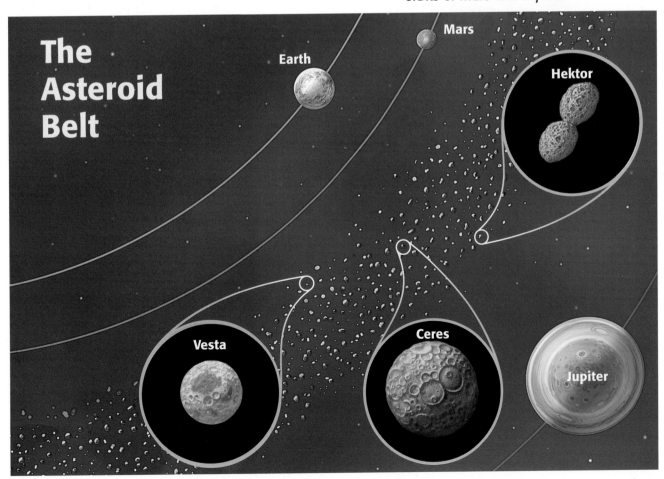

The Asteroid Belt

Earth

Mars

Hektor

Vesta

Ceres

Jupiter

Meteoroids

A **meteoroid** is a small, rocky body orbiting the sun. Meteoroids are similar to asteroids, but they are much smaller. In fact, most meteoroids probably come from asteroids. If a meteoroid enters Earth's atmosphere and strikes the ground, it is then called a **meteorite.** When a meteoroid falls into Earth's atmosphere, it is usually traveling at such a high speed that its surface heats up and melts. As it burns up, the meteoroid glows red hot and gives off an enormous amount of light. From the ground, we see a spectacular streak of light, or a shooting star. The bright streak of light caused by a meteoroid or comet dust burning up in the atmosphere is called a **meteor.**

Meteor Showers Many of the meteors that we see come from very small (dust-sized to pebble-sized) rocks and can be seen on almost any night if you are far enough away from the city to avoid the glare of its lights. At certain times of the year, you can see large numbers of meteors, as shown in **Figure 39.** These events are called *meteor showers.* Meteor showers occur when Earth passes through the dusty debris left behind in the orbit of a comet.

Types of Meteorites Like their relatives the asteroids, meteorites have a variety of compositions. The three major types of meteorites—stony, metallic, and stony-iron—are shown in **Figure 40.** Many of the stony meteorites probably come from carbon-rich asteroids and may contain organic materials and water. Scientists use meteorites to study the early solar system. Like comets and asteroids, meteoroids are some of the building blocks of planets.

Figure 39 *Meteors are the streaks of light caused by meteoroids as they burn up in Earth's atmosphere.*

Figure 40 *There are three major types of meteorites.*

Stony meteorite
rocky material

Metallic meteorite
iron and nickel

Stony-iron meteorite
rocky material, iron, and nickel

The Role of Impacts in the Solar System

Planets and moons that have no atmosphere have many more impact craters than those that do have atmospheres. Look at **Figure 41.** The Earth's moon has many more impact craters than the Earth because it has no atmosphere or tectonic activity. Fewer objects land on Earth because Earth's atmosphere acts like a shield. Smaller bodies burn up before they ever reach the surface. On the moon, there is nothing to stop them! Also, most craters left on Earth have been erased due to weathering, erosion, and tectonic activity.

Figure 41 *The surface of the moon preserves a record of billions of years of cosmic impacts.*

Impacts on Earth Objects smaller than about 10 m across usually burn up in the atmosphere, causing a meteor. Larger objects are more likely to strike Earth's surface. In order to estimate the risk of cosmic impacts, we need to consider how often large impacts occur.

The number of large objects that could collide with Earth is relatively small. Scientists estimate that impacts powerful enough to cause a natural disaster might occur once every few thousand years. An impact large enough to cause a global catastrophe—such as the extinction of the dinosaurs—is estimated to occur once every 30 million to 50 million years on average.

SECTION REVIEW

1. Why is the study of comets, asteroids, and meteoroids important in understanding the formation of the solar system?

2. Why do a comet's two tails often point in different directions?

3. Describe one reason asteroids may become a natural resource in the future.

4. **Analyzing Viewpoints** Do you think the government should spend money on programs to search for asteroids and comets with Earth-crossing orbits? Discuss why.

internet connect

sci LINKS

NSTA

TOPIC: Comets, Asteroids, and Meteoroids
GO TO: www.scilinks.org
*sci*LINKS NUMBER: HSTE500

Making Models Lab

Eclipses

As Earth and the moon revolve around the sun, the Earth and the moon both cast shadows into space. An eclipse happens when one planetary body passes through the shadow of another. You can demonstrate how an eclipse happens by using clay models of planetary bodies.

MATERIALS

- modeling clay
- metric ruler
- sheet of notebook paper
- small flashlight

Procedure

1. Make two balls out of the modeling clay. One ball should have a diameter of about 4 cm and will represent the Earth. The other should have a diameter of about 1 cm and will represent the moon.

2. Place the two balls about 15 cm apart on the sheet of paper.

3. Hold the flashlight approximately 15 cm away from the larger ball. The flashlight and the two balls should be in a straight line. Keep the flashlight at about the same level as the clay. When the whole class is ready, your teacher will turn off the lights.

4. Turn on your flashlight. Shine the light on the closer ball, and sketch your model in your ScienceLog. Include the beam of light in your drawing.

5. Move the flashlight to the opposite side of the paper. The flashlight should now be about 15 cm away from the smaller clay ball. Repeat step 4.

Analysis

6. What does the flashlight in your model represent?

7. As viewed from Earth, what event did your model represent in step 4? in step 5?

8. As viewed from the moon, what event did your model represent in step 4? in step 5?

9. According to your model, how often would solar and lunar eclipses happen? Is this accurate? Explain.

Discovery Lab

Phases of the Moon

When the moon is full, it's easy to see. But you may have wondered exactly what happens when the moon appears as a crescent or when you cannot see the moon at all. Does the Earth cast its shadow on the moon? In this activity, you will discover how and why the moon appears as it does in each phase.

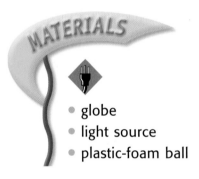

MATERIALS

- globe
- light source
- plastic-foam ball

Procedure

1. Place your globe near the light source. Be sure that the North Pole is tilted toward the light. Rotate the globe so that the state of Texas faces the light.

2. Using the ball as your model of the moon, move the moon between the Earth (the globe) and the sun (the light). The side of the moon that faces the Earth will be in darkness. Write your observations of this new-moon phase in your ScienceLog.

3. Continue to move the moon in its orbit around the Earth. When part of the moon is illuminated by the light, as viewed from Earth, the moon is in the crescent phase. Add your observations to your ScienceLog.

4. If you have time, you may draw your own moon-phase diagram.

Analysis

5. About two weeks after the new moon, the entire moon is visible in the sky. Move the ball to show this event.

6. What other phases can you add to your diagram? For example, when do the quarter moons appear?

7. Explain why the moon sometimes appears as a crescent to viewers on Earth.

Chapter Highlights

Vocabulary

astronomical unit (AU) *(p. 64)*
terrestrial planets *(p. 65)*
prograde rotation *(p. 66)*
retrograde rotation *(p. 66)*
gas giants *(p. 70)*

Section Notes

- The solar system has nine planets.
- Distances within the solar system can be expressed in astronomical units (AU) or in light-minutes.
- The inner four planets, called the terrestrial planets, are small and rocky.
- The outer planets, with the exception of Pluto, are gas giants.

- By learning about the properties of the planets, we get a better understanding of global processes on Earth.

Labs

Why Do They Wander? *(p. 164)*

Vocabulary

satellite *(p. 75)*
phases *(p. 77)*
eclipse *(p. 78)*

Section Notes

- Earth's moon probably formed from a giant impact on Earth.
- The moon's phases are caused by the moon's orbit around the Earth. At different times of the month, we view different amounts of sunlight on the moon because of the moon's position relative to the sun and the Earth.
- Lunar eclipses occur when the Earth's shadow falls on the moon.

☑ Skills Check

Math Concepts

INTERPLANETARY DISTANCES The distances between planets are so vast that scientists have invented new units of measurement to describe them. One of these units is the astronomical unit (AU). One AU is equal to the average distance between the Earth and the sun—about 150 million kilometers. If you wanted to get to the sun from the Earth in 10 hours, you would have to travel at a rate of 15,000,000 km/h!

$$\frac{150 \text{ million kilometers}}{15 \text{ million kilometers/hour}} = 10 \text{ hours}$$

Visual Understanding

AXIAL TILT A planet's axis of rotation is an imaginary line that runs through the center of the planet and comes out its north and south poles. The tilt of a planet's axis is the angle between the planet's axis and the plane of the planet's orbit around the sun.

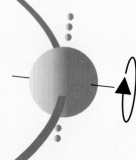

SECTION 2

- Solar eclipses occur when the moon is between the sun and the Earth, causing the moon's shadow to fall on the Earth.

- The plane of the moon's orbit around the Earth is tilted by 5° relative to the plane of the Earth's orbit around the sun.

SECTION 3

Vocabulary

comet *(p. 83)*

asteroid *(p. 85)*

asteroid belt *(p. 85)*

meteoroid *(p. 86)*

meteorite *(p. 86)*

meteor *(p. 86)*

Section Notes

- Comets are small bodies of water ice and cosmic dust left over from the formation of the solar system.

- When a comet is heated by the sun, the ices convert to gases that leave the nucleus and form an ion tail. Dust also comes off a comet to form a second kind of tail called a dust tail.

- All orbits are ellipses—circles that have been stretched out.

- Asteroids are small, rocky bodies that orbit the sun between the orbits of Mars and Jupiter.

- Meteoroids are small, rocky bodies that probably come from asteroids.

- Meteor showers occur when Earth passes through the dusty debris along a comet's orbit.

- Impacts that cause natural disasters occur once every few thousand years, but impacts large enough to cause global extinctions occur once every 30 million to 50 million years.

---

internetconnect

GO TO: go.hrw.com

Visit the **HRW** Web site for a variety of learning tools related to this chapter. Just type in the keyword:

KEYWORD: HSTFAM

GO TO: www.scilinks.org

Visit the **National Science Teachers Association** on-line Web site for Internet resources related to this chapter. Just type in the *sci*LINKS number for more information about the topic:

TOPIC: The Nine Planets	*sci*LINKS NUMBER: HSTE480
TOPIC: Studying Earth from Space	*sci*LINKS NUMBER: HSTE485
TOPIC: The Earth's Moon	*sci*LINKS NUMBER: HSTE490
TOPIC: The Moons of Other Planets	*sci*LINKS NUMBER: HSTE495
TOPIC: Comets, Asteroids, and Meteoroids	*sci*LINKS NUMBER: HSTE500

Chapter Review

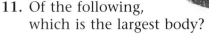

USING VOCABULARY

For each pair of terms, explain the difference in their meaning.

1. terrestrial planet/gas giant

2. asteroid/comet

3. meteor/meteorite

4. satellite/moon

5. Kuiper belt/Oort cloud

To complete the following sentences, choose the correct term from each pair of terms listed below:

6. The average distance between the sun and the Earth is 1 __?__ . (*light-minute,* or *AU*)

7. A small rock in space is called a __?__ . (*meteor* or *meteoroid*)

8. The time it takes for the Earth to __?__ around the sun is one year. (*rotate* or *revolve*)

9. Most lunar craters are the result of __?__ . (*volcanoes* or *impacts*)

UNDERSTANDING CONCEPTS

Multiple Choice

10. When do annular eclipses occur?
    a. every solar eclipse
    b. when the moon is closest to the Earth
    c. only during full moon
    d. when the moon is farthest from the Earth

11. Of the following, which is the largest body?
    a. the moon
    b. Pluto
    c. Mercury
    d. Ganymede

12. Which is not true about impacts?
    a. They are very destructive.
    b. They can bring water to dry worlds.
    c. They only occurred as the solar system formed.
    d. They can help us do remote geology.

13. Which of these planets does not have any moons?
    a. Mercury
    b. Mars
    c. Uranus
    d. none of the above

14. What is the most current theory for the formation of Earth's moon?
    a. The moon formed from a collision between another body and the Earth.
    b. The moon was captured by the Earth.
    c. The moon formed at the same time as the Earth.
    d. The moon formed by spinning off from the Earth early in its history.

15. Liquid water cannot exist on the surface of Mars because
    a. the temperature is too hot.
    b. liquid water once existed there.
    c. the gravity of Mars is too weak.
    d. the atmospheric pressure is too low.

16. Which of the following planets is not a terrestrial planet?
    a. Mercury
    b. Mars
    c. Earth
    d. Pluto

17. All of the gas giants have ring systems.
    a. true
    b. false

18. A comet's ion tail consists of
    a. dust.
    b. electrically charged particles of gas.
    c. light rays.
    d. comet nuclei.

Short Answer

19. Do solar eclipses occur at the full moon or at the new moon? Explain why.

20. How do we know there are small meteoroids and dust in space?

21. Which planets have retrograde rotation?

Concept Mapping

22. Use the following terms to create a concept map: solar system, terrestrial planets, gas giants, moons, comets, asteroids, meteoroids.

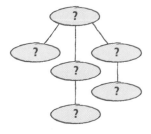

CRITICAL THINKING AND PROBLEM SOLVING

23. Even though we haven't yet retrieved any rock samples from Mercury's surface for radiometric dating, we know that the surface of Mercury is much older than that of Earth. How do we know this?

24. Where in the solar system might we search for life, and why?

25. Is the far side of the moon always dark? Explain your answer.

26. If we could somehow bring Europa as close to the sun as the Earth is, 1 AU, what do you think would happen?

MATH IN SCIENCE

27. Suppose you have an object that weighs 200 N (45 lbs.) on Earth. How much would that same object weigh on each of the other terrestrial planets?

INTERPRETING GRAPHICS

The graph below shows density versus mass for Earth, Uranus, and Neptune. Mass is given in Earth masses—the mass of Earth equals one. The relative volumes for the planets are shown by the size of each circle.

Density vs. Mass for Earth, Uranus, and Neptune

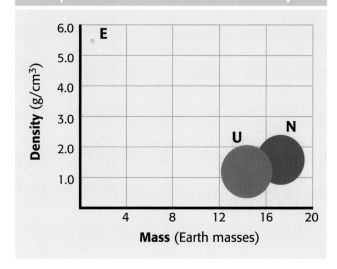

28. Which planet is denser, Uranus or Neptune? How can you tell?

29. You can see that although Earth has the smallest mass, it has the highest density. How can Earth be the densest of the three when Uranus and Neptune have so much more mass?

Reading Check-up

Take a minute to review your answers to the Pre-Reading Questions found at the bottom of page 62. Have your answers changed? If necessary, revise your answers based on what you have learned since you began this chapter.

Is Pluto Really a Planet?

We have all learned that Pluto is the planet farthest from the sun in our solar system. Since it was discovered in 1930, astronomers have grouped it with the outer planets. However, Pluto has not been a perfect fit in this group. Unlike the other outer planets, which are large and gaseous, Pluto is small and made of rock and ice. Pluto also has a very elliptical orbit that is unlike its neighboring planets. These and other factors once fueled a debate as to whether Pluto should be classified as a planet.

◀ *A composite drawing of Pluto, Charon, Triton, and Halley's comet*

Kuiper Belt

In the early 1990s, astronomers discovered a belt of comets outside the orbit of Neptune. The belt was named the Kuiper Belt in honor of Gerard Kuiper, a Dutch-born American astronomer. So what does this belt have to do with Pluto? Given its proximity to Pluto, some astronomers thought Pluto might actually be a large comet that escaped the Kuiper Belt.

Comet?

Comets are basically dirty snowballs made of ice and cosmic dust. Pluto is about 30 percent ice and 70 percent rock. This is much more rock than is in a normal comet. Also, at 2,390 km in diameter, Pluto is much larger than a comet. For example, Halley's comet is only about 20 km in diameter. Even so, Pluto's orbit is very similar to that of a comet. Both have orbits that are very elliptical.

Escaped Moon?

Pluto and its moon, Charon, have much in common with Neptune's moon, Triton. All three have atmospheres made of nitrogen and methane, which suggests that they share a similar origin. And because Triton has a "backward" orbit compared with Neptune's other moons, it may have been captured by Neptune's gravity. Some astronomers thought Pluto might also have been captured by Neptune but broke free by some cataclysmic event.

New Category of Planet?

Some astronomers suggested that perhaps we should create a new subclass of planets, such as the ice planets, to add to the gas-giant and terrestrial classification we currently use. Pluto would be the only planet in this class, but scientists think we are likely to find others.

As there are more new discoveries, astronomers will likely continue to debate these issues. To date, however, Pluto is still officially considered a planet. This decision is firmly grounded by the fact that Pluto has been called a planet since its discovery.

You Decide

▶ Do some additional research about Pluto, the Kuiper Belt, and comets. What do you think Pluto should be called?

Science Fiction

"The Mad Moon"

by Stanley Weinbaum

The third largest satellite of Jupiter, called Io, can be a hard place to live. Although living comfortably is possible in the small cities at the polar regions, most of the moon is hot, humid, and jungle-like. There is also *blancha,* a kind of tropical fever that causes hallucinations, weakness, and vicious headaches. Without proper medication a person with *blancha* can go mad or even die.

Just 2 years ago, Grant Calthorpe was a wealthy hunter and famous sportsman. Then the gold market crashed, and he lost his entire fortune. What better way for an experienced hunter and explorer to get a fresh start than to set out for a little space travel? The opportunity to rekindle his fortune by gathering ferva leaves so that they can be converted into useful human medications lures Calthorpe to Io.

There he meets the loonies—creatures with balloon heads and silly grins atop *really* long necks. The three-legged parcat Oliver quickly becomes Calthorpe's pet and helps him cope with the loneliness and the slinkers. The slinkers, well, they would just as soon *not* have Calthorpe around at all, but they are pretty good at making even this famous outdoorsman wonder why he ever took this job.

In "The Mad Moon," you'll discover a dozen adventures with Grant Calthorpe as he struggles to stay alive—and sane. Read Stanley Weinbaum's story "The Mad Moon" in the *Holt Anthology of Science Fiction.* Enjoy your trip!

The Universe Beyond

Pre-Reading
Questions

1. Why do stars shine?
2. What is a galaxy?
3. How did the universe begin, and how will it end? or will it?

GALAXIES GALORE

If you had a telescope, what would you look for? In the 1920s, astronomer Edwin Hubble chose to look for galaxies much like the NGC 3031 galaxy shown here. Basically, a galaxy is a large group of stars. In 1995 the Hubble Space Telescope was used to develop the single image called the Hubble Deep Field shown below. The segment of sky in that image contains nearly 2,000 galaxies! In this chapter, you will learn about the different types of galaxies.

Hubble Deep Field image

EXPLORING GALAXIES IN THE UNIVERSE

Galaxies are large groupings of millions of stars. But not all galaxies are the same. In this activity, you will explore some of these differences.

Procedure

1. Look at the different galaxies in the Hubble Deep Field image on page 96. (The bright spot with spikes is a star that is much closer to Earth; you can ignore it.)

2. Can you find different types of galaxies? In your ScienceLog, make sketches of at least three different types. Make up a name that describes each type of galaxy.

3. In your ScienceLog, construct a chart to classify, compare, and describe the different characteristics you see in these galaxies.

Analysis

4. Why did you classify the galaxies the way you did?

5. Compare your types of galaxies with those of your classmates. Are there similarities?

Terms to Learn

spectrum
apparent magnitude
absolute magnitude
light-year
parallax

What You'll Do

◆ Describe how color indicates temperature.

◆ Compare absolute magnitude with apparent magnitude, and discuss how each measures brightness.

◆ Describe the difference between the apparent motion of stars and the real motion of stars.

Figure 1 *Because Betelgeuse is red and Rigel is blue, astronomers know that Rigel is the hotter star.*

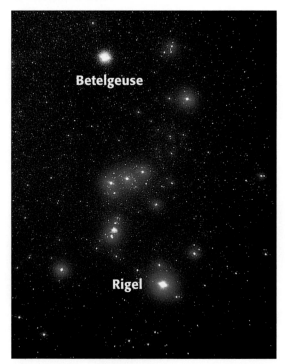

Betelgeuse

Rigel

Stars

Most stars look like faint dots of light in the night sky. But stars are actually huge, hot, brilliant balls of gas trillions of kilometers away from Earth. How do astronomers learn about stars when they are too far away to visit? They study starlight!

Color of Stars

Look closely at the flames on the candle and the Bunsen burner shown here. Which one has the hotter flame? How can you tell? Although artists may speak of *red* as a "hot" color, to a scientist, *red* is a "cool" color. The blue flame of the Bunsen burner is much hotter than the yellow flame of the candle. In the same way, the candle's yellow flame is hotter than the red glowing embers of a campfire.

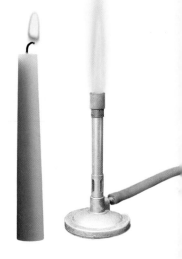

If you look carefully at the night sky, you might notice the different colors of some familiar stars. Betelgeuse (BET uhl jooz), which is red, and Rigel (RIE juhl), which is blue, are the stars that form two corners of the constellation Orion, shown in **Figure 1.** This constellation is easy to see in the evenings during the winter months. Because these two stars are different colors, we can infer that they have different temperatures.

Composition of Stars

When you look at white light through a glass prism, you see a rainbow of colors called a **spectrum.** The spectrum consists of millions of colors, including the ones we recognize as red, orange, yellow, green, blue, indigo, and violet. A hot solid object, like the glowing wire inside a light bulb, gives off a *continuous spectrum*—one that shows all the colors. Astronomers use an instrument called a *spectrograph* to spread starlight out into its colors, just as you might use a prism to spread sunlight. Stars, however, don't have continuous spectra. Because they are not solid objects, stars give off spectra that are different from those of light bulbs.

Hot, Dense Gas Stars are made of various gases that are so dense that they act like a hot solid. For this reason, the "surface" of a star, or the part that we see, gives off a continuous spectrum. But the light we see passes through the star's "atmosphere," which is made of cooler gases than the star itself. A star therefore produces a spectrum with various lines in it. To understand what these lines are, let's look at something you might be more familiar with than stars.

Making an ID Many restaurants use neon signs to attract customers. The gas in a neon sign glows orange-red when an electric current flows through it. If we were to look at the sign with an astronomer's spectrograph, we would not see a continuous spectrum. Instead we would see *emission lines*. Emission lines are bright lines that are made when certain wavelengths of light are given off, or emitted, by hot gases. Only some colors in the spectrum show up, while all of the other colors are missing. Every tube of neon gas, for example, emits light with the same emission lines. Each element has its own unique set of emission lines. Emission lines are like fingerprints for the elements. You can see some of these "fingerprints" in **Figure 2.**

Physics

C O N N E C T I O N

Police use spectrographs to "fingerprint" cars. Automobile manufacturers put trace elements in the paint of cars. Each make of car has its own special paint and therefore its own combination of trace elements. When a car is involved in a hit-and-run accident, the police can identify the make of the car by the paint that is left behind.

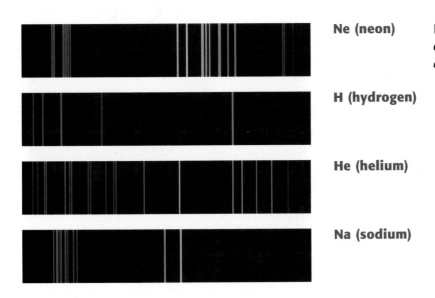

Ne (neon)

H (hydrogen)

He (helium)

Na (sodium)

Figure 2 *Neon gas produces its own characteristic pattern of emission lines, as do hydrogen, helium, and sodium.*

Trapping the Light The spectrum produced by a star is not continuous, nor is it made of bright lines similar to those of the elements you saw above. Because a star's atmosphere is cooler than the star itself, the gases in its atmosphere absorb some of the star's light. The cooler gases in a star's atmosphere remove certain colors of light from the continuous spectrum of the hot star. In fact, the colors that the atmosphere absorbs are the same colors it would emit if heated.

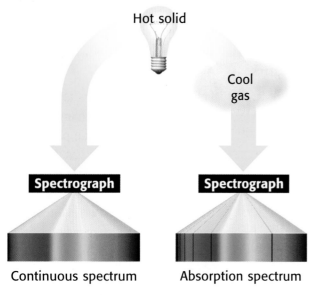

Hot solid

Cool gas

Spectrograph   Spectrograph

Continuous spectrum   Absorption spectrum

Figure 3 *An absorption spectrum (right) is produced when light passes through a cooler gas. Notice the dark lines in the spectrum.*

Biology
C O N N E C T I O N

Our eyes are not sensitive to colors when light levels are low. There are two types of light-sensitive cells inside the eye: rods and cones. Rods are good at distinguishing shades of light and dark as well as shape and movement. Cones are good for distinguishing colors. Cones, however, do not work well in low light. This is why it is hard to distinguish between star colors.

Cosmic Detective Work If light from a hot solid passes through a cooler gas, it produces an *absorption spectrum*—a continuous spectrum with dark lines where less light gets through. Take a look at **Figure 3.** Can you identify the element in the gas by comparing the position of the dark lines in its spectrum with the bright lines in Figure 2?

An astronomer's spectrum of a star shows an absorption spectrum. The pattern of lines shows some of the elements that are in the star's atmosphere. If a star were made of just one element, it would be simple to identify the element. But stars are a mixture of things, and all the different sets of lines for its elements appear together in a star's spectrum. Sorting out the patterns is often a puzzle.

Classifying Stars

In the 1800s, people started to collect the spectra of lots of stars and tried to classify them. At first, letters were assigned to each type of spectra. Stars with spectra that had very noticeable hydrogen patterns were classified as A type stars. Other stars were classified as B, and so on. Later, scientists realized that the stars were classified in the wrong order.

Differences in Temperature Stars are now classified by how hot they are. We see the temperature differences as colors. The original class O stars are blue—they are very hot, the hottest of all stars. If you arrange the letters in order of temperature, they are no longer in alphabetical order. The resulting order of star classes—OBAFGKM—is shown in the table on the next page.

If you see a certain pattern of absorption lines in a star, you know that a certain element or molecule is in the star or its atmosphere. But the absence of a pattern doesn't mean the element isn't there; the temperature might not be high enough or low enough to produce absorption lines.

Types of Stars				
Class	Color	Surface temperature (°C)	Elements detected	Examples of stars
O	blue	above 30,000	helium	10 Lacertae
B	blue-white	10,000–30,000	helium and hydrogen	Rigel, Spica
A	blue-white	7,500–10,000	hydrogen	Vega, Sirius
F	yellow-white	6,000–7,500	hydrogen and heavier elements	Canopus, Procyon
G	yellow	5,000–6,000	calcium and other metals	the sun, Capella
K	orange	3,500–5,000	calcium and molecules	Arcturus, Aldebaran
M	red	less than 3,500	molecules	Betelgeuse, Antares

Differences in Brightness With only their eyes to aid them, ancient astronomers also came up with a system to classify stars based on their brightness. They called the brightest stars in the sky *first magnitude* stars and the faintest stars *sixth magnitude* stars. But when they began to use telescopes, astronomers were able to see many stars that had previously been too faint to see. Rather than replace the old system of magnitudes, they added to it—positive numbers for dimmer stars and negative numbers for brighter stars. For example, with large telescopes, astronomers can see stars as dim as 29th magnitude. And the brightest star in the sky, Sirius, has a magnitude of –1.4.

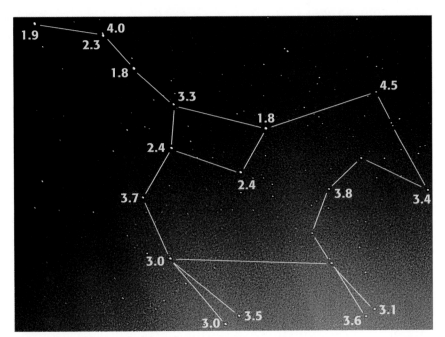

Figure 4 *The constellation Ursa Major, or the Great Bear, contains both bright and faint stars. Numbers indicate their relative brightness. What is the magnitude of the brightest star?*

MATH BREAK

Starlight, Star Bright

Magnitude is used to indicate how bright one object is compared with another. Five magnitudes equal a factor of 100 times in brightness. The brightest blue stars, for example, have an absolute magnitude of −10. The sun is about +5. How much brighter is a blue star than the sun? Since each five magnitudes is a factor of 100 and the blue star and the sun are 15 magnitudes different, the blue star must be 100 × 100 × 100 times brighter than the sun. This is 1,000,000 (one million) times!

How Bright Is That Star?

If you look at a row of street lights along a highway, like those shown in **Figure 5,** do they all look exactly the same? Does the light you are standing under look the same as a light several blocks away? Of course not! The nearest ones look bright, and the farthest ones look dim.

Apparent Magnitude How bright a light looks, or appears, is called **apparent magnitude.** If you measure the brightness of a street light with a light meter, you will find that its brightness depends on the square of the distance between them. For example, a light that is 10 m away will appear four (2×2 or 2^2) times as bright as a light that is 20 m away. The same light will appear nine (3×3 or 3^2) times as bright as a light that is 30 m away.

Figure 5 *You can estimate how far away each street light is by looking at its apparent brightness. Does this work with stars?*

✓ Self-Check

If two identical stars are located the same distance away from Earth, what can you say about their apparent magnitudes? *(See page 200 to check your answer.)*

Environment
C O N N E C T I O N

And speaking of street lights . . . Someone looking at the night sky in a city would not see as many stars as someone looking at the sky in the country. Light pollution is a big problem for astronomers and backyard stargazers alike. Certain types of lighting can help reduce glare, but there will continue to be a conflict between lighting buildings at night and seeing the stars.

But unlike street lights, some stars are brighter than others because of their size or energy output, not their distance from Earth. So how can you tell the difference?

Absolute Magnitude Astronomers use a star's apparent magnitude (how bright it seems to be) and its distance from Earth to calculate its absolute magnitude. **Absolute magnitude** is the actual brightness of a star. In other words, if all stars could be placed the same distance away, their absolute magnitudes would be the same as their apparent magnitudes and the brighter stars would look brighter. The sun, for example, has an absolute magnitude of +4.8—pretty ordinary for a star. But because the sun is so close to Earth, its apparent magnitude is −26.8, making it the brightest object in the sky.

Distance to the Stars

Because they are so far away, astronomers use light-years to give the distances to the stars. A **light-year** is the distance that light travels in one year. Because the speed of light is about 300,000 km/s, it travels almost 9.5 trillion kilometers in one year. Obviously it would be easier to give the distance to the North Star as 431 light-years than 4,080,000,000,000,000 km. But how do astronomers measure a star's distance?

To get a clue, take a look at the QuickLab at right. Just as your thumb appeared to move, stars near the Earth seem to move compared with more-distant stars as Earth revolves around the sun, as shown in **Figure 6.** This apparent shift in position is called **parallax.** While this shift can be seen only through telescopes, using parallax and simple trigonometry (a type of math), astronomers can find the actual distance to stars that are close to Earth.

Quick Lab

Not All Thumbs!

1. Hold your **thumb** in front of your face at arm's length.

2. Close one **eye** and focus on an **object** some distance behind your thumb.

3. Slowly move your **head** back and forth a small amount, and notice how your thumb seems to be moving compared with the background you are looking at.

4. Now move your thumb in close to your face and move your head the same amount. Notice how much more your thumb moves.

TRY at HOME

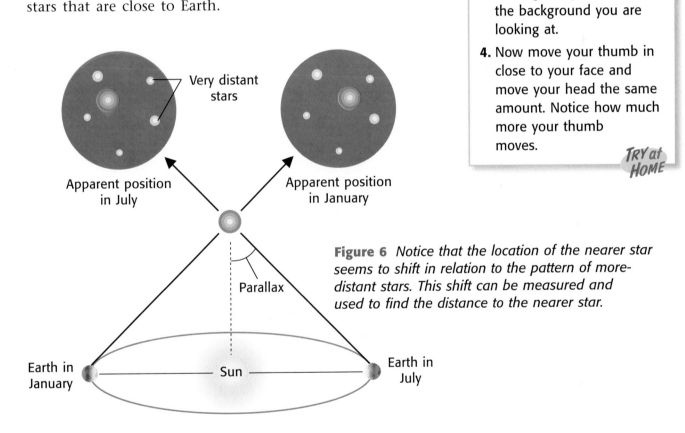

Figure 6 *Notice that the location of the nearer star seems to shift in relation to the pattern of more-distant stars. This shift can be measured and used to find the distance to the nearer star.*

Motions of Stars

As you know, the Earth rotates on its axis. As the Earth turns, different parts of its surface face the sun. This is why we have days and nights. The Earth also revolves around the sun. At different times of the year, you see different stars in the night sky. This is because the side of Earth that is away from the sun at night faces a different part of the universe.

To learn more about parallax, turn to page 166 in the LabBook.

Figure 7 *As Earth rotates on its axis, stars set in the western horizon.*

Apparent Motion Because of Earth's rotation, the sun appears to move across the sky. Likewise, if you look at the night sky long enough, the stars also appear to move. In fact, at night we can observe that the whole sky is rotating above us. As shown in **Figure 7,** the rest of the stars appear to rotate around Polaris, the North Star, which is directly above Earth's north pole. Because of Earth's rotation, all of the stars in the sky appear to make one complete circle around Polaris every 24 hours.

Actual Motion You now know that the apparent motion of the sun and stars in our sky is due to Earth's rotation. But each star is also really moving in space. Because stars are so distant, however, their real motion is hard to observe. If you could watch stars over thousands of years, their movement would be obvious. As shown in **Figure 8,** you would see that familiar star patterns slowly change their shapes.

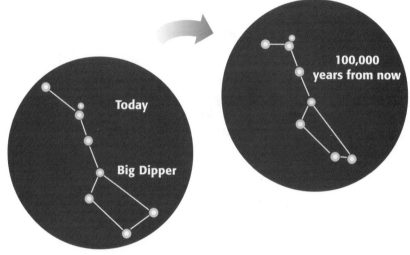

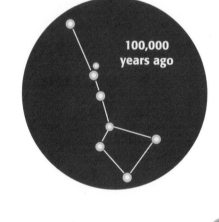

Figure 8 *Over time, the shapes of the constellations and other star groups change.*

SECTION REVIEW

1. Is a yellow star, such as the sun, hotter or cooler than an orange star? Explain.

2. Suppose you see two stars that have the same apparent magnitude. If one star is actually four times as far away as the other, how much brighter is the farther star?

3. **Interpreting Illustrations** Look back at Figure 7. How many hours passed between the first image and the second image? How can you tell?

The Life Cycle of Stars

Terms to Learn

H-R diagram	supernova
main sequence	neutron star
white dwarf	pulsar
red giant	black hole

What You'll Do

◆ Describe the quantities that are plotted in the H-R diagram.

◆ Explain how stars at different stages in their life cycle appear on different parts of the H-R diagram.

Quick Lab

Plotting Pairs

Compare your classmates by making a graph of two different characteristics that each student has. Choose variables that you can assign a number to, such as age and shoe size.

1. Decide on two variables.

2. Collect the data from your classmates.

3. Construct your graph, plotting one variable against the other.

4. Do you see a pattern in your graph? What does the graph tell you about how the two variables you chose are related?

Just like people, stars are born, grow old, and eventually die. But unlike people, stars exist for billions of years. They are born when clouds of gas and dust come together and become very hot and dense. As stars get older, they lose some of their material. Usually this is a gradual change, but sometimes it happens in a big explosion. Either way, when a star dies, much of its material returns to space. There some of it combines with more gas and dust to form new stars. How do scientists know these things about stars? Read on to find out.

The Diagram That Did It!

In 1911, a Danish astronomer named Ejnar Hertzsprung (IE nahr HUHRTZ sprung) compared the temperature and brightness of stars on a graph. Two years later, American astronomer Henry Norris Russell made some similar graphs. Although they used different data, these astronomers had similar results. The combination of their ideas is now called the *Hertzsprung-Russell,* or *H-R, diagram.* The **H-R diagram** is a graph showing the relationship between a star's surface temperature and its absolute magnitude. Russell's original diagram is shown in **Figure 9.**

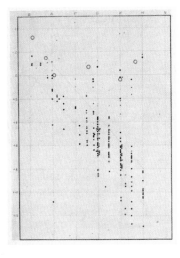

Figure 9 *Notice that a pattern begins to appear from the lower right to the upper left of the graph. Although it may not look like much, this graph began a revolution in astronomy.*

Over the years, the H-R diagram has become a tool for studying the nature of stars. It not only shows how stars are classified by temperature and brightness but also is a good way to illustrate how stars change over time. Turn the page to see a modern version of this diagram.

The H-R Diagram

Look closely at the diagram on these two pages. Temperature is given along the bottom of the diagram. Absolute magnitude, or brightness, is given along the left side. Hot (blue) stars are located on the left, and cool (red) stars are on the right. Bright stars are at the top, and faint stars are at the bottom. The brightest stars are a million times brighter than the sun. The faintest are 1/10,000 as bright as the sun. As you can see, there seems to be a band of stars going from the top left to the bottom right corner. This diagonal pattern of stars is called the **main sequence.** A star spends most of its lifetime as a main-sequence star and then changes into one of the other types of stars shown here.

Main-sequence
Stars in the main sequence form a band that runs along the middle of the H-R diagram. The sun is a main-sequence star. Stars similar to the sun are called *dwarfs.* The sun has been shining for about 5 billion years. Scientists think the sun is in midlife and that it will remain on the main sequence for another 5 billion years.

Absolute magnitude is measured upside down. That means the larger the number, the dimmer the star. At +5, the sun is not as bright as a −7 star.

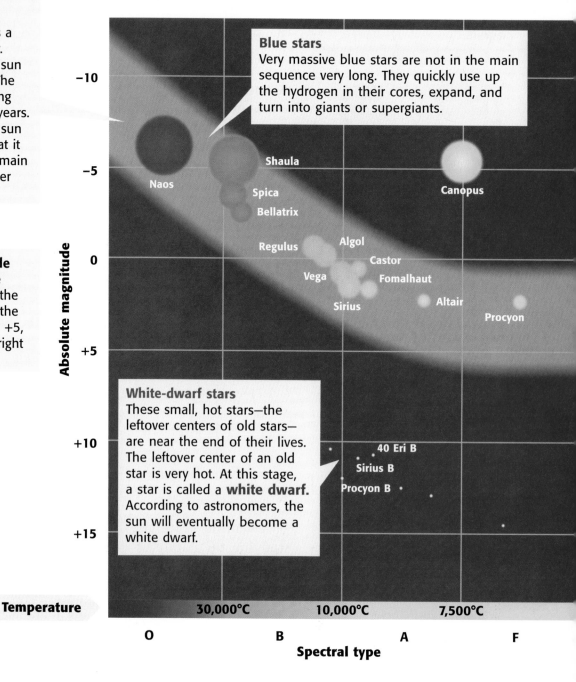

Blue stars
Very massive blue stars are not in the main sequence very long. They quickly use up the hydrogen in their cores, expand, and turn into giants or supergiants.

White-dwarf stars
These small, hot stars—the leftover centers of old stars—are near the end of their lives. The leftover center of an old star is very hot. At this stage, a star is called a **white dwarf.** According to astronomers, the sun will eventually become a white dwarf.

All stars begin as a ball of gas and dust in space as gravity pulls the gas and dust together into a sphere. As the sphere becomes denser, it gets hotter. When it is hot enough in the center, hydrogen turns into helium in a process called nuclear fusion and lots of energy is given off. A star is born!

Stars spend most of their lives on the main-sequence. Small-mass stars tend to be located at the lower right end of the main-sequence; more massive stars are found at the left end. As main-sequence stars age, they move up and to the right on the H-R diagram to become giants or supergiants. Such stars can then lose their atmospheres, leaving small cores behind, which end up in the lower left corner of the diagram as white dwarfs.

Giants and supergiants

When a star runs out of hydrogen in its core, the center of the star shrinks inward and the outer parts expand outward. In a star the size of our sun, the atmosphere will grow very large and cool. When this happens, the star becomes a **red giant.** If the star is very massive, it becomes a *supergiant.*

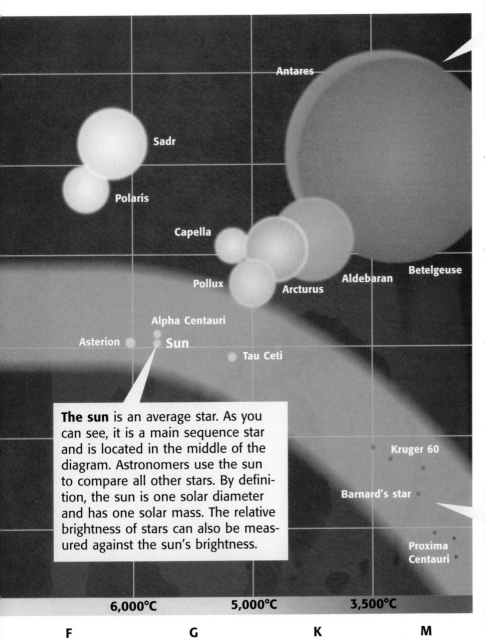

The sun is an average star. As you can see, it is a main sequence star and is located in the middle of the diagram. Astronomers use the sun to compare all other stars. By definition, the sun is one solar diameter and has one solar mass. The relative brightness of stars can also be measured against the sun's brightness.

Red-dwarf stars

At the lower end of the main sequence are the red dwarf stars. Red dwarfs are low-mass stars. Low-mass stars remain on the main sequence a long time. The lowest mass stars may be some of the oldest stars in the galaxy.

When Stars Get Old

While stars may stay on the main sequence for a long time, they don't stay there forever. Average stars, such as the sun, turn into red giants and then white dwarfs. But when massive stars get old, they may leave the main sequence in a more spectacular fashion. Stars much larger than the sun may explode with such violence that they turn into a variety of strange new objects. Let's take a look at some of these objects.

Supernovas Massive blue stars use up their hydrogen much faster than stars like the sun. This means they make a lot more energy, which makes them very hot and therefore blue! And compared with other stars, they don't last long. At the end of its life, a blue star may explode in a tremendous flash of light called a *supernova*. A **supernova** is basically the death of a large star by explosion. A supernova explosion is so powerful that it can be brighter than an entire galaxy for several days. Heavy elements, such as silver, gold, and lead, are formed by supernova explosions.

The ringed structure shown in **Figure 10** is the result of a supernova explosion that was first observed in February 1987. The star, located in a nearby galaxy, actually exploded before civilization began here on Earth, but it took 169,000 years for the light from the explosion to reach our planet!

Before (1984)

During (1987)

Figure 10 *Supernova 1987A was the first supernova visible to the unaided eye in 400 years. The first image shows what the original star must have looked like only a few hours before the explosion. Today its remains form a double ring of gas and dust, shown at right.*

After (Hubble Space Telescope close-up, 1994)

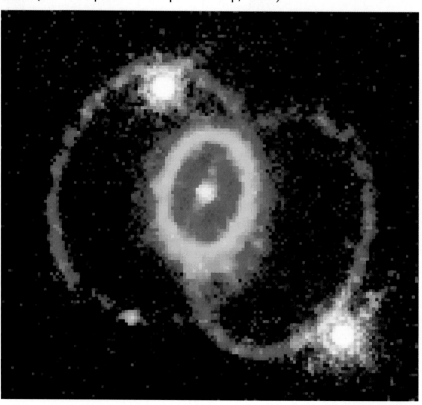

Neutron Stars So what happens to a star that becomes a supernova? The leftover materials in the center of a supernova are squeezed together to form a star of about two solar masses. But the star is only about 20 km in diameter. The particles inside the star become neutrons, so this star is called a **neutron star.** A neutron star is so dense that if you brought a teaspoon of it back to Earth, it would weigh nearly a billion metric tons!

Pulsars If a neutron star is spinning, it is called a **pulsar.** A pulsar sends out beams of radiation that also spin around very rapidly. These beams are much like the beams from a lighthouse. The beams are detected as rapid clicks or pulses by radio telescopes.

Black Holes Sometimes the leftovers of a supernova are so massive that they collapse to form a *black hole.* A **black hole** is an object with more than three solar masses squeezed into a ball only 10 km across—100 football fields long. A black hole's gravity is so strong that not even light can escape. That is why it is called a *black* hole. Contrary to some movie depictions, a black hole doesn't gobble up other stars. But if a star is nearby, some gas or dust from the star will spiral into the black hole, as shown in **Figure 11,** giving off X rays. It is by these X rays that astronomers can detect the existence of black holes.

Figure 11 *A black hole's gravity is so strong that it can pull in material from a nearby star, as shown in this artist's drawing.*

SECTION REVIEW

1. Are blue stars young or old? How can you tell?

2. In main-sequence stars, what is the relationship between brightness and temperature?

3. Arrange the following in order of their appearance in the life cycle of a star: white dwarf, red giant, main-sequence star. Explain your answer.

4. **Applying Concepts** Given that there are more low-mass stars than high-mass stars in the universe, do you think there are more white dwarfs or more black holes? Explain.

internet**connect**

SC*i*LINKS

NSTA

TOPIC: Supernovas
GO TO: www.scilinks.org
*sci*LINKS NUMBER: HSTE515

Terms to Learn

galaxy   nebula
spiral galaxy   open cluster
elliptical galaxy globular cluster
irregular galaxy quasar

What You'll Do

◆ Identify the various types of galaxies from pictures.
◆ Describe the contents of galaxies.
◆ Explain why looking at distant galaxies reveals what early galaxies looked like.

Galaxies

Stars don't exist alone in space. They belong to larger groups that are held together by the attraction of gravity. The most common groupings are galaxies. **Galaxies** are large groupings of stars in space. Galaxies come in a variety of sizes and shapes. The largest galaxies contain more than a trillion stars. Some of the smaller ones have only a few million. Astronomers don't count the stars, of course; they estimate from the size and brightness of the galaxy how many sun-sized stars the galaxy might have.

Types of Galaxies

Edwin Hubble, the astronomer for whom the Hubble Space Telescope is named, began to classify galaxies in the 1920s, mostly by their shapes. We still use the galaxy names that Hubble originally assigned.

Figure 12 *The Milky Way galaxy is thought to be a spiral galaxy similar to the galaxy in Andromeda, shown here.*

Spiral Galaxies Spiral galaxies are what most people think of when you say *galaxy.* **Spiral galaxies** have a bulge at the center and very distinctive spiral arms. Hot blue stars in the spiral arms make the arms in spiral galaxies appear blue. The central region appears yellow because it contains cooler stars. **Figure 12** shows a spiral galaxy tilted, so you can see its pinwheel shape. Other spiral galaxies appear to be "edge-on." It is hard to tell what type of galaxy we are in because the gas, dust, and stars keep us from having a good view. It is like trying to figure out what pattern a marching band is making while you are in the band. Observing other galaxies and making measurements inside our galaxy lead astronomers to think that Earth is in a spiral galaxy.

Elliptical Galaxies About one-third of all galaxies are simply massive blobs of stars, as shown in **Figure 13.** Many look like spheres, while others are more elongated. Because we don't know how they are oriented, some of these galaxies could be cucumber shaped, with the round end facing us. These galaxies are called *elliptical galaxies.* **Elliptical galaxies** have very bright centers and very little dust and gas. Because there is so little gas, there are no new stars forming, and therefore elliptical galaxies contain only old stars. Some elliptical galaxies, like M87, at right, are huge and are therefore called *giant elliptical galaxies.* Others are much smaller and are called *dwarf elliptical galaxies.* There are probably lots of dwarf ellipticals, but because they are small and faint, they are very hard to detect.

Figure 13 *Unlike the Milky Way, the galaxy known as M87 has no spiral arms.*

Irregular Galaxies When Hubble first classified galaxies, he had a group of leftovers. He named them "irregulars." **Irregular galaxies** are galaxies that don't fit into any other class. As their name suggests, their shape is irregular. Many of these galaxies, such as the Large Magellanic Cloud, shown in **Figure 14,** are close companions of large spiral galaxies, whose gravity may be distorting the shape of their smaller neighbors.

Figure 14 *The Large Magellanic Cloud, an irregular galaxy, is located within our own galactic neighborhood.*

Contents of Galaxies

Galaxies are composed of billions and billions of stars. But besides the stars and the planetary systems many of them probably have, there are larger features within galaxies that are made up of stars or the material of stars. Among these are gas clouds and star clusters.

Gas Clouds The Latin word for "cloud" is *nebula*. In space, **nebulas** (or *nebulae*) are giant clouds of gas and dust. Some types of nebulas glow by themselves, while others absorb light and hide stars. Still others reflect starlight, producing some amazing images. Some nebulas are regions where new stars form. **Figure 15** shows part of the Eagle nebula. Spiral galaxies generally contain nebulas, but elliptical galaxies don't.

Globular Clusters **Globular clusters** are groups of older stars. A globular cluster looks like a ball of stars, as shown in **Figure 16**. There may be 20,000 to 100,000 stars in an average globular cluster. Globular clusters are located in a spherical *halo* that surrounds spiral galaxies such as the Milky Way. Globular clusters are also common around giant elliptical galaxies.

Open Clusters **Open clusters** are groups of stars that are usually located along the spiral disk of a galaxy. Newly formed open clusters have many bright blue stars, as shown in **Figure 17.** There may be a few hundred to a few thousand stars in an open cluster.

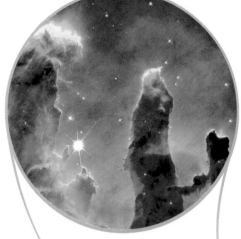

Figure 15 *Part of a nebula in which stars are born is shown above. The finger-like shape to the left of the bright star is slightly wider than our solar system.*

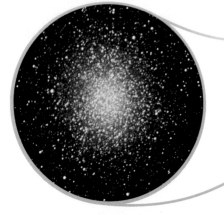

Figure 16 *With 5 to 10 million stars, Omega Centauri is the largest globular cluster in the Milky Way Galaxy.*

Figure 17 *The open cluster Pleiades is just visible without a telescope.*

Origin of Galaxies

How did galaxies form in the first place? To answer this question, astronomers must travel back in time, exploring the early universe through telescopes. Scientists investigate the early universe by observing objects that are extremely far away in space. Because it takes time for light to travel through space, looking through a telescope is like looking back in time. The farther out one looks, the further back in time one travels.

Looking at distant galaxies reveals what early galaxies looked like. This helps give scientists an idea of how galaxies evolve through time and perhaps what caused them to form in the first place. Scientists have already found some very strange looking objects in the early universe.

Quasars Among the most distant objects are **quasars,** which look like tiny points of light. But because they are very far away, they must be extremely bright for their size. Quasars are among the most powerful energy sources in the universe. They may be young galaxies with massive black holes at their centers. Some scientists think that what we see as quasars are galaxies in the process of forming. In **Figure 18,** you can see a quasar that is 6 billion light-years away. You are seeing it as it was 6 billion years ago—long before the Earth even existed!

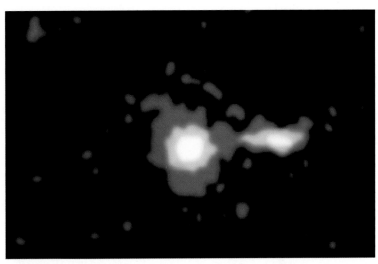

Figure 18 *The quasar known as PKS 0637-752 is as powerful as 10 trillion suns.*

SECTION REVIEW

1. Arrange these galaxies in order of decreasing size: spiral, giant elliptical, dwarf elliptical, irregular.

2. Describe the difference between an elliptical galaxy and a globular cluster.

3. **Analyzing Relationships** Suppose the quasar in Figure 18 suddenly underwent some dramatic change. How long would we have to wait to see this change? Explain.

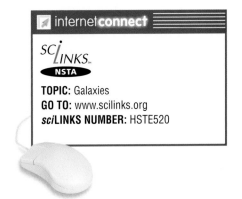

internet**connect**

SC*i*LINKS.
NSTA

TOPIC: Galaxies
GO TO: www.scilinks.org
*sci***LINKS NUMBER:** HSTE520

Terms to Learn

cosmology
big bang theory
cosmic background radiation

What You'll Do

- ◆ Describe the big bang theory.
- ◆ Explain evidence used to show support for the big bang theory.
- ◆ Explain how the expansion of the universe is explained by the big bang theory.

Formation of the Universe

So far you've learned about the contents of the universe. But what about its history? How did the universe begin? How might it end? Questions like these are a special part of astronomy called *cosmology*. **Cosmology** is the study of the origin and future of the universe. Like other scientific theories, theories about the beginning and end of the universe must be tested by observations or experiments.

The Big Bang Theory

One of the most important theories in cosmology is the big bang theory. The **big bang theory** states that the universe began with a tremendous explosion. According to the theory, 12 to 15 billion years ago, all the contents of the universe were gathered together under extreme pressure, temperature, and density in a very tiny spot. Then, for some reason, it rapidly expanded. In the early moments of the universe, some of the expanding energy turned into matter that eventually became the galaxies, as shown in **Figure 19.**

A Big Crunch? As the galaxies move apart, they get older and eventually stop forming stars. What happens next depends on how much matter is contained in the universe. If there is enough matter, gravity will slow and eventually stop the expansion of the universe. The universe may even start collapsing to its original state, causing a "big crunch."

If there is not enough matter to stop the expansion, then as stars age and die, the universe will eventually become cold and dark. Recent observations suggest that there may not be enough matter to stop the universe from expanding forever, but the answer is still uncertain.

Figure 19 *The big bang caused the universe to expand in all directions.*

Supporting the Theory So how do we know if the big bang really happened? In 1964, two scientists, using the antenna shown in **Figure 20,** accidentally found radiation coming from all directions in space. One explanation for this radiation is that it is **cosmic background radiation** left over from the big bang.

Think about what happens when an oven door is left open after the oven has been used. Thermal energy is transferred throughout the kitchen and the oven cools. Eventually the room and the oven are the same temperature. According to the big bang theory, thermal energy from the original explosion was distributed in every direction as the universe expanded. This cosmic background radiation—corresponding to a temperature of −270°C—now fills all of space.

Figure 20 *Robert Wilson (left) and Arno Penzias (right) discovered the cosmic background radiation, giving a big boost to the big bang theory.*

Universal Expansion

Today, the big bang theory is widely accepted by astronomers. But where did the idea of a big bang come from? The answer is found in deep space. No matter what direction we look, galaxies are moving away from us, as shown in **Figure 21.** This observation may make it seem like our galaxy is the center of the universe, with all other galaxies moving away from our own. But this is not the case. Careful measurements have shown that all distant galaxies are moving away from all other galaxies.

With the discovery that the universe is expanding, scientists began to wonder what it would be like to watch the universe evolve backwards through time. In reverse, the universe would appear to be contracting, not expanding. All matter would eventually come together to a single point. Thinking about what would happen if all of the matter in the universe were squeezed into such a small space led scientists to the big bang theory.

Figure 21 *The big bang theory explains the expansion of the universe we observe as galaxies move outward in all directions.*

A Raisin-Bread Model

Imagine a loaf of raisin bread before it is baked. Inside the dough, each raisin is a certain distance from every other raisin. As the dough gets warm and rises, it expands and all of the raisins begin to move away from each other. No matter which raisin you observe, the other raisins are moving farther from it.

The universe itself is like the rising bread dough—it is expanding in all directions. And like the raisins, every distant galaxy is moving away from our galaxy as well as every other galaxy. In other words, there isn't any way to find the "center" of the universe.

How Old Is the Universe? One way scientists can measure the age of the universe is by measuring the distance to the farthest galaxies. Because light travels at a certain speed, the amount of time it takes light to travel this distance is a measure of the age of the universe. Another way to estimate the age of the universe is to calculate the ages of old, nearby stars. Because the universe must be at least as old as the oldest stars it contains, their ages provide a clue to the age of the universe. But according to these calculations, some stars are older than the universe itself! Astronomers continue to search for evidence that will solve this puzzle.

APPLY

Graphing Expansion

Suppose you decide to make some raisin bread. You would form a lump of dough, as shown in the top image. The lower image represents dough that has been rising for 2 hours. Look at raisin **B** in the top image. Measure how far it is from each of the other raisins—**A, C, D, E, F,** and **G**—in millimeters. Now measure how far each raisin has moved away from **B** in the lower image. Make a graph of speed (in units of mm/h) versus original distance (in mm). Remember that speed equals distance divided by time. For example, if raisin **E** was originally 15 mm from raisin **B** and is now 30 mm away, it moved 15 mm in 2 hours. Its speed is therefore 7.5 mm/h. Repeat the procedure, starting with raisin **D**. Plot your results on the same graph, and compare the two results. What can you conclude from the information you graphed?

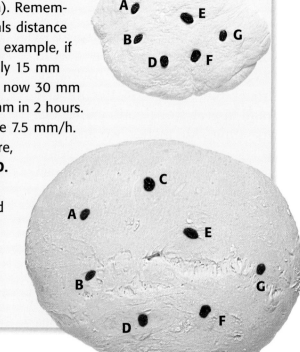

Structure of the Universe

The universe is an amazing place. From our home on planet Earth, it stretches out farther than we can see with our most sensitive instruments. It contains a variety of objects, some of which you have just learned about. But these objects are not simply scattered through the universe at random. The universe has a structure that is repeated over and over again.

A Cosmic Repetition You already know that the Earth is a planet. But planets are part of planetary systems. Our solar system is the one we are most familiar with, but recently planets have been detected in orbit around other stars. Scientists think that planetary systems are actually quite common in the universe. Stars are grouped in larger systems, ranging from star clusters to galaxies. Galaxies themselves are arranged in groups that are bound together by gravity. Even galaxy groups form galaxy clusters and superclusters, as shown in **Figure 22.**

Multiple Universes? Farther than the eye can see, the universe continues with this pattern, with great collections of galaxy clusters and vast empty regions of space in between. But is the universe itself alone? Some cosmologists think that our universe is only one of a great many other universes, perhaps similar to ours or perhaps not. At present, we cannot observe other universes. But someday, who knows? Maybe students in future classrooms will have much more to study!

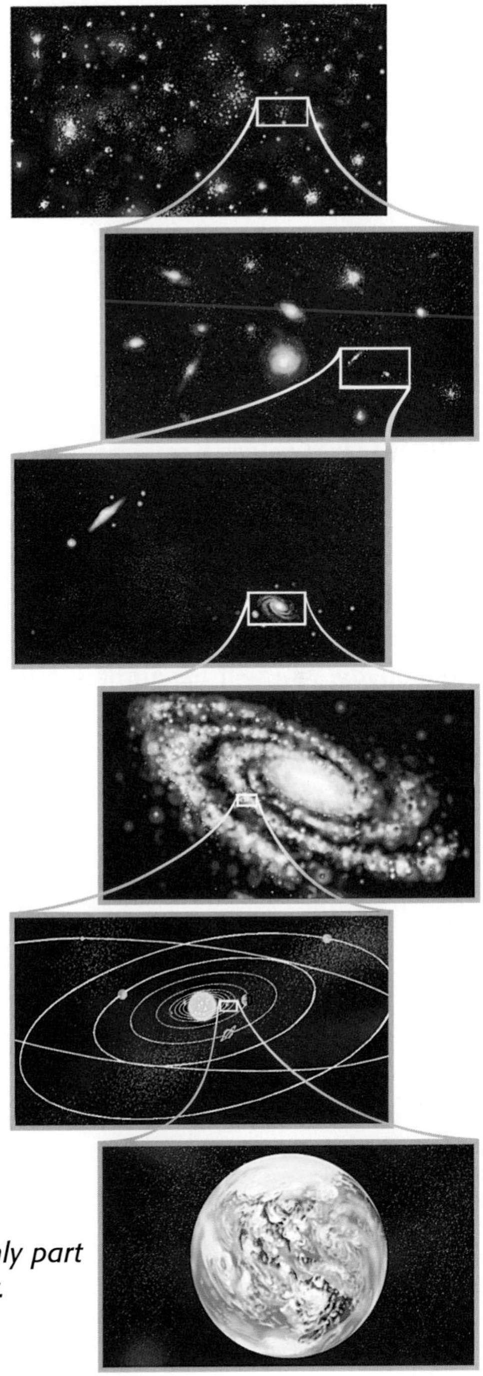

Figure 22 *The Earth is only part of a vast system of matter.*

SECTION REVIEW

1. Name one observation that supports the big bang theory.

2. How does the big bang theory explain the observed expansion of the universe?

3. **Understanding Technology** Large telescopes gather more light than small telescopes gather. Why are large telescopes used to study very distant galaxies?

Discovery Lab

Red Hot, or Not?

When you look at the night sky, some stars are brighter than others. Some are even different colors from what you might expect. For example, one star in the constellation Orion glows red. Sirius, the brightest star in the sky, glows a bluish white. Astronomers use these colors to estimate the temperature of the stars. In this activity, you will experiment with a light bulb and some batteries to discover what the color of a glowing object reveals about the temperature of the object.

MATERIALS

- electrical tape
- 2 conducting wires
- weak D cell
- flashlight bulb
- 2 fresh D cells

Ask a Question

1 How are the color and temperature of a star related?

Form a Hypothesis

2 In your ScienceLog, change the question above into a statement giving your best guess about what the relationship is between a star's color and temperature.

Test the Hypothesis

3 Tape one end of a conducting wire to the positive pole of the weak D cell. Tape one end of the second conducting wire to the negative pole.

4. Touch the free end of each wire to the light bulb. Hold one of the wires against the bottom tip of the light bulb. Hold the second wire against the side of the metal portion of the bulb. The bulb should light.

Make Observations

5. In your ScienceLog, record the color of the filament in the light bulb. Carefully touch your hand to the bulb. Observe the temperature of the bulb. Record your observations in your ScienceLog.

6. Repeat steps 3–5 with one fresh D cell.

7. Use the electrical tape to connect the two fresh D cells in a continuous circuit so that the positive pole of the first cell is connected to the negative pole of the second cell.

8. Repeat steps 3–5 using two fresh D cells.

Analyze Results

9. How did the color of the filament change in the three trials? How did the temperature change?

10. What information does the color of a star provide?

11. What color are stars with relatively high surface temperatures? What color are stars with relatively low surface temperatures?

Draw Conclusions

12. Arrange the following stars in order from highest to lowest surface temperature: Sirius is bluish white. Aldebaran is orange. Procyon is yellow-white. Capella is yellow. Betelgeuse is red.

Betelgeuse

Rigel

Chapter Highlights

SECTION 1

Vocabulary

spectrum *(p. 98)*

apparent magnitude *(p. 102)*

absolute magnitude *(p. 102)*

light-year *(p. 103)*

parallax *(p. 103)*

Section Notes

- The color of a star depends on its temperature. Hot stars are blue. Cool stars are red.

- The spectra of stars indicate their composition. Spectra are also used to classify stars.

- The magnitude of a star is a measure of its brightness.

- Apparent magnitude is how bright a star appears from Earth.

- Absolute magnitude is how bright a star actually is. Lower absolute magnitude numbers indicate brighter stars.

- Distance to nearby stars can be measured by their movement relative to stars farther away.

Labs

I See the Light! *(p. 166)*

SECTION 2

Vocabulary

H-R diagram *(p. 105)*

main sequence *(p. 106)*

white dwarf *(p. 106)*

red giant *(p. 107)*

supernova *(p. 108)*

neutron star *(p. 109)*

pulsar *(p. 109)*

black hole *(p. 109)*

Section Notes

- New stars form from the material of old stars that have gone through their life cycles.

- The H-R diagram relates the temperature and brightness of a star. It also illustrates the life cycle of stars.

- Most stars are main-sequence stars. Red giants and white dwarfs are later stages in a star's life cycle.

- Massive stars become supernovas. Their cores turn into neutron stars or black holes.

☑ Skills Check

Math Concepts

SQUARING THE DIFFERENCE The difference in brightness (apparent magnitude) between a pair of similar stars depends on the difference in their distances from Earth. Compare a star that is 10 light-years away with a star that is 5 light-years away. One star is twice as close, so it is $2 \times 2 = 4$ times brighter than the other star. The star that is 5 light-years away is also 3^2, or 9, times brighter than one that is 15 light-years away.

Visual Understanding

READING BETWEEN THE LINES The composition of a star is determined by the absorption spectra it displays. Dark lines in the spectrum of a star indicate which elements are present. Look back at Figure 3 to review.

SECTION 3

Vocabulary

galaxy *(p. 110)*

spiral galaxy *(p. 110)*

elliptical galaxy *(p. 111)*

irregular galaxy *(p. 111)*

nebula *(p. 112)*

open cluster *(p. 112)*

globular cluster *(p. 112)*

quasar *(p. 113)*

Section Notes

- Edwin Hubble classified galaxies according to their shape. Major types include spiral, elliptical, and irregular galaxies.

- A nebula is a cloud of gas and dust. New stars are born in some nebulas.

- Open clusters are groups of stars located along the spiral disk of a galaxy. Globular star clusters are found in the halos of spiral galaxies and in elliptical galaxies.

- Because light travels at a certain speed, observing distant galaxies is like looking back in time. Scientists look at distant galaxies to learn what early galaxies looked like.

SECTION 4

Vocabulary

cosmology *(p. 114)*

big bang theory *(p. 114)*

cosmic background radiation *(p. 115)*

Section Notes

- The big bang theory states that the universe began with an explosion about 12 to 15 billion years ago.

- Cosmic background radiation fills the universe with radiation that is left over from the big bang. It is supporting evidence for the big bang theory.

- Observations show that the universe is expanding outward. There is no measurable center and no apparent edge.

- All matter in the universe is a part of larger systems, from planets to superclusters of galaxies.

---

internet**connect**

GO TO: go.hrw.com

Visit the **HRW** Web site for a variety of learning tools related to this chapter. Just type in the keyword:

KEYWORD: HSTUNV

GO TO: www.scilinks.org

Visit the **National Science Teachers Association** on-line Web site for Internet resources related to this chapter. Just type in the *sci*LINKS number for more information about the topic:

TOPIC: The Hubble Space Telescope	*sci*LINKS NUMBER: HSTE505
TOPIC: Stars	*sci*LINKS NUMBER: HSTE510
TOPIC: Supernovas	*sci*LINKS NUMBER: HSTE515
TOPIC: Galaxies	*sci*LINKS NUMBER: HSTE520
TOPIC: Structure of the Universe	*sci*LINKS NUMBER: HSTE525

Chapter Review

USING VOCABULARY

For each pair of terms, explain the difference in their meanings.

1. absolute magnitude/apparent magnitude

2. spectrum/parallax

3. main-sequence star/red giant

4. white dwarf/black hole

5. elliptical galaxy/spiral galaxy

6. big bang/cosmic background radiation

UNDERSTANDING CONCEPTS

Multiple Choice

7. The majority of stars in our galaxy are
   a. blue.
   b. white dwarfs.
   c. main-sequence stars.
   d. red giants.

8. Which would be seen as the brightest star in the following group?
   a. Alcyone—apparent magnitude of 3
   b. Alpheratz—apparent magnitude of 2
   c. Deneb—apparent magnitude of 1
   d. Rigel—apparent magnitude of 0

9. A cluster of stars forms in a nebula. There are red stars, blue stars, yellow stars, and white stars. Which stars are most like the sun?
   a. red   c. blue
   b. yellow   d. white

10. Individual stars are moving in space. How long will it take to see a noticeable difference without using a telescope?
    a. 24 hours   c. 100 years
    b. 1 year   d. 100,000 years

11. You visited an observatory and looked through the telescope. You saw a ball of stars through the telescope. What type of object did you see?
    a. a spiral galaxy
    b. an open cluster
    c. a globular cluster
    d. an irregular galaxy

12. In which part of a spiral galaxy do you expect to find nebulas?
    a. the spiral arms
    b. the central region
    c. the halo
    d. all parts of the galaxy

13. Which statement about the big bang theory is accurate?
    a. The universe will never end.
    b. New matter is being continuously created in the universe.
    c. The universe is filled with radiation coming from all directions in space.
    d. We can locate the center of the universe.

Short Answer

14. Describe how the apparent magnitude of a star varies with its distance from Earth.

15. Name six types of astronomical objects in the universe. Arrange them by size.

16. Which contains more stars on average, a globular cluster or an open cluster?

17. What does the big bang theory have to say about how the universe will end?

Concept Mapping

18. Use the following terms to create a concept map: black hole, neutron star, main-sequence star, red giant, nebula, white dwarf.

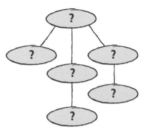

CRITICAL THINKING AND PROBLEM SOLVING

Write one or two sentences to answer the following questions:

19. If a certain star displayed a large parallax, what could you say about its distance from Earth?

20. Two M-type stars have the same apparent magnitude. Their spectra show that one is a red giant and the other is a red-dwarf star. Which one is farther from Earth? Explain your answer.

21. Look back at the H-R diagram in Section 2. Why do astronomers use absolute magnitudes to plot the stars? Why don't they use apparent magnitudes?

22. While looking at a galaxy through a nearby university's telescope, you notice that there are no blue stars present. What kind of galaxy is it most likely to be?

MATH IN SCIENCE

23. An astronomer observes two stars of about the same temperature and size. Alpha Centauri B is about 4 light-years away, and Sigma² Eridani A is about 16 light-years away. How much brighter does Alpha Centauri B appear?

INTERPRETING GRAPHICS

The following graph illustrates the Hubble law relating the distances of galaxies and their speed away from us.

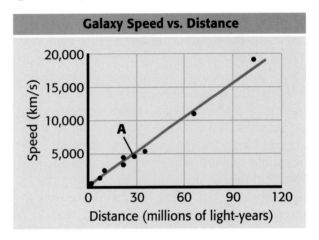

Galaxy Speed vs. Distance

24. Look at the galaxy marked **A** in the graph. What is its speed and distance?

25. If a new galaxy with a speed of 15,000 km/s were found, at what distance would you expect it to be?

Reading Check-up

Take a minute to review your answers to the Pre-Reading Questions found at the bottom of page 96. Have your answers changed? If necessary, revise your answers based on what you have learned since you began this chapter.

WEIRD SCIENCE

HOLES WHERE STARS ONCE WERE

An invisible phantom lurks in outer space, ready to swallow up everything that comes near it. Once trapped in its grasp, matter is stretched, torn, and crushed into oblivion. Does this sound like a horror story? Guess again! Scientists call it a black hole.

Born of a Collapsing Star

As a star runs out of fuel, it cools and eventually collapses under the force of its own gravity. If the collapsing star is massive enough, it may shrink enough to become a black hole. The resulting gravitational attraction is so enormous that even light cannot escape!

Scientists predict that at the center of the black hole is a *singularity,* a tiny point of incredible density, temperature, and pressure. The area around the singularity is called the *event horizon.* The event horizon represents the boundary of the black hole. Anything that crosses the event horizon, including light, will eventually be pulled into the black hole. As matter comes near the event horizon, the matter begins to swirl in much the same way that water swirls down a drain.

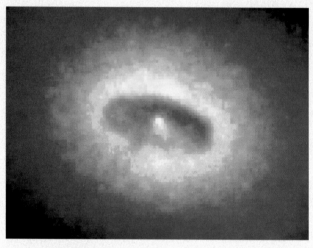

▲ *This photograph of M87 was taken by the Hubble Space Telescope.*

The Story of M87

For years, scientists had theorized about black holes but hadn't actually found one. Then in 1994, scientists found something strange at the core of a galaxy called M87. Scientists detected a disk-shaped cloud of gas with a diameter of 60 light-years, rotating at about 2 million kilometers per hour. When scientists realized that a mass more than 2 billion times that of the sun was crammed into a space no bigger than our solar system, they knew that something was pulling in the gases at the center of the galaxy.

Many astronomers think that black holes, such as the one in M87, lie at the heart of many galaxies. Some scientists suggest that there is a giant black hole at the center of our own Milky Way galaxy. But don't worry. The Earth is too far away to be caught.

Modeling a Black Hole

▶ Make a model to show how a black hole pulls in the matter surrounding it. Indicate the singularity and event horizon.

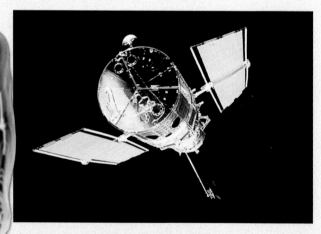

▲ *The Hubble Space Telescope*

CAREERS

ASTROPHYSICIST

Jocelyn Bell-Burnell became fascinated with astronomy at an early age. As a research student at Cambridge University, Bell-Burnell discovered pulsars, celestial objects that emit radio waves at short and regular intervals. Today Bell-Burnell is a leading expert in the field of astrophysics and the study of stars. She is currently head of the physics department at the Open University, in Milton Keynes, England.

At Cambridge University in 1967, Bell-Burnell and her adviser, Antony Hewish, completed work on a gigantic radio telescope designed to pick up signals from quasars. Bell-Burnell's job was to operate the telescope and analyze the "chart paper" recordings of the telescope on a graph. Each day, the telescope recorded 29.2 m of chart paper! After a month of operating the telescope, Bell-Burnell noticed a few "bits of scruff" that she could not explain—they were very short, pulsating radio signals. The signals were only 6.3 mm long, and they occurred only once every 4 days. What Bell-Burnell had accidentally found was a needle in a cosmic haystack!

LGM 1

Bell-Burnell and Hewish struggled to find the source of this mysterious new signal. They double-checked the equipment and began eliminating all of the possible sources of the signal, such as satellites, television, and radar. Because they could not rule out that the signal was coming from aliens, Bell-Burnell and Hewish called it LGM 1. Can you guess why? LGM stood for "Little Green Men"!

The Answer: Neutron Stars

Shortly after finding the first signal, Bell-Burnell discovered yet another strange, pulsing signal within the vast quantity of chart paper. This signal was similar to the first, except that it came from the other side of the sky. To Bell-Burnell, this second signal was exciting because it meant that her first signal was not of local origin and that she had stumbled on a new and unknown signal from space! By January 1968, Bell-Burnell had discovered two more pulsating signals. In March of that year, her findings were published, to the amazement of the scientific community. The scientific press coined the term *pulsars,* from pulsating radio stars. Bell-Burnell and other scientists reached the conclusion that her "bits of scruff" were caused by rapidly spinning neutron stars!

Star Tracking

▶ Pick out a bright star in the sky, and keep a record of its position in relation to a reference point, such as a tree or building. Each night, record what time the star appears at this point in the sky. Do you notice a pattern?

▲ *An artist's depiction of a pulsar*

Pre-Reading Questions

1. What's the difference between a satellite and a space probe?

2. How has the space program benefited our daily lives?

3. How are humans preparing to live in space?

A SHUTTLE TO OUTER SPACE

The space shuttle was developed to take people into outer space. Because the shuttle can be reused, it lowers the cost of space launches by up to 90 percent. The lower cost of getting to outer space has opened a new era of space exploration in which space missions are more common. From these missions, scientists are able to gather important information that will eventually help humans adapt to living and working in space. In this chapter, you will see how technology and space exploration are connected and how they both impact us on Earth.

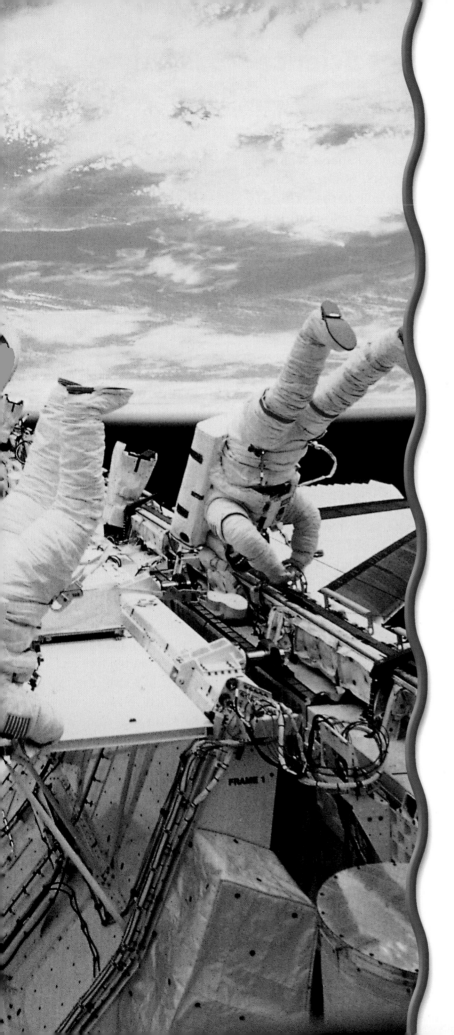

ROCKET FUN

Rockets are used to send people into space. Rockets work by forcing hot gas out one end of a tube. As this gas escapes in one direction, the rocket moves in the opposite direction. While you may have let a full balloon loose many times before, here you will use a balloon to learn about the principles of rocket propulsion.

Procedure

1. Thread a **string** through a **drinking straw,** and tie the string between two things that won't move, such as chairs. Make sure that the string is tight.

2. Blow into a large **balloon** until it is the size of a grapefruit. Hold the neck of the balloon closed.

3. **Tape** the balloon to the straw so that the opening of the balloon points toward one end of the string.

4. Move the balloon and straw to one end of the string, and then release the neck of the balloon. Record what happens in your ScienceLog.

5. Fill the balloon until it is almost twice the size it was in step 2, and repeat steps 3 and 4. Again record your observations.

Analysis

6. What happened during the second test that was different from the first? Can you figure out why?

Rocket Science

Terms to Learn

rocket   orbital velocity
NASA   escape velocity
thrust

What You'll Do

◆ Outline the early development of rocket technology.
◆ Explain how a rocket works.
◆ Explain the difference between orbital velocity and escape velocity.

How would you get to the moon? Before the invention of rockets, people could only dream of going into outer space. Science fiction writers, such as Jules Verne, were able to dress those dreams in scientific clothing by using what seemed like reasonable means of getting into space. For example, in a story he wrote in 1865, some of Verne's characters rode a capsule to the moon shot from a giant 900 ft long cannon.

But, as growing knowledge about the heavens was stimulating the imagination of writers and readers alike, an invention was slowly being developed that would become the key to exploring space. This was the rocket. A **rocket** is a machine that uses escaping gas to move.

The Beginning of Rocket Science

Around the year 1900, a Russian high school teacher named Konstantin Tsiolkovsky (KAHN stan teen TSEE uhl KAHV skee) began trying to understand the reasoning behind the motion of rockets. Tsiolkovsky's inspiration came from the fantastic, imaginative stories of Jules Verne. Tsiolkovsky believed that rockets were the key to space exploration. In his words, "The Earth is the cradle of mankind. But one does not have to live in the cradle forever." Tsiolkovsky is considered the father of rocket theory.

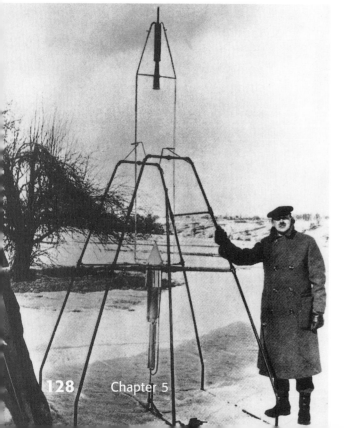

Figure 1 *Robert Goddard tests one of his early rockets.*

Although Tsiolkovsky explained how rockets work, he never built any rockets himself. That was left to American physicist Robert Goddard, who became known as the father of modern rocketry.

Modern Rocketry Gets a Boost Goddard, shown in **Figure 1,** conducted many rocket experiments in Massachusetts from 1915 to 1930. He then moved to New Mexico, where deserts provided enough room to conduct his tests safely. Between 1930 and 1941, Goddard tested more than 150 rocket engines, and by the time of World War II, his work was receiving much attention, most notably from the United States military.

From Rocket Bombs to Rocket Ships

During World War II, Germany developed the V-2 rocket, shown in **Figure 2,** and used it to bomb England. The design for the V-2 rocket came from Wernher von Braun, a young Ph.D. student whose research was being supported by the German military. In 1945, near the end of the war, von Braun and his entire research team surrendered to the advancing Americans. The United States thus gained 127 of the best German rocket scientists, and rocket research in the United States boomed in the 1950s.

Figure 2 *The V-2 rocket is the direct ancestor of all modern space vehicles.*

The Birth of NASA The end of World War II marked the beginning of the Cold War—the arms race between the United States and the Soviet Union. The Soviet Union was made up of Russia and 15 other countries, forming a superpower that supported a military rivaling that of the United States.

On July 29, 1958, in response to the alarm Americans felt over a possible Soviet superiority in space, the National Aeronautics and Space Administration, or **NASA,** was formed. This organization combined all of the separate rocket-development teams in the United States. Their combined efforts led to the development of a series of rockets, including the Saturn V rocket and those used to launch the space shuttle, as shown in **Figure 3.**

Figure 3 *Some of the space vehicles developed by NASA during its first 40 years are shown here to scale.*

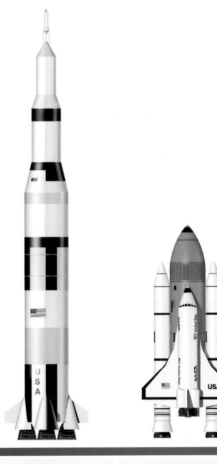

Mercury-Atlas	Delta	Titan IV	Saturn V	Space shuttle and boosters
1,400 kg payload	1,770 kg payload	18,000 kg payload	129,300 kg payload	29,500 kg payload
29 m tall	36 m tall	62 m tall	111 m tall	56 m tall

How Rockets Work

Rockets work on a simple physical principle, known as *Newton's third law of motion*. This principle states that for every action there is an equal reaction in the opposite direction. For example, the air rushing backward from a balloon (the action) is paired with the forward motion of the balloon itself (the reaction).

In the case of rockets, however, the equality between the action and the reaction may not be obvious. This is because the mass of a rocket—which includes all of the fuel it carries—is much more than the mass of the hot gases as they come out of the exhaust nozzle. Because the hot gases are under extreme pressure, however, they exert a tremendous amount of force. The force that accelerates a rocket is called **thrust**. To learn more about how this works, look at **Figure 4.**

Figure 4 *Rockets work according to Newton's third law of motion.*

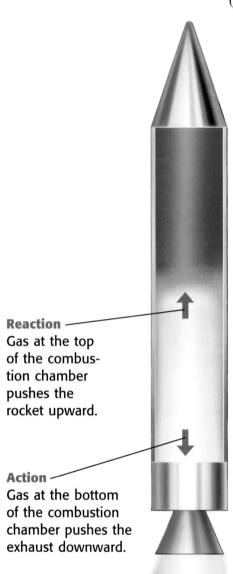

Reaction
Gas at the top of the combustion chamber pushes the rocket upward.

Action
Gas at the bottom of the combustion chamber pushes the exhaust downward.

Combustion All rockets have a combustion chamber in which hot gases are under very high pressure. As long as there is no opening for the gas to escape, the rocket remains at rest. In this state, the force that the gas exerts outward is the same as the force that the walls of the combustion chamber exert inward.

Pressure When the pressurized gas is released in only one direction—out the tail end of the rocket—the force of the hot gas against the top of the combustion chamber becomes greater than the opposing force of the air outside. As a result, the gas is forced out of the rocket nozzle.

Thrust If the force of the gas pushing against the top of the combustion chamber (thrust) becomes greater than the force of gravity holding the rocket down (the weight of the rocket), the rocket begins to move skyward.

How Fast Is Fast Enough? It is not enough for a rocket to have sufficient thrust to just move upward. It must have enough thrust to achieve *orbital velocity*. **Orbital velocity** is the speed and direction a rocket must have in order to orbit the Earth. The lowest possible speed a rocket may go and still orbit the Earth is about 8 km/s.

For Earth, all speeds less than about 8 km/s are *suborbital*. If the rocket goes any slower, it will fall back to Earth. If a rocket travels fast enough, however, it can attain *escape velocity*. **Escape velocity** is the speed and direction a rocket must travel in order to completely break away from a planet's gravitational pull. As you can see in **Figure 5,** the speed a rocket must attain to escape the Earth is about 11 km/s.

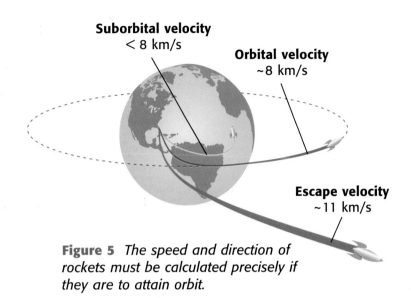

Figure 5 *The speed and direction of rockets must be calculated precisely if they are to attain orbit.*

You Need More Than Rocket Fuel . . . Rockets burn fuel to provide the thrust that propels them forward. But in order for something to burn, oxygen must be present. The earliest rocket fuel was gunpowder, which burns because oxygen is present in the atmosphere. Goddard was the first to use liquid fuel for rockets, which also burns in the presence of oxygen. But while oxygen is plentiful at the Earth's surface, in the upper atmosphere and in outer space, there is little or no oxygen. For this reason, rockets that go into outer space must carry enough oxygen with them to be able to burn their fuel. Otherwise the escaping gas would not create enough thrust to propel the rocket forward.

MATH BREAK

It's Just Rocket Science

As a burning gas (*g*) rushes out the back of a rocket (*r*), it provides thrust to move the rocket. The mass (*m*) and speed (*v*) of the gas and rocket are given by the following equation:

$$m_g \times v_g = m_r \times v_r$$

If the mass of a rocket is 100,000 kg, the speed of the gas leaving the rocket is 1,000 m/s, and the mass of the gas leaving the rocket is 1,000 kg, how fast will the rocket move?

SECTION REVIEW

1. What force must we overcome to reach outer space?

2. How does a rocket engine work?

3. What is the difference between orbital velocity and escape velocity?

4. **Making Inferences** How did World War II help us get into space exploration earlier than we otherwise would have?

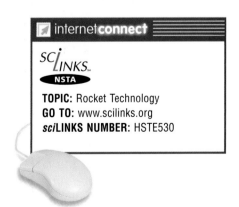

internet**connect**

SC*i*LINKS
NSTA

TOPIC: Rocket Technology
GO TO: www.scilinks.org
*sci*LINKS NUMBER: HSTE530

Artificial Satellites

Terms to Learn

artificial satellite
low Earth orbit
geosynchronous orbit

What You'll Do

◆ Describe how the launch of the first satellite started the space race.

◆ Explain why some orbits are better than others for communications satellites.

◆ Describe how the satellite program has given us a better understanding of the Earth as a global system.

In 1955, President Dwight D. Eisenhower announced that the United States would launch an artificial satellite as part of America's contribution to international space science. An **artificial satellite** is any human-made object placed in orbit around a body in space, such as Earth. The Soviets were also working on a satellite program—and launched their satellite first!

The Space Race Begins

On October 4, 1957, a Soviet satellite became the first object to be placed in orbit around the Earth. *Sputnik 1,* shown in **Figure 6,** carried instruments to measure the properties of Earth's upper atmosphere. Less than a month later, the Soviets launched *Sputnik 2.* This satellite carried a dog named Laika.

Two months later, the U.S. Navy attempted to launch its own satellite by using a Vanguard rocket, which was originally intended for launching weather instruments into the atmosphere. To the embarrassment of the United States, the rocket rose only 1 m into the air and exploded.

The U.S. Takes a Close Second In the meantime, the U.S. Army was also busy modifying its military rockets to send a satellite into space, and on January 31, 1958, *Explorer 1,* the first United States satellite, was successfully launched. The space race was on!

Explorer 1, shown in **Figure 7,** carried scientific instruments to measure cosmic rays and small dust particles and to record temperatures of the upper atmosphere. *Explorer 1* discovered the Van Allen radiation belts around the Earth. These are regions in the Earth's magnetic field where charged particles from the sun have been trapped.

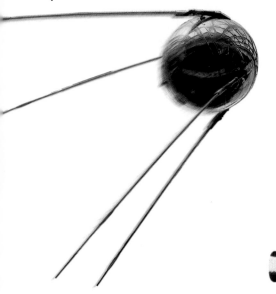

Figure 6 Sputnik 1 *was the first artificial satellite successfully placed in Earth orbit.*

Figure 7 *From left to right, NASA scientists William Pickering, James Van Allen, and Wernher von Braun show off a model of the first successfully launched American artificial satellite,* Explorer 1.

Into the Information Age

The first United States weather satellite, *Tiros 1,* was launched in April 1960 and gave meteorologists their first look at the Earth and its clouds from above. Weather satellites have given us an understanding of how storms develop and change by helping us study wind patterns and ocean currents. You now can see weather satellite images on your television at almost any time of the day or night or download them from the Internet.

Just a few months after *Tiros 1* began returning signals to Earth, the United States launched its first communications satellite, *Echo 1.* This satellite bounced signals from the ground to other areas on Earth, as shown in **Figure 8.** Within 3 years, sophisticated communications-satellite networks were sending TV signals from continent to continent.

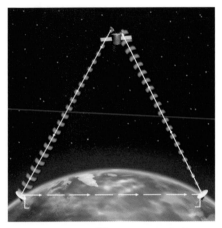

Figure 8 *Satellites can send signals beyond the curve of the Earth's surface, enabling communication around the world.*

Choose Your Orbit

All of the early satellites were placed in **low Earth orbit** (LEO), a few hundred kilometers above the Earth's surface. This location, while considered space, is still within the outermost part of Earth's atmosphere. A satellite in LEO travels around the Earth very quickly, which can place it out of contact much of the time.

Science fiction writer Arthur C. Clarke suggested a much higher orbit than LEO for weather and communications satellites. In this orbit, called a **geosynchronous orbit** (GEO), a satellite travels around the Earth at a speed that exactly matches the rotational speed of the Earth. This keeps the satellite positioned above the same spot on Earth at all times. Today there are many communications satellites in GEO. Ground stations are in continuous contact with these satellites, so your television program or phone call is not interrupted.

✓ Self-Check

The space station being built by the United States and other countries is in LEO. What is one advantage of this location? *(See page 200 to check your answer.)*

Anything GOES

The height above the Earth's surface for a geosynchronous orbit is 35,862 km. Today, a network of Geostationary Operational Environment Satellites (GOES) provides us with an international network of weather satellites. What would happen if a GOES satellite were placed in LEO rather than in GEO? How would that adversely affect the information the satellite was able to collect?

Not all satellites look down on Earth. Among the most important satellites to astronomers, for example, are the Hubble Space Telescope and the Chandra X-ray Observatory, both of which look out toward the stars.

Results of the Satellite Programs

Satellites gather information by *remote sensing*. Remote sensing is the gathering of images and data from high above the Earth's surface. The images and data help us investigate the Earth's surface by measuring the light and other forms of energy that reflect off Earth. Some satellites use radar, which bounces high-frequency radio waves off the surface of objects and measures the returned signal.

Military Satellites   The United States military, which has a keen interest in satellites for defense and spying purposes, recognized that LEO was a perfect location for placing powerful telescopes that could be turned toward the Earth to photograph activities on the ground anywhere in the world.

The period from the late 1940s to the late 1980s is known as the Cold War. During that time, the United States and the former Soviet Union built up their military forces in order to ensure that neither nation became more powerful than the other. Both countries monitored each other using spy satellites. **Figure 9** shows an image of part of the United States taken by a Soviet spy satellite during the Cold War.

The military also launches satellites into GEO to aid in navigation and to serve as early warning systems against missiles launched toward the United States. Even though the Cold War is over, spy satellites continue to play an important role in the United States's military defense.

Figure 9 *This image was taken in 1989 by a Soviet spy satellite in LEO about 220 km above the city of San Francisco. Can you identify any objects on the ground?*

Eyes on the Environment

Satellites have given us a new vantage point for looking at the Earth. By getting above the Earth's atmosphere and looking down, we have been able to study the Earth in ways that were never before possible.

One of the most successful remote-sensing projects was the Landsat program, which began in 1972 and continues today. It has given us the longest continuous record of Earth's surface as seen from space. The newest Landsat satellite (number 7) was launched in 1999. It will gather images in several frequencies—from visible light that we can see to infrared. The Landsat program has produced millions of images that are being used to identify and track global and regional changes on Earth, as shown in **Figure 10.**

Remote sensing has allowed scientists to perform large-scale mapping, look at changes in patterns of vegetation growth, map the spread of urban development, help with mineral exploration, and study the effect of humans on the global environment.

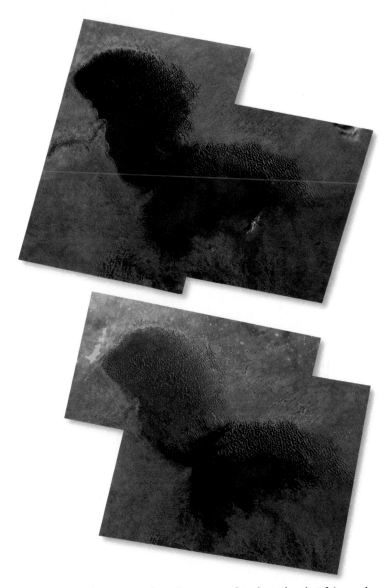

Figure 10 *These Landsat images of Lake Chad, Africa, show how environmental changes can be monitored from orbit. The top image was taken in 1973, and the bottom image was taken in 1987. Can you tell what changed?*

SECTION REVIEW

1. What types of satellites did the United States first place in orbit?

2. List two ways that satellites have benefited human society.

3. **Applying Concepts** The Hubble Space Telescope is located in LEO. Will the telescope move faster or slower around the Earth compared with a geosynchronous weather satellite? Explain.

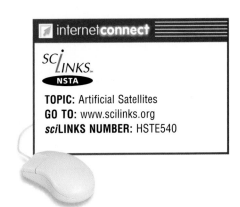

Terms to Learn

space probe

What You'll Do

◆ Describe some of the discoveries made by space probes.

◆ Explain how space-probe missions help us better understand the Earth.

◆ Describe how future space-probe missions will differ from the original missions to the planets.

Space Probes

The 1960s and early 1970s are known as the golden era of space exploration. The Soviets were the first to successfully launch a space probe. A **space probe** is a vehicle that carries scientific instruments to planets or other bodies in space. Unlike satellites, which stay in Earth orbit, space probes travel away from Earth. The early space probes gave us our first close encounters with the other planets and their moons.

Visits to Our Planetary Neighborhood

Because the Earth's moon and the inner planets of the solar system are so much closer to us than any other celestial bodies, they were the first to be targeted for exploration by the Soviet Union and the United States. Launched by the Soviets, *Luna 1* was the first space probe. In January of 1959, it flew past the moon. Two months later, an American space probe—*Pioneer 4*—accomplished the same feat. Follow along the next few pages to learn about space-probe missions since *Luna 1*.

The Moon

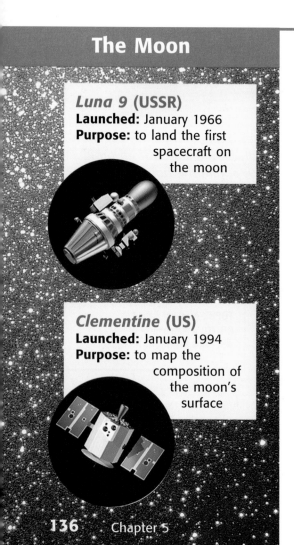

Luna 9 (USSR)
Launched: January 1966
Purpose: to land the first
spacecraft on
the moon

Clementine (US)
Launched: January 1994
Purpose: to map the
composition of
the moon's
surface

The Luna 9 and Clementine Missions *Luna 9,* a Soviet probe, made the first soft landing on the moon's surface. During the next 10 years, there were more than 30 lunar missions made by the Soviet Union and the United States. Thousands of images of the moon's surface were taken.

In 1994, the probe *Clementine* discovered possible evidence of water at the south pole of the moon. The image below was taken by the *Clementine* space probe and shows the area surrounding the south pole of the moon. You can see that some of the craters at the pole are permanently in shadow. Elsewhere on the moon, sunlight would cause any ice to vaporize. Ice may have been left by comet impacts. If this frozen water exists, it will be very valuable to humans seeking to colonize the moon.

Lunar South Pole

The Venera 9 Mission The Soviet Union landed the first probe on Venus. The probe, called *Venera 9*, parachuted into Venus's atmosphere and transmitted the first images of the surface. *Venera 9* found that surface temperature and atmospheric pressure on Venus are much higher than on Earth. It also found that the chemistry of the surface rocks is similar to that of rocks on Earth. Perhaps most importantly, *Venera 9* and earlier missions showed us a planet with a severe greenhouse effect. Scientists study Venus's atmosphere to learn about how greenhouse gases released into Earth's atmosphere trap thermal energy.

The Magellan Mission In 1989, the United States launched the *Magellan* probe, which used radar to map 98 percent of the surface of Venus. The Magellan mission showed that, in many ways, the geology of Venus is similar to that of Earth. Venus has features that suggest some type of plate tectonics occurs, as it does on Earth. Venus also has volcanoes, some of which may have been active recently. The diagram at below left shows the *Magellan* probe using radar to penetrate the thick cloud layer. The radar data were then transmitted back to Earth, where computers were able to use the data to generate three-dimensional maps like the one at below right.

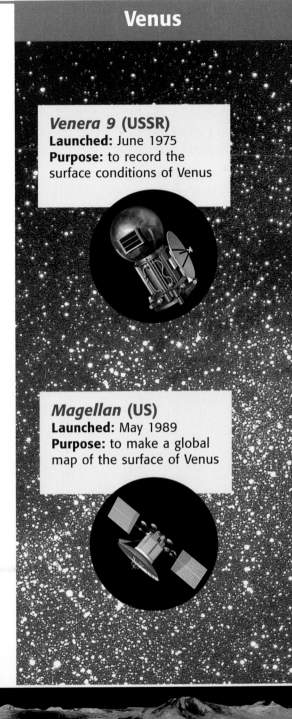

Venus

Venera 9 (USSR)
Launched: June 1975
Purpose: to record the surface conditions of Venus

Magellan (US)
Launched: May 1989
Purpose: to make a global map of the surface of Venus

Mars

The Viking Missions In 1975, the United States sent a pair of probes—*Viking 1* and *Viking 2*—to Mars. Because the surface of Mars is more like the Earth's surface than that of any other planet, one of the main goals of the Viking missions was to look for signs of life. The probes contained instruments designed to collect soil samples and test them for evidence of life. However, no hard evidence was found. The Viking missions did find evidence that Mars was once much warmer and wetter than it is now. The probes sent back images of dry water channels on the planet's surface. This discovery led scientists to ask even more questions about Mars. Why and when did the Martian climate change?

Viking 2 (US)
Launched: September 1975
Purpose: to search for life on the surface of Mars

Mars Pathfinder (US)
Launched: December 1996
Purpose: to use inexpensive technology to study the surface of Mars

The Mars Pathfinder Mission More than 20 years later, in 1997, the surface of Mars was visited again by a NASA space probe. The goal of the Mars Pathfinder mission was to show that Martian exploration is possible at a lower cost than that of the larger Viking mission. The *Mars Pathfinder* successfully landed on Mars and deployed the *Sojourner* rover, which traveled across the planetary surface for almost 3 months, collecting data and recording images of the Martian surface, as shown at left.

The Pioneer and Voyager Missions The *Pioneer 10* and *Pioneer 11* space probes were the first to visit the outer planets. Among other things, these probes sampled the *solar wind*—the flow of particles coming from the sun. The Pioneer probes also found that the dark belts on Jupiter are warmer than the light belts and that these dark belts provide deeper views into Jupiter's atmosphere. In June of 1983, *Pioneer 10* became the first space probe to travel past the orbit of Pluto, the outermost planet.

The Voyager space probes were the first to detect Jupiter's faint rings, and *Voyager 2* was the first space probe to fly by the four gas giant planets—Jupiter, Saturn, Uranus, and Neptune. The paths of the Pioneer and Voyager space probes are shown below. Today they are all near the edge of the solar system and are still sending back information.

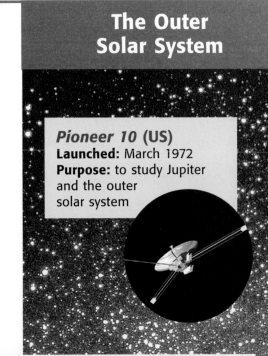

Pioneer 10 (US)
Launched: March 1972
Purpose: to study Jupiter and the outer solar system

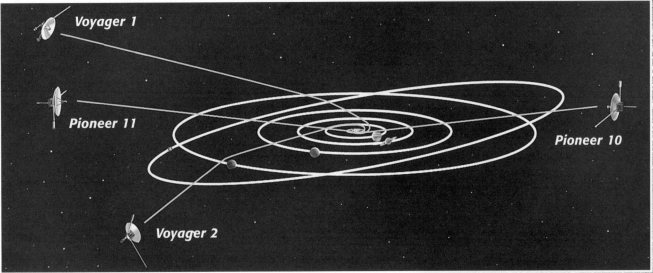

The Galileo Mission The *Galileo* space probe arrived at Jupiter in 1995. While *Galileo* itself began a long tour of Jupiter's moons, it sent a smaller probe into Jupiter's atmosphere to measure composition, density, temperature, and cloud structure. During its tour, *Galileo* gathered data that allowed scientists to study the geology of Jupiter's major moons and to examine Jupiter's magnetic properties more closely. The moons of Jupiter proved to be far more exciting than the earlier Pioneer and Voyager images had suggested. The *Galileo* probe discovered that two of Jupiter's moons have magnetic fields and that one of its moons, Europa, may have an ocean of liquid water lying under its icy surface.

Galileo (US)
Launched: October 1989
Purpose: to study Jupiter and its moons

Space Probes—A New Approach

NASA has a vision for missions that are "faster, cheaper, and better." The original space probes were very large, complex, and costly. Probes such as *Voyager 2* and *Galileo* took years to develop and carry out. One new program, called Discovery, seeks proposals for smaller science programs. The missions are supposed to bring faster results at much lower costs. The first six approved Discovery missions included sending small space probes to asteroids, another Mars landing, studies of the moon, the return of comet dust to Earth, collecting samples of the solar wind, and a tour of three comets.

Stardust—Comet Detective

Launched in 1999, the *Stardust* space probe is a NASA Discovery mission and the first to focus only on a comet. As shown in **Figure 11,** it will arrive at the comet in 2004 and gather samples of the comet's dust tail, returning them to Earth in 2006. It will be the first time that material from beyond the orbit of the moon has been brought back to Earth. The comet dust should help scientists better understand the evolution of the sun and the planets.

Figure 11 Stardust *will visit a comet and collect samples of its dust tail.*

***Deep Space 1*—The New Kid in Town** Another NASA project is the New Millennium program. Its purpose is to test new and risky technologies so that they can be used with confidence in the years to come. *Deep Space 1,* shown in **Figure 12,** undertook the first mission of this program. It is a space probe with an ion-propulsion system. Rather than burning chemical fuel, an ion rocket uses charged particles that exit the vehicle at high speed. An ion rocket still follows Newton's third law of motion, but it does so using a different source of propulsion.

Figure 12 Deep Space 1 *uses a revolutionary type of propulsion—an ion drive.*

The Last of the Big Boys On October 15, 1997, the *Cassini* space probe was launched on a 7-year journey to Saturn. This is the last of the large old-style missions. The *Cassini* space probe will make a grand tour of Saturn's system of moons, much as *Galileo* toured Jupiter's system. As shown in **Figure 13,** a smaller probe, called the *Huygens probe,* will detach itself from *Cassini* and descend into the atmosphere of Saturn's moon Titan to study its chemistry.

Biology CONNECTION

The atmosphere of Titan, Saturn's largest moon, may be similar to Earth's early atmosphere. Scientists hope to study the chemistry of Titan's atmosphere for clues to how life developed on Earth.

Figure 13 *An artist's view of* Cassini *at Saturn, with* Huygens *falling toward Saturn's moon Titan.*

Future Missions Proposals for future missions include a first-ever space-probe visit to Pluto, an orbiter for Jupiter's moon Europa that will use radar to determine whether it has a liquid ocean, and a possible Mercury orbiter to survey the planet closest to the sun. These are just a few of the many exciting international missions planned for the future—opening up a new golden era of planetary exploration.

SECTION REVIEW

1. List three discoveries that have been made by space probes.

2. Which two planets best help us understand Earth's environment? Explain.

3. What are the advantages of the new Discovery program over the older space-probe missions?

4. **Inferring Conclusions** Why did we need space probes to discover water channels on Mars or ice on Europa?

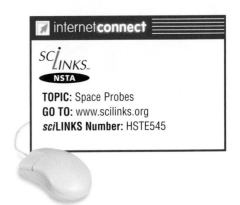

internet**connect**

*sci*LINKS
NSTA

TOPIC: Space Probes
GO TO: www.scilinks.org
*sci*LINKS Number: HSTE545

Living and Working in Space

Terms to Learn

space shuttle
space station

What You'll Do

◆ Summarize the benefits of the manned space program.
◆ Explain how large projects such as the Apollo program and the *International Space Station* developed.
◆ Identify future possibilities for human exploration of space.

Although sending human explorers into space was an early goal of the space program, it had to come in small steps. The first steps were to test the control of spacecraft with rocket-powered airplanes. Test flights in high-speed aircraft through the upper atmosphere became the beginnings of the Mercury program. The goal of the Mercury program was to put a man in orbit and to test his ability to function in space. Test flights began in 1959, but the dates for manned flight kept getting delayed because of unreliable rockets.

Human Space Exploration

On April 12, 1961, a Soviet cosmonaut named Yuri Gagarin became the first human to orbit the Earth. The United States didn't achieve its first suborbital flight until May 5, 1961, when Alan Shepard reached space but not orbit. Because the Soviets were first once again, they appeared to be winning the Cold War. As a result, many Americans began to consider the military advantages of a strong presence in space. On May 25, 1961, an announcement was made that would set the tone for American space policy for the next 10 years.

Figure 14 *In 1962, John Glenn flew aboard* Friendship 7, *the first NASA spacecraft to orbit the Earth.*

"I believe that this nation should commit itself to achieving the goal, before this decade is out, of landing a man on the moon and returning him safely to the Earth. No single space project in this period will be more impressive to mankind, or more important for the long-range exploration of space; and none will be so difficult or expensive to accomplish."

— *John F. Kennedy, President of the United States*

Many people were expecting the simple announcement of an accelerated space program, but Kennedy's proclamation took everyone by surprise—especially the leaders at NASA. Go to the moon? The United States had not even achieved Earth orbit yet! But the American people took the challenge seriously, and by February 1962, a new spaceport site in Florida was purchased, a manned space-center site was bought, and John Glenn, shown in **Figure 14,** was successfully launched into orbit around the Earth.

The Dream Comes True On July 20, 1969, the President's challenge was met. The *Apollo 11* landing module—the *Eagle*, shown in **Figure 15**—landed on the moon. Astronaut Neil Armstrong became the first human to set foot on a world other than Earth, forever changing the way we view ourselves and our planet.

Although the primary reason for the Apollo program was political (national pride), the Apollo missions also contributed to the advancement of science and technology. *Apollo 11* returned nearly 22 kg of moon rocks to Earth for study. Its crew also put devices on the moon to monitor moonquake activity and the solar wind. The results from these samples and studies completely changed our view of the solar system.

The Space Shuttle

The dream of human space flight and Kennedy's challenge were great for getting us into space, but they could not be the motivation for the continued political support of space exploration. The huge rockets required for launching spacecraft into orbit were just too expensive.

Early in the manned program, Wernher von Braun had suggested that a reusable space transportation system would be needed. Proposals for reusable launch vehicles were made in the 1950s and 1960s, but the Kennedy challenge overshadowed other efforts, and these ideas were not given serious attention. Finally in 1972, President Richard Nixon announced a space shuttle program to the American public, saying that this would be an economical way to get into space regularly. A **space shuttle** is a reusable vehicle that takes off like a rocket and lands like an airplane, as shown in **Figure 16**.

Figure 15 *Astronaut Neil Armstrong took this photo of Edwin "Buzz" Aldrin as he was about to become the second human being to step onto the moon.*

Figure 16 Columbia *was one of NASA's original shuttles.*

The first shuttle was launched on April 12, 1981, and was followed by two dozen successful missions until 1986, when tragedy struck. On January 28, 1986, the booster rocket on the space shuttle *Challenger* exploded just after takeoff, killing all seven of its astronauts. On board was Christa McAuliffe, who would have been the first teacher in space. All shuttle flights were suspended until this disaster could be explained. Finally in 1988, the space shuttle program resumed with the return of shuttle *Discovery* to space.

Commuter Shuttle? Currently efforts are underway to make space travel easier and cheaper. New space vehicles are being developed for more efficient space travel. The *X-33*, shown in **Figure 17,** was the first space plane that scientists attempted to develop. Although the *X-33* became too costly to complete, research continues on the next generation of space vehicles. Once in operation, space planes may lower the cost of getting material to LEO by 90 percent. New types of rockets and rocket fuels, as well as other means of sending vehicles into space, are being considered.

Figure 17 *Future space vehicles may provide inexpensive transportation not only between Earth and outer space but around the world.*

Biology
C O N N E C T I O N

When a human body stays in space for long periods of time without having to work against gravity, the bones lose mass and muscles become weaker. Long space-station missions, which can last for months, are very important in order to study whether humans can survive voyages to Mars and other planets. These missions will last for several years.

Space Stations—People Working in Space
On April 19, 1971, the Soviets became the first to successfully place a manned space station in low Earth orbit. A **space station** is a long-term orbiting platform from which other vehicles can be launched or scientific research can be carried out. In June of the same year, a crew of three Soviet cosmonauts entered *Salyut 1* to conduct a 23-day mission. By 1982, the Soviets had put up a total of seven space stations. Because of this experience, the Soviet Union became the world leader in space-station development and in the study of the effects of weightlessness on humans. Their discoveries will be important for future manned flights to other planets— journeys that will take years to complete.

A Home Away from Home *Skylab,* the United States's first space station, was a science and engineering lab that orbited the Earth in LEO at a height of 435 km. The lab, shown in **Figure 18,** was used to conduct a wide variety of scientific studies, including astronomy, biological experiments, and experiments in space manufacturing. Three different crews spent a total of 171 days on board *Skylab.*

All objects in LEO, including *Skylab,* eventually spiral toward Earth. Even at several hundred kilometers above the Earth, there is still a very small amount of atmosphere. The atmosphere slows down any object in orbit unless something periodically pushes the object in the opposite direction. *Skylab*'s orbit began to decay in 1979. A space shuttle was supposed to return the lab to a higher orbit, but delays in the shuttle program prevented the rescue of *Skylab,* and it fell into the Indian Ocean.

Figure 18 Skylab, *in orbit above Earth, was lifted into space by a Saturn V rocket.*

From Russia with Peace In 1986, the Soviets began to launch the pieces for a much more ambitious space station called *Mir* (meaning "peace"). The Soviets, and later the Russians, used *Mir* to conduct astronomy experiments, provide biological and Earth orbital observations, and study manufacturing technologies in space. When completed, *Mir* had seven modules and measured 33 m long and 27 m wide.

Astronauts from the United States and other countries eventually became visitors to *Mir,* as shown in **Figure 19.** Almost continuously inhabited between 1987 and 1999, *Mir* became the inspiration to build the next generation of space station—the International Space Station.

Figure 19 Mir *provided an opportunity for American astronauts and Russian cosmonauts to live and work together in space.*

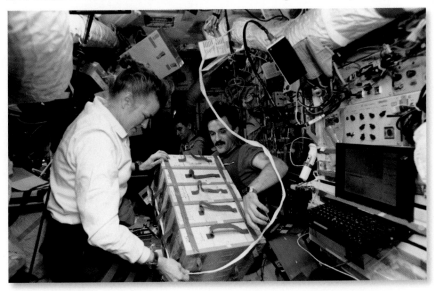

Science
CONNECTION

Working together to live in space? To learn more about the latest station in orbit, turn to page 154.

BRAIN FOOD

It will take more than 40 shuttle flights and 6 years to lift into space the 400 tons of materials needed for the construction of the *International Space Station.*

The International Space Station

In 1993, a design for a new space station was proposed that called for international involvement and a collaboration between the newly formed Russian Republic and the United States. The new space station is called the *International Space Station (ISS)*. A drawing of the station when completed is shown in **Figure 20.**

The station is being assembled in LEO with materials brought up on the space shuttle or by Russian rockets. The United States is providing lab modules, the supporting truss, solar panels for power, living quarters, and a biomedical laboratory. The Russians are contributing a service module, docking modules, life support and research modules, and transportation to and from the station. Other components will come from Japan, Canada, and several European countries.

The *ISS* will provide many benefits—some of which we cannot even predict. What we do know is that it will be a good place to perform space-science experiments and perhaps to invent new technologies. Hopefully the *ISS* will also promote cooperation among countries and continue the pioneering spirit of the first astronauts and cosmonauts.

Figure 20 *This artist's view of the* International Space Station *shows what the station will look like once it is completed.*

The Moon, Mars, and Beyond

We may eventually need resources and living space beyond what Earth can provide. Space can provide abundant mineral resources. One interesting resource is a rare form of helium that can be found on the moon. Used as a fuel for nuclear reactors, it leaves no radioactive waste!

We have seen that there are also many scientific benefits to space exploration. For example, the far side of the moon can be 100 times darker than any observatory site on Earth. The moon also could be a wonderful place to locate factories that require a vacuum to process materials, as shown in **Figure 21.** A base in Earth orbit can produce materials that require low gravity. A colony or base on the moon or on Mars could be an important link to bringing space resources to Earth. The key will be to make these missions economically worthwhile.

Activity

Technological improvements intended for space exploration have often led to the invention of new products that improve our lives here on Earth. NASA has a special program that transfers these new ideas and technology to the public. Find out more about NASA's technology transfers on the Internet and about how many everyday technologies had their beginnings in the space program.

Figure 21 *Humans may eventually colonize the moon for scientific, economic, and perhaps even recreational reasons.*

SECTION REVIEW

1. How was the race to explore our solar system influenced by the Cold War?

2. How did missions to the moon benefit space science?

3. How will space stations help in the exploration of space?

4. **Making Inferences** Why did the United States quit sending people to the moon after the Apollo program ended?

internet**connect**

SC*I*LINKS.
NSTA

TOPIC: Space Exploration and Space Stations
GO TO: www.scilinks.org
*sci*LINKS NUMBER: HSTE550

Making Models Lab

USING SCIENTIFIC METHODS

Reach for the Stars

Have you ever thought about living and working in space? Well, in order for you to do so, you would have to learn to deal with the new environment. Astronauts must adjust to the conditions of space. Meanwhile, they are also dealing with special tools used to repair and build space stations. In this activity, you will get the chance to model one tool that might help astronauts work in space.

MATERIALS

- cardboard box
- scissors
- metric ruler
- hole punch
- 2 brads
- metal wire
- 2 jumbo paper clips
- plastic-foam ball

Ask a Question

1 How can I build a piece of equipment that models how astronauts work in space?

Form a Hypothesis

2 Before you begin, write a hypothesis that answers the question in step 1. Explain your reasoning.

Test the Hypothesis

3 Cut three strips from the cardboard box. Each strip should be about 5 cm wide. The strips should be at least 20 cm long but not longer than 40 cm.

4 Punch holes near the center of each end of the three cardboard strips. The holes should be about 3 cm from the end of each strip.

5 Lay the strips end to end along your table. Slide the second strip toward the first strip so that a hole in the first strip lines up with a hole in the second strip. Slip a brad through the holes, and bend its ends out to attach the cardboard strips.

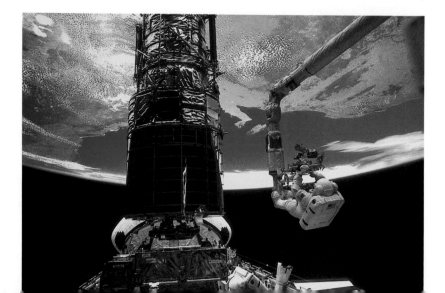

6 Use another brad to attach the third cardboard strip to the free end of the second strip. Now you have your mechanical arm. The brads form joints where the cardboard strips meet.

7 Straighten the wire, and slide it through the hole in one end of your mechanical arm. Bend about 3 cm of the wire in a 90° angle so that it will not slide back out of the hole.

8 Try to move the arm by holding the free ends of the cardboard and wire. The arm should bend and straighten at the joints. If the arm is hard to move, adjust the design. Consider loosening the brads, for example.

9 Now your mechanical arm needs a hand. Otherwise, it won't be able to pick things up! Straighten one paper clip, and slide it through the hole where you attached the wire in step 7. Bend one end of the paper clip to form a loop around the cardboard, and bend the other end to form a hook. You will use this hook to pick up things.

10 Bend a second paper clip into a U-shape. Stick the straight end of this paper clip into the foam ball. Leave the ball on your desk.

11 Move the arm so that you can lift the foam ball. The paper-clip hook on the arm will have to catch the paper clip on the ball.

Analyze the Results

12 Did you have any trouble moving the arm in step 8? What changes did you make?

13 Did you have trouble picking up the foam ball? What might have made this step easier?

Draw Conclusions

14 What changes could you make to your mechanical arm that might make it easier to use?

15 How would a tool like this one help people work in space?

Going Further

Adjust the design for your mechanical arm. Can you find a way to lift anything other than the foam ball? For example, can you lift heavier objects or ones that do not have a loop attached? How?

Research the tools that astronauts use on space stations and on the space shuttle. How do their tools help them work in the conditions of space?

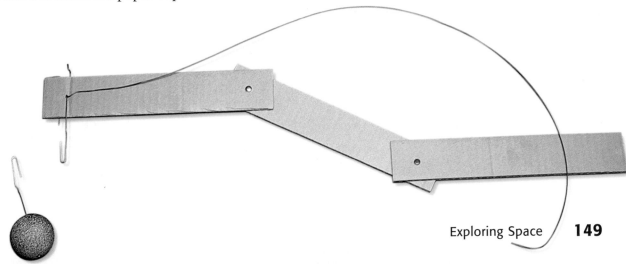

Chapter Highlights

SECTION 1

Vocabulary

rocket (*p. 128*)

NASA (*p. 129*)

thrust (*p. 130*)

orbital velocity (*p. 131*)

escape velocity (*p. 131*)

Section Notes

- Two pioneers of rocketry were Konstantin Tsiolkovsky and Robert Goddard.

- Rockets work according to Newton's third law of motion—for every action there is an equal and opposite reaction.

- NASA was formed in 1958, combining rocket research from several programs. It was originally formed to compete with the Soviet Union's rocket program.

Labs

Water Rockets Save the Day! (*p. 168*)

SECTION 2

Vocabulary

artificial satellite (*p. 132*)

low Earth orbit (*p. 133*)

geosynchronous orbit (*p. 133*)

Section Notes

- The Soviet Union launched the first Earth-orbiting satellite in 1957. The first United States satellite went up in 1958.

- Low Earth orbits (LEOs) are located a few hundred kilometers above the Earth's surface. Satellites in geosynchronous orbits (GEOs) have an orbit period of 24 hours and remain over one spot.

- Satellite programs are used for weather observations, communications, mapping the Earth, and tracking ocean currents, crop growth, and urban development.

- One great legacy of the satellite program has been an increase in our awareness of the Earth's fragile environment.

☑ Skills Check

Math Concepts

THE ROCKET EQUATION Suppose the mass of a certain rocket is 1,000 kg and the mass of the gas leaving the rocket is 100 kg. If the speed that the gas leaves the rocket is 50 m/s, the rocket will move at a speed of 5 m/s. Rearranging the rocket equation:

$$m_g \times v_g = m_r \times v_r$$

as $v_r = m_g \times v_g / m_r$

gives $v_r = \dfrac{100 \text{ kg} \times 50 \text{ m/s}}{1{,}000 \text{ kg}} = 5 \text{ m/s}$

Visual Understanding

GLOBAL COMMUNICATION As you saw on page 133, satellites can relay television, radio, and telephone signals around the world. Because they remain in GEO, these satellites are always above the same spot on Earth, letting them relay our signals without interruption.

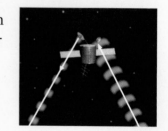

SECTION 3

Vocabulary

space probe *(p. 136)*

Section Notes

• Planetary exploration with space probes began with missions to the moon. The next targets of exploration were the inner planets: Venus, Mercury, and Mars.

• The United States has been the only country to explore the outer solar system, beginning with the Pioneer and Voyager missions.

• Space-probe science has given us information about how planets form and develop, helping us better understand our own planet Earth.

SECTION 4

Vocabulary

space shuttle *(p. 143)*
space station *(p. 144)*

Section Notes

• The great race to get a manned flight program underway and to reach the moon was politically motivated.

• The United States beat the Soviets to a manned moon landing with the Apollo moon flights in 1969.

• During the 1970s, the United States focused on developing the space shuttle. The Soviets focused on developing orbiting space stations.

• The United States, Russia, and 14 other international partners are currently developing the *International Space Station.*

• Because of scientific, economic, and even recreational reasons, humans may eventually live and work on other planets and moons.

internet connect

GO TO: go.hrw.com

Visit the **HRW** Web site for a variety of learning tools related to this chapter. Just type in the keyword:

KEYWORD: HSTEXP

GO TO: www.scilinks.org

Visit the **National Science Teachers Association** on-line Web site for Internet resources related to this chapter. Just type in the *sci*LINKS number for more information about the topic:

TOPIC:	Rocket Technology	*sci*LINKS NUMBER: HSTE530
TOPIC:	The History of NASA	*sci*LINKS NUMBER: HSTE535
TOPIC:	Artificial Satellites	*sci*LINKS NUMBER: HSTE540
TOPIC:	Space Probes	*sci*LINKS NUMBER: HSTE545
TOPIC:	Space Exploration and Space Stations	*sci*LINKS NUMBER: HSTE550

Chapter Review

For each pair of terms, explain the difference in their meaning:

1. geosynchronous orbit/low Earth orbit

2. space probe/space shuttle

3. artificial satellite/moon

To complete the following sentences, choose the correct term from each pair of terms listed below:

4. The force that accelerates a rocket is called ___?___. (*escape velocity* or *thrust*)

5. Rockets need to have ___?___ in order to burn their fuel. (*oxygen* or *nitrogen*)

UNDERSTANDING CONCEPTS

Multiple Choice

6. The father of modern rocketry is considered to be
   a. K. Tsiolkovsky.   c. W. von Braun.
   b. R. Goddard.   d. D. Eisenhower.

7. Rockets work according to Newton's
   a. first law of motion.
   b. second law of motion.
   c. third law of motion.
   d. law of universal gravitation.

8. The first artificial satellite to orbit the Earth was
   a. *Pioneer 4.*   c. *Voyager 2.*
   b. *Explorer 1.*   d. *Sputnik 1.*

9. Satellites are able to transfer TV signals across and between continents because satellites
   a. are located in LEOs.
   b. relay signals past the horizon.
   c. travel quickly around Earth.
   d. can be used during the day and night.

10. GEOs are better orbits for communications because satellites in GEO
    a. remain in position over one spot.
    b. are farther away from Earth's surface.
    c. do not revolve around the Earth.
    d. are only a few hundred kilometers high.

11. Which space probe discovered evidence of water at the moon's south pole?
    a. *Luna 9*
    b. *Viking 1*
    c. *Clementine*
    d. *Magellan*

12. When did humans first set foot on the moon?
    a. 1949   c. 1969
    b. 1959   d. 1979

13. Which one of these planets has not yet been visited by space probes?
    a. Mercury
    b. Neptune
    c. Mars
    d. Pluto

14. Of the following, which space probe is about to leave our solar system?
    a. *Galileo*   c. *Mariner 10*
    b. *Magellan*   d. *Pioneer 10*

15. Based on space-probe data, which of the following is the most likely place in our solar system to find liquid water?
    a. the moon   c. Europa
    b. Mars   d. Venus

Short Answer

16. Describe how Newton's third law of motion relates to the movement of rockets.

17. What is one disadvantage that objects in LEO have?

18. Why did the United States develop the space shuttle?

19. During which period were spy satellites first used?

Concept Mapping

20. Use the following terms to create a concept map: orbital velocity, thrust, LEO, artificial satellites, escape velocity, space probes, GEO, rockets.

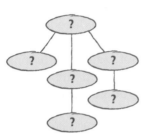

CRITICAL THINKING AND PROBLEM SOLVING

Write one or two sentences to answer the following questions:

21. What is the difference between speed and velocity?

22. Why must rockets that travel in outer space carry oxygen with them?

23. How will data from space probes help us understand the Earth's environment?

24. Why is it necessary for several nations to work together to create the *ISS*?

MATH IN SCIENCE

25. In order to escape Earth's gravity, a rocket must travel at least 11 km/s. This is pretty fast! If you could travel to the moon at this speed, how many hours would it take you to get there? (The moon is about 384,000 km away from Earth.) Round your answer to the nearest whole number.

INTERPRETING GRAPHICS

The map below was made using satellite data. It indicates the different amounts of chlorophyll in the ocean. Chlorophyll, in turn, identifies the presence of marine plankton. The blues and purples show the smallest amount of chlorophyll, and the reds and oranges show the most. Examine the map, and answer the questions that follow:

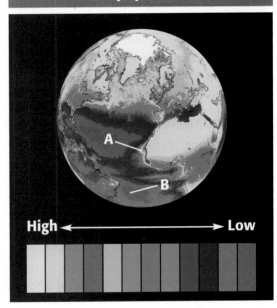

Chlorophyll Content

High ← → Low

26. At which location, **A** or **B**, are more plankton concentrated?

27. What do you conclude about the conditions in which plankton prefer to live?

Reading Check-up

Take a minute to review your answers to the Pre-Reading Questions found at the bottom of page 126. Have your answers changed? If necessary, revise your answers based on what you have learned since you began this chapter.

International Space Station

On a June day in 1995, the space shuttle *Atlantis* docked at the Russian space station, *Mir,* and picked up three passengers. These passengers, one from the United States and two from Russia, had completed a 3-month stay at the space station. This mission was the first in a series of missions to develop construction techniques for assembling the *International Space Station.* These missions are considered to be phase one of the process.

An International Place in Space

Sixteen nations plan to build the *International Space Station (ISS)* by the year 2004. These nations are the United States, Russia, Canada, Brazil, Japan, Denmark, Germany, France, Italy, Belgium, the Netherlands, Switzerland, the United Kingdom, Spain, Norway, and Sweden.

The *ISS* will be made up of cylindrical rooms called *modules.* Each of these components will be built on the ground and then assembled 274 km above Earth. The current plan calls for more than 40 space flights to carry the parts of the space station into orbit. Once the *ISS* is completed, a seven-member crew will be able to live and work there.

Life Aboard

One of the strange things about living in space is the reduced effect of gravity known as *free fall.* Everything inside the space station that is not fastened down, including the astronauts, will float! The designers of the *ISS*'s habitation module have come up with some intriguing solutions to this problem. For example, each astronaut will sleep in a sack similar to a sleeping bag that is fastened to the module. The sack will keep the astronauts from floating around while they sleep. Astronauts will shower with a hand-held nozzle that squirts water onto their body. Afterward, the water droplets will be vacuumed up so that they won't float around. Other problems being studied include how to prepare and serve food, how to design an effective toilet, and how to dispose of waste.

Ready to Go

Phase two began with the actual construction of the *ISS* in orbit. In November and December of 1998, two modules, *Zarya* and *Unity,* were launched into orbit. In early 2000, a three-person crew began living on board—the first of many crews expected to inhabit the *International Space Station.*

Address the Gravity of a Situation

▶ Create a sketch for a device that will help the space-station crew cope with free fall. Pick a problem to solve such as brushing teeth, getting exercise, or washing hair.

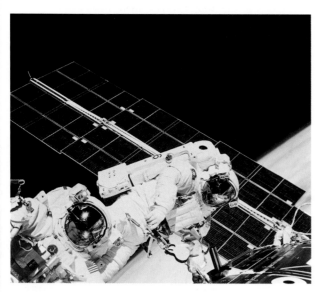

▲ *Parts of the* International Space Station *are being assembled in space.*

Science Fiction

"Why I Left Harry's All-Night Hamburgers"

by Lawrence Watt-Evans

At 16, he needed a job. His dad was out of work and his family needed money. Right around the corner from his house was Harry's All-Night Hamburgers. With a little persistence, he talked Harry into giving him a job.

He worked from midnight to 7:30 A.M. so he could still go to school. He was the counterman, waiter, busboy, and janitor, all in one. Harry's was pretty quiet most nights, especially because the interstate was 8 mi away and nobody wanted to drive to Harry's. Most of the time, the customers were pretty normal.

There were some, though, who were unusual. For instance, one guy came in dressed for Arctic winter, even though it was April and it was 60°F outside. Then there were the folks who parked a very strange vehicle right out in the parking lot for anyone to see.

Pretty soon, the captivated waiter starts asking questions. What he learns startles and fascinates him. Soon he's thinking about leaving Harry's. Find out why by reading "Why I Left Harry's All-Night Hamburgers," by Lawrence Watt-Evans, in the *Holt Anthology of Science Fiction.*

Exploring, inventing, and investigating are essential to the study of science. However, these activities can also be dangerous. To make sure that your experiments and explorations are safe, you must be aware of a variety of safety guidelines.

You have probably heard of the saying, "It is better to be safe than sorry." This is particularly true in a science classroom where experiments and explorations are being performed. Being uninformed and careless can result in serious injuries. Don't take chances with your own safety or with anyone else's.

Following are important guidelines for staying safe in the science classroom. Your teacher may also have safety guidelines and tips that are specific to your classroom and laboratory. Take the time to be safe.

Safety Rules!

Start Out Right

Always get your teacher's permission before attempting any laboratory exploration. Read the procedures carefully, and pay particular attention to safety information and caution statements. If you are unsure about what a safety symbol means, look it up or ask your teacher. You cannot be too careful when it comes to safety. If an accident does occur, inform your teacher immediately, regardless of how minor you think the accident is.

Safety Symbols

All of the experiments and investigations in this book and their related worksheets include important safety symbols to alert you to particular safety concerns. Become familiar with these symbols so that when you see them, you will know what they mean and what to do. It is important that you read this entire safety section to learn about specific dangers in the laboratory.

If you are instructed to note the odor of a substance, wave the fumes toward your nose with your hand. Never put your nose close to the source.

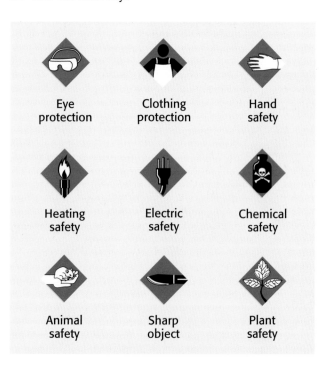

Eye protection

Clothing protection

Hand safety

Heating safety

Electric safety

Chemical safety

Animal safety

Sharp object

Plant safety

Eye Safety

Wear safety goggles when working around chemicals, acids, bases, or any type of flame or heating device. Wear safety goggles any time there is even the slightest chance that harm could come to your eyes. If any substance gets into your eyes, notify your teacher immediately, and flush your eyes with running water for at least 15 minutes. Treat any unknown chemical as if it were a dangerous chemical. Never look directly into the sun. Doing so could cause permanent blindness.

Avoid wearing contact lenses in a laboratory situation. Even if you are wearing safety goggles, chemicals can get between the contact lenses and your eyes. If your doctor requires that you wear contact lenses instead of glasses, wear eye-cup safety goggles in the lab.

Safety Equipment

Know the locations of the nearest fire alarms and any other safety equipment, such as fire blankets and eyewash fountains, as identified by your teacher, and know the procedures for using them.

Be extra careful when using any glassware. When adding a heavy object to a graduated cylinder, tilt the cylinder so the object slides slowly to the bottom.

Neatness

Keep your work area free of all unnecessary books and papers. Tie back long hair, and secure loose sleeves or other loose articles of clothing, such as ties and bows. Remove dangling jewelry. Don't wear open-toed shoes or sandals in the laboratory. Never eat, drink, or apply cosmetics in a laboratory setting. Food, drink, and cosmetics can easily become contaminated with dangerous materials.

Certain hair products (such as aerosol hair spray) are flammable and should not be worn while working near an open flame. Avoid wearing hair spray or hair gel on lab days.

Sharp/Pointed Objects

Use knives and other sharp instruments with extreme care. Never cut objects while holding them in your hands. Place objects on a suitable work surface for cutting.

Heat

Wear safety goggles when using a heating device or a flame. Whenever possible, use an electric hot plate as a heat source instead of an open flame. When heating materials in a test tube, always angle the test tube away from yourself and others. In order to avoid burns, wear heat-resistant gloves whenever instructed to do so.

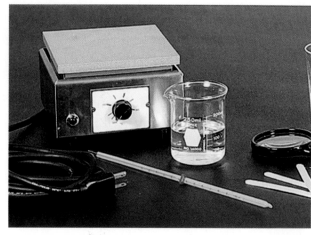

Electricity

Be careful with electrical cords. When using a microscope with a lamp, do not place the cord where it could trip someone. Do not let cords hang over a table edge in a way that could cause equipment to fall if the cord is accidentally pulled. Do not use equipment with damaged cords. Be sure your hands are dry and that the electrical equipment is in the "off" position before plugging it in. Turn off and unplug electrical equipment when you are finished.

Chemicals

Wear safety goggles when handling any potentially dangerous chemicals, acids, or bases. If a chemical is unknown, handle it as you would a dangerous chemical. Wear an apron and safety gloves when working with acids or bases or whenever you are told to do so. If a spill gets on your skin or clothing, rinse it off immediately with water for at least 5 minutes while calling to your teacher.

Never mix chemicals unless your teacher tells you to do so. Never taste, touch, or smell chemicals unless you are specifically directed to do so. Before working with a flammable liquid or gas, check for the presence of any source of flame, spark, or heat.

Animal Safety

Always obtain your teacher's permission before bringing any animal into the school building. Handle animals only as your teacher directs. Always treat animals carefully and with respect. Wash your hands thoroughly after handling any animal.

Plant Safety

Do not eat any part of a plant or plant seed used in the laboratory. Wash hands thoroughly after handling any part of a plant. When in nature, do not pick any wild plants unless your teacher instructs you to do so.

Glassware

Examine all glassware before use. Be sure that glassware is clean and free of chips and cracks. Report damaged glassware to your teacher. Glass containers used for heating should be made of heat-resistant glass.

The Sun's Yearly Trip Through the Zodiac

During the course of a year, the sun appears to move through a circle of twelve constellations in the sky. The twelve constellations make up a "belt" in the sky called the *zodiac.* Each month, the sun appears to be in a different constellation. The ancient Babylonians developed a 12-month calendar based on the idea that the sun moved through this circle of constellations as it revolved around the Earth. They believed that the constellations of stars were fixed in position and that the sun and planets moved past the stars. Later, Copernicus developed a model of the solar system in which the Earth and the planets revolve around the sun. But how can Copernicus's model of the solar system be correct when the sun appears to move through the zodiac?

Materials

- 12 chairs
- 12 index cards
- roll of masking tape
- inflated ball
- large cardboard box

Ask a Question

1. If the sun is at the center of the solar system, why does it appear to move with respect to the stars in the sky?

Conduct an Experiment

2. Set the chairs in a large circle so that the backs of the chairs all face the center of the circle. Make sure that the chairs are equally spaced, like the numbers on the face of a clock.

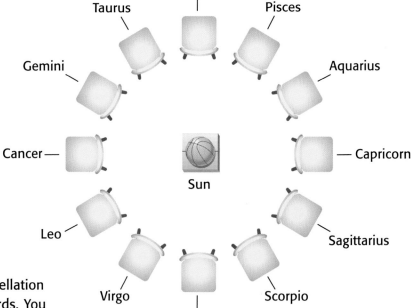

3. Write the name of each constellation in the zodiac on the index cards. You should have one card for each constellation.

4. Stand inside the circle with the masking tape and the index cards. Moving counterclockwise, attach the cards to the backs of the chairs in the following order: Aries, Taurus, Gemini, Cancer, Leo, Virgo, Libra, Scorpio, Sagittarius, Capricorn, Aquarius, and Pisces.

5. Use masking tape to label the ball "Sun."

6. Place the large closed box in the center of the circle. Set the roll of masking tape flat on top of the box.

7. Place the ball on top of the roll of masking tape so that the ball stays in place.

8. Stand inside of the circle of chairs. You will represent the Earth. As you move around the ball, you will model the Earth's orbit around the sun. Notice that even though only the "Earth" is moving, as seen from the Earth, the sun appears to move through the entire zodiac!

9. Stand in front of the chair labeled "Aries." Look at the ball representing the sun. Then look past the ball to the chair at the opposite side of the circle. Where in the zodiac does the sun appear to be?

10. Move to the next chair on your right (counterclockwise). Where does the sun appear to be? Is it in the same constellation? Explain your answer.

11. Repeat step 10 until you have observed the position of the sun from each chair in the circle.

Analyze the Results

12. Did the sun appear to move through the 12 constellations, even though the Earth was orbiting around the sun? How can you explain this?

Draw Conclusions

13. How does Copernicus's model of the solar system explain the apparent movement of the sun through the constellations of the zodiac?

Through the Looking Glass

Have you ever looked toward the horizon or up into the sky and wished you could see farther? Think a telescope might help? Astronomers use huge telescopes to study the universe. You can build your very own telescope to get a glimpse of what astronomers see with their incredible equipment.

Materials

- masking tape
- 2 convex lenses, 3 cm in diameter
- desk lamp
- sheet of construction paper
- metric ruler
- cardboard wrapping-paper tube
- cardboard toilet-paper tube
- scissors
- modeling clay

Procedure

1. Use modeling clay to form a base to hold one of the lenses upright on your desktop. When the lights are turned off, your teacher will turn on a lamp at the front of the classroom. Rotate your lens so that the light from the lamp passes through it.

2. Hold the construction paper so that the light passing through the lens lands on the paper. Slowly move the paper closer to or farther from the lens until you see the sharpest image of the light on the paper. Hold the paper in this position.

3. With the metric ruler, measure the distance between the lens and the paper. Record this distance in your ScienceLog.

4. How far is the paper from the lens? This distance, called the *image distance,* is how far the paper has to be from the lens in order for the image to be in focus.

5. Repeat steps 1–4 with the other lens.

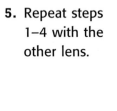

6. From one end of the long cardboard tube, measure and mark the image distance of the lens with the longer image distance. Place a mark 2 cm past this line toward the other end of the tube, and label the mark "cut."

7. From one end of the short cardboard tube, measure and mark the image distance of the lens with the shorter image distance. Place a mark 2 cm past this line toward the other end of the tube, and label the mark "cut."

8. Shorten the tubes by cutting along the marks labeled "cut."

9. Tape the lens with the longer image distance to one end of the longer tube. Tape the other lens to one end of the shorter tube. Slip one tube inside the other. Be sure the lenses are at each end of this new, longer tube.

10. Congratulations! You have just constructed a telescope! To use your telescope, look through the short tube (the eyepiece), and point the long end at various objects in the room. You can focus the telescope by adjusting its length. Are the images right side up, or upside down? Observe birds, insects, trees, or other outside objects.
Caution: Never look directly at the sun! This could cause permanent blindness.

Analysis

11. Which type of telescope did you just construct—a refracting telescope or a reflecting telescope? What makes it one type and not the other?

12. Would upside-down images negatively affect astronomers looking at stars through their telescopes? Explain your answer.

Using Scientific Methods

Why Do They Wander?

Before the discoveries of Nicholas Copernicus in the early 1500s, most people thought that the planets and the sun revolve around the Earth and that the Earth was the center of the solar system. But Copernicus observed that the sun is the center of the solar system and that all the planets, including Earth, revolve around the sun. He also explained a puzzling aspect of the movement of planets across the night sky.

If you watch a planet every night for several months, you'll notice that it appears to "wander" among the stars. While the stars remain in fixed positions relative to each other, the planets appear to move independently of the stars. First Mars travels to the left, then it goes back to the right a little, and finally it reverses direction and travels again to the left. No wonder the early Greeks called the planets wanderers!

In this lab you will make your own model of part of the solar system to find out how Copernicus's model of the solar system explained this zigzag motion of the planets.

Materials

- drawing compass
- white paper
- metric ruler
- colored pencils

Ask a Question

1. Why do the planets appear to move back and forth in the Earth's night sky?

Conduct an Experiment

2. Use the compass to draw a circle with a diameter of 9 cm on the paper. This circle will represent the orbit of the Earth around the sun. (Note: The orbits of the planets are actually slightly elliptical, but circles will work for this activity.)

3. Using the same center point, draw a circle with a diameter of 12 cm. This circle will represent the orbit of Mars.

4. Using a blue pencil, draw three parallel lines in a diagonal across one end of your paper, as shown at right. These lines will help you plot the path Mars appears to travel in Earth's night sky. Turn your paper so that the diagonal lines are at the top of the page.

5. Place 11 dots on your Earth orbit, as shown on the next page, and number them 1 through 11. These dots will represent Earth's position from month to month.

6. Now place 11 dots along the top of your Mars orbit, as shown below. Number the dots as shown. These dots will represent the position of Mars at the same time intervals. Notice that Mars travels slower than Earth.

7. Use a green line to connect the first dot on Earth's orbit to the first dot on Mars's orbit, and extend the line all the way to the first diagonal line at the top of your paper. Place a green dot where this green line meets the first blue diagonal line, and label the green dot *1*.

8. Now connect the second dot on Earth's orbit to the second dot on Mars's orbit, and extend the line all the way to the first diagonal at the top of your paper. Place a green dot where this line meets the first blue diagonal line, and label this dot *2*.

9. Continue drawing green lines from Earth's orbit through Mars's orbit and finally to the blue diagonal lines. Pay attention to the pattern of dots you are adding to the diagonal lines. When the direction of the dots changes, extend the green line to the next diagonal, and add the dots to that line instead.

10. When you are finished adding green lines, draw a red line to connect all the dots on the blue diagonal lines in the order you drew them.

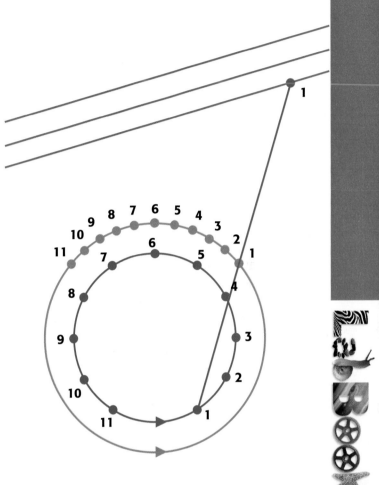

Analyze the Results

11. What do the green lines connecting points along Earth's orbit and Mars's orbit represent?

12. What does the red line connecting the dots along the diagonal lines look like? How can you explain this?

Draw Conclusions

13. What does this demonstration show about the motion of Mars?

14. Why do planets appear to move back and forth across the sky?

15. Were the Greeks justified in calling the planets wanderers? Explain.

I See the Light!

How do you find the distance to an object you can't reach? You can do it by measuring something you can reach, finding a few angles, and using mathematics. In this activity, you'll practice measuring the distances of objects here on Earth. When you get used to it, you can take your skills to the stars!

Materials

- 16 × 16 cm piece of poster board
- metric ruler
- protractor
- scissors
- sharp pencil
- 30 cm string
- transparent tape
- meterstick
- metric measuring tape
- scientific calculator

Procedure

1. Draw a line 4 cm away from the edge of one side of the piece of poster board. Fold the poster board along this line.

2. Tape the protractor to the poster board with its flat edge against the fold, as shown in the photo below.

3. Use a sharp pencil to carefully punch a hole through the poster board along its folded edge at the center of the protractor.

4. Thread the string through the hole, and tape one end to the underside of the poster board. The other end should be long enough to hang off the far end of the poster board.

5. Carefully punch a second hole in the smaller area of the poster board halfway between its short sides. The hole should be directly above the first hole and should be large enough for the pencil to fit through. This is the viewing hole of your new parallax device. This device will allow you to measure the distance of faraway objects.

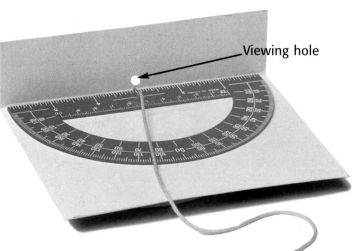

Viewing hole

6. Find a location outside that is at least 50 steps away from a tall, narrow object, such as the school's flagpole or a tall tree. (This object will represent background stars.) Set the meterstick on the ground with one of its long edges facing the flagpole.

7. Ask your partner, who represents a nearby star, to take 10 steps toward the flagpole, starting at the left end of the meterstick. You will be the observer. When you stand at the left end of the meterstick, which represents the location of the sun, your partner's nose should be lined up with the flag pole.

8. Move to the other end of the meterstick, which represents the location of Earth. Does your partner appear to the left or right of the flagpole? Record your observations in your ScienceLog.

9. Hold the string so that it runs straight from the viewing hole to the 90° mark on the protractor. Using one eye, look through the viewing hole along the string and point the device at your partner's nose.

10. Holding the device still, slowly move your head until you can see the flagpole through the viewing hole. Move the string so that it lines up between your eye and the flagpole. Make sure the string is taut, and hold it tightly against the protractor.

11. Read and record the angle made by the string and the string's original position at 90° (count the number of degrees between 90° and the string's new position).

12. Use the measuring tape to find and record the distance from the left end of the meterstick to your partner's nose.

13. Now find a place outside that is at least 100 steps away from the flagpole. Set the meterstick on the ground as before, and repeat steps 7–12.

Analysis

14. The angle you recorded in step 11 is called the *parallax angle.* The distance from one end of the meterstick to the other is called the *baseline.* With this angle and the length of your baseline, you can calculate the distance to your partner.

15. To calculate the distance (*d*) to your partner, use the following equation:

$$d = b/\tan A$$

In this equation, *A* is the parallax angle and *b* is the length of the baseline (1 m). (Tan *A* means the tangent of angle *A*, which you will learn more about in high school math classes.)

16. To find *d*, enter 1 (the length of your baseline in meters) into the calculator, press the "divide" key, enter the value of *A* (the parallax angle you recorded), then press the "tan" key. Finally, press the "equals" key.

17. Record this result in your ScienceLog. It is the distance in meters between the left end of the meterstick and your partner. You may want to use a table like the one shown at right.

18. How close is this calculated distance to the distance you measured in step 12?

19. Repeat steps 15–17 using the angle you found when the flagpole was 100 steps away.

Conclusions

20. At which position, 50 steps or 100 steps from the flagpole, did your calculated distance better match the actual distance as measured in step 12?

21. What do you think would happen if you were even farther from the flagpole?

22. When astronomers use parallax, their "flagpole" is the very distant stars. How might this affect the accuracy of their parallax readings?

Distance by Parallax Versus Measuring Tape		
	At 50 steps	At 100 steps
Parallax angle		
Distance (calculated)		
Distance (measured)		

DO NOT WRITE IN BOOK

Water Rockets Save the Day!

Imagine that for the big Fourth of July celebration you and your friends had planned a full day of swimming, volleyball, and fireworks at the lake. You've just learned however, that the city passed a law that bans all fireworks within city limits. But you are not one to give up so easily on having fun. Last year at summer camp you learned how to build water rockets. And you kept the launcher in your garage all this time! With a little bit of creativity, you and your friends are going to celebrate with a splash!

Materials

- 2 L soda bottle with cap
- foam board
- modeling clay
- duct tape
- scissors
- water
- bucket, 5-gal
- rocket launcher
- watch or clock that indicates seconds

Ask a Question

1. How can I use water and a soda bottle to build a rocket?

Conduct an Experiment

2. Decide how you want your rocket to look. Draw a sketch in your ScienceLog.

3. Using only the materials listed, decide how to build your rocket. Describe your design in your ScienceLog. Keep in mind that you will need to leave the opening of your bottle clear. It will be placed over a rubber stopper on the rocket launcher.

4. Fins are often used to stabilize rockets. Do you want fins on your water rocket? Decide on the best shape for the fins, and then decide how many fins your rocket needs. Use the foam board to construct the fins.

5. Your rocket must be heavy enough to fly along a controlled pathway. Consider using clay in the body of your rocket to provide some additional weight and stability.

6. Pour water into your rocket until it is one-third to one-half full.

7. Your teacher will provide the launcher and assist you during blastoff. Attach your rocket to the launcher by placing its opening on the rubber stopper.

8. When the rocket is in place, clear the immediate area and begin pumping air into your rocket. Watch the pump gauge, and take note of how much pressure is needed for liftoff.
   Caution: Be sure to step back from the launch site. You should be several meters away from the bottle when you launch it.

9. Use the watch to time your rocket's flight. (How long was your rocket in the air?)

10. Make small changes in your rocket design that you think will improve the rocket's performance. Consider using different amounts of water and clay or experimenting with different fins. You may also want to compare your design with those of your classmates.

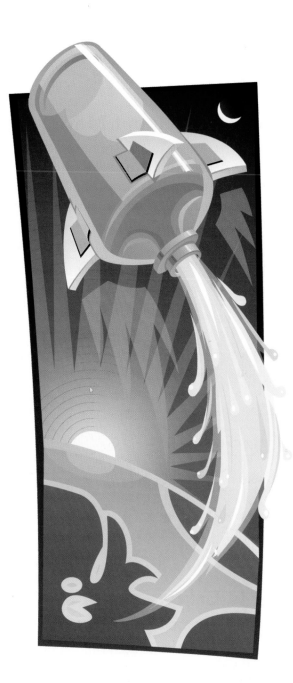

Analyze the Results

11. How did your rocket perform? If you used fins, do you think they helped your flight? Explain.

12. What do you think propelled your rocket? Use Newton's third law of motion to justify your answer.

13. How did the amount of water in your rocket affect the launch?

Newton's third law of motion: For every action there is an equal and opposite reaction.

Draw Conclusions

14. What modifications made your rocket fly for the longest time? How did the design help the rockets fly so far?

15. Which group's rockets were the most stable? How did the design help the rockets fly straight?

16. How can you improve your design to make your rocket perform even better?

Concept Mapping: A Way to Bring Ideas Together

What Is a Concept Map?

Have you ever tried to tell someone about a book or a chapter you've just read and found that you can remember only a few isolated words and ideas? Or maybe you've memorized facts for a test and then weeks later discovered you're not even sure what topics those facts covered.

In both cases, you may have understood the ideas or concepts by themselves but not in relation to one another. If you could somehow link the ideas together, you would probably understand them better and remember them longer. This is something a concept map can help you do. A concept map is a way to see how ideas or concepts fit together. It can help you see the "big picture."

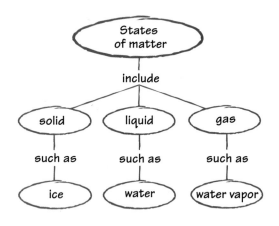

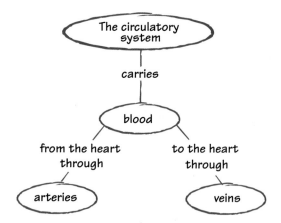

How to Make a Concept Map

① **Make a list of the main ideas or concepts.**

It might help to write each concept on its own slip of paper. This will make it easier to rearrange the concepts as many times as necessary to make sense of how the concepts are connected. After you've made a few concept maps this way, you can go directly from writing your list to actually making the map.

② **Arrange the concepts in order from the most general to the most specific.**

Put the most general concept at the top and circle it. Ask yourself, "How does this concept relate to the remaining concepts?" As you see the relationships, arrange the concepts in order from general to specific.

③ **Connect the related concepts with lines.**

④ **On each line, write an action word or short phrase that shows how the concepts are related.**

Look at the concept maps on this page, and then see if you can make one for the following terms:

plants, water, photosynthesis, carbon dioxide, sun's energy

One possible answer is provided at right, but don't look at it until you try the concept map yourself.

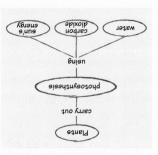

SI Measurement

The International System of Units, or SI, is the standard system of measurement used by many scientists. Using the same standards of measurement makes it easier for scientists to communicate with one another.

SI works by combining prefixes and base units. Each base unit can be used with different prefixes to define smaller and larger quantities. The table below lists common SI prefixes.

SI Prefixes			
Prefix	Abbreviation	Factor	Example
kilo-	k	1,000	kilogram, 1 kg = 1,000 g
hecto-	h	100	hectoliter, 1 hL = 100 L
deka-	da	10	dekameter, 1 dam = 10 m
		1	meter, liter
deci-	d	0.1	decigram, 1 dg = 0.1 g
centi-	c	0.01	centimeter, 1 cm = 0.01 m
milli-	m	0.001	milliliter, 1 mL = 0.001 L
micro-	μ	0.000 001	micrometer, 1 μm = 0.000 001 m

SI Conversion Table		
SI units	From SI to English	From English to SI
Length		
kilometer (km) = 1,000 m	1 km = 0.621 mi	1 mi = 1.609 km
meter (m) = 100 cm	1 m = 3.281 ft	1 ft = 0.305 m
centimeter (cm) = 0.01 m	1 cm = 0.394 in.	1 in. = 2.540 cm
millimeter (mm) = 0.001 m	1 mm = 0.039 in.	
micrometer (μm) = 0.000 001 m		
nanometer (nm) = 0.000 000 001 m		
Area		
square kilometer (km^2) = 100 hectares	1 km^2 = 0.386 mi^2	1 mi^2 = 2.590 km^2
hectare (ha) = 10,000 m^2	1 ha = 2.471 acres	1 acre = 0.405 ha
square meter (m^2) = 10,000 cm^2	1 m^2 = 10.765 ft^2	1 ft^2 = 0.093 m^2
square centimeter (cm^2) = 100 mm^2	1 cm^2 = 0.155 in.^{2}	1 in.^{2} = 6.452 cm^2
Volume		
liter (L) = 1,000 mL = 1 dm^3	1 L = 1.057 fl qt	1 fl qt = 0.946 L
milliliter (mL) = 0.001 L = 1 cm^3	1 mL = 0.034 fl oz	1 fl oz = 29.575 mL
microliter (μL) = 0.000 001 L		
Mass		
kilogram (kg) = 1,000 g	1 kg = 2.205 lb	1 lb = 0.454 kg
gram (g) = 1,000 mg	1 g = 0.035 oz	1 oz = 28.349 g
milligram (mg) = 0.001 g		
microgram (μg) = 0.000 001 g		

Scientific Method

The series of steps that scientists use to answer questions and solve problems is often called the **scientific method.** The scientific method is not a rigid procedure. Scientists may use all of the steps or just some of the steps of the scientific method. They may even repeat some of the steps. The goal of the scientific method is to come up with reliable answers and solutions.

Six Steps of the Scientific Method

1 **Ask a Question** Good questions come from careful **observations.** You make observations by using your senses to gather information. Sometimes you may use instruments, such as microscopes and telescopes, to extend the range of your senses. As you observe the natural world, you will discover that you have many more questions than answers. These questions drive the scientific method.

Questions beginning with *what, why, how,* and *when* are very important in focusing an investigation, and they often lead to a hypothesis. (You will learn what a hypothesis is in the next step.) Here is an example of a question that could lead to further investigation.

Question: How does acid rain affect plant growth?

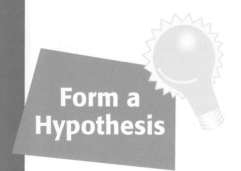

2 **Form a Hypothesis** After you come up with a question, you need to turn the question into a **hypothesis.** A hypothesis is a clear statement of what you expect the answer to your question to be. Your hypothesis will represent your best "educated guess" based on your observations and what you already know. A good hypothesis is testable. If observations and information cannot be gathered or if an experiment cannot be designed to test your hypothesis, it is untestable, and the investigation can go no further.

Here is a hypothesis that could be formed from the question, "How does acid rain affect plant growth?"

Hypothesis: Acid rain causes plants to grow more slowly.

Notice that the hypothesis provides some specifics that lead to methods of testing. The hypothesis can also lead to predictions. A **prediction** is what you think will be the outcome of your experiment or data collection. Predictions are usually stated in an "if . . . then" format. For example, **if** meat is kept at room temperature, **then** it will spoil faster than meat kept in the refrigerator. More than one prediction can be made for a single hypothesis. Here is a sample prediction for the hypothesis that acid rain causes plants to grow more slowly.

Prediction: If a plant is watered with only acid rain (which has a pH of 4), then the plant will grow at half its normal rate.

3 **Test the Hypothesis** After you have formed a hypothesis and made a prediction, you should test your hypothesis. There are different ways to do this. Perhaps the most familiar way is to conduct a **controlled experiment.** A controlled experiment tests only one factor at a time. A controlled experiment has a **control group** and one or more **experimental groups.** All the factors for the control and experimental groups are the same except for one factor, which is called the **variable.** By changing only one factor, you can see the results of just that one change.

Sometimes, the nature of an investigation makes a controlled experiment impossible. For example, dinosaurs have been extinct for millions of years, and the Earth's core is surrounded by thousands of meters of rock. It would be difficult, if not impossible, to conduct controlled experiments on such things. Under such circumstances, a hypothesis may be tested by making detailed observations. Taking measurements is one way of making observations.

4 **Analyze the Results** After you have completed your experiments, made your observations, and collected your data, you must analyze all the information you have gathered. Tables and graphs are often used in this step to organize the data.

5 **Draw Conclusions** Based on the analysis of your data, you should conclude whether or not your results support your hypothesis. If your hypothesis is supported, you (or others) might want to repeat the observations or experiments to verify your results. If your hypothesis is not supported by the data, you may have to check your procedure for errors. You may even have to reject your hypothesis and make a new one. If you cannot draw a conclusion from your results, you may have to try the investigation again or carry out further observations or experiments.

Draw Conclusions

Do they support your hypothesis?

No

Yes

6 **Communicate Results** After any scientific investigation, you should report your results. By doing a written or oral report, you let others know what you have learned. They may want to repeat your investigation to see if they get the same results. Your report may even lead to another question, which in turn may lead to another investigation.

Communicate Results

Scientific Method in Action

The scientific method is not a "straight line" of steps. It contains loops in which several steps may be repeated over and over again, while others may not be necessary. For example, sometimes scientists will find that testing one hypothesis raises new questions and new hypotheses to be tested. And sometimes, testing the hypothesis leads directly to a conclusion. Furthermore, the steps in the scientific method are not always used in the same order. Follow the steps in the diagram below, and see how many different directions the scientific method can take you.

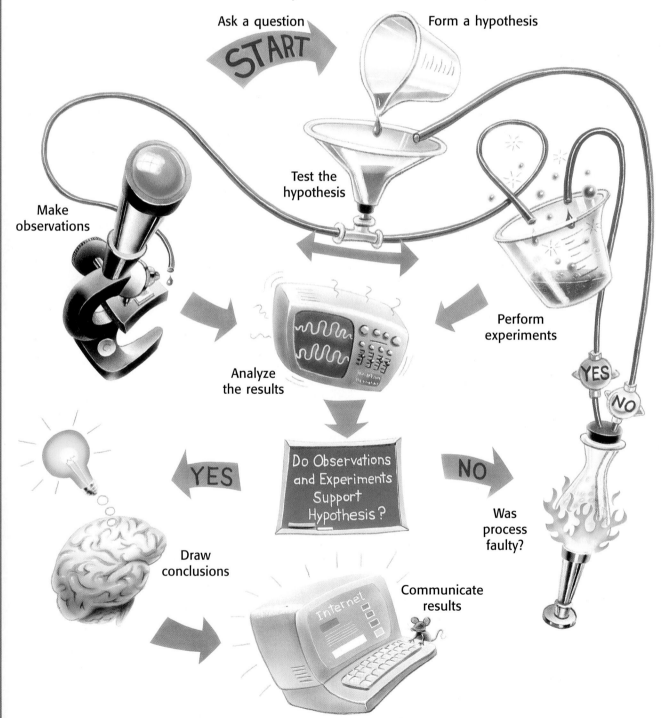

Ask a question
START

Form a hypothesis

Test the hypothesis

Make observations

Analyze the results

Perform experiments

Do Observations and Experiments Support Hypothesis?

YES

NO

Draw conclusions

Communicate results

Was process faulty?

Making Charts and Graphs

Circle Graphs

A circle graph, or pie chart, shows how each group of data relates to all of the data. Each part of the circle represents a category of the data. The entire circle represents all of the data. For example, a biologist studying a hardwood forest in Wisconsin found that there were five different types of trees. The data table at right summarizes the biologist's findings.

Wisconsin Hardwood Trees	
Type of tree	Number found
Oak	600
Maple	750
Beech	300
Birch	1,200
Hickory	150
Total	3,000

How to Make a Circle Graph

1 In order to make a circle graph of this data, first find the percentage of each type of tree. To do this, divide the number of individual trees by the total number of trees and multiply by 100.

$$\frac{600 \text{ oak}}{3,000 \text{ trees}} \times 100 = 20\%$$

$$\frac{750 \text{ maple}}{3,000 \text{ trees}} \times 100 = 25\%$$

$$\frac{300 \text{ beech}}{3,000 \text{ trees}} \times 100 = 10\%$$

$$\frac{1,200 \text{ birch}}{3,000 \text{ trees}} \times 100 = 40\%$$

$$\frac{150 \text{ hickory}}{3,000 \text{ trees}} \times 100 = 5\%$$

2 Now determine the size of the pie shapes that make up the chart. Do this by multiplying each percentage by 360°. Remember that a circle contains 360°.

$20\% \times 360° = 72°$ $25\% \times 360° = 90°$
$10\% \times 360° = 36°$ $40\% \times 360° = 144°$
$5\% \times 360° = 18°$

3 Then check that the sum of the percentages is 100 and the sum of the degrees is 360.

$20\% + 25\% + 10\% + 40\% + 5\% = 100\%$
$72° + 90° + 36° + 144° + 18° = 360°$

4 Use a compass to draw a circle and mark its center.

5 Then use a protractor to draw angles of 72°, 90°, 36°, 144°, and 18° in the circle.

6 Finally, label each part of the graph, and choose an appropriate title.

A Community of Wisconsin Hardwood Trees

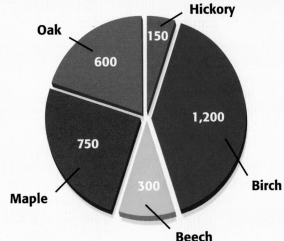

Population of Appleton, 1900–2000	
Year	Population
1900	1,800
1920	2,500
1940	3,200
1960	3,900
1980	4,600
2000	5,300

Line Graphs

Line graphs are most often used to demonstrate continuous change. For example, Mr. Smith's science class analyzed the population records for their hometown, Appleton, between 1900 and 2000. Examine the data at left.

Because the year and the population change, they are the *variables*. The population is determined by, or dependent on, the year. Therefore, the population is called the **dependent variable**, and the year is called the **independent variable**. Each set of data is called a **data pair**. To prepare a line graph, data pairs must first be organized in a table like the one at left.

How to Make a Line Graph

1 Place the independent variable along the horizontal (x) axis. Place the dependent variable along the vertical (y) axis.

2 Label the x-axis "Year" and the y-axis "Population." Look at your largest and smallest values for the population. Determine a scale for the y-axis that will provide enough space to show these values. You must use the same scale for the entire length of the axis. Find an appropriate scale for the x-axis too.

3 Choose reasonable starting points for each axis.

4 Plot the data pairs as accurately as possible.

5 Choose a title that accurately represents the data.

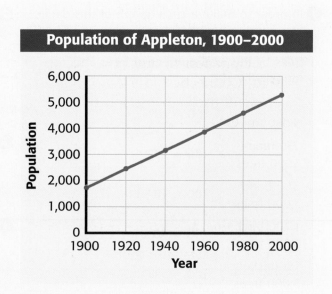
Population of Appleton, 1900–2000

How to Determine Slope

Slope is the ratio of the change in the y-axis to the change in the x-axis, or "rise over run."

1 Choose two points on the line graph. For example, the population of Appleton in 2000 was 5,300 people. Therefore, you can define point a as (2000, 5,300). In 1900, the population was 1,800 people. Define point b as (1900, 1,800).

2 Find the change in the y-axis. (y at point a) − (y at point b) 5,300 people − 1,800 people = 3,500 people

3 Find the change in the x-axis. (x at point a) − (x at point b) 2000 − 1900 = 100 years

4 Calculate the slope of the graph by dividing the change in y by the change in x.

$$slope = \frac{change\ in\ y}{change\ in\ x}$$

$$slope = \frac{3,500\ people}{100\ years}$$

slope = 35 people per year

In this example, the population in Appleton increased by a fixed amount each year. The graph of this data is a straight line. Therefore, the relationship is **linear**. When the graph of a set of data is not a straight line, the relationship is **nonlinear**.

Using Algebra to Determine Slope

The equation in step 4 may also be arranged to be:

$$y = kx$$

where y represents the change in the y-axis, k represents the slope, and x represents the change in the x-axis.

$$\text{slope} = \frac{\text{change in } y}{\text{change in } x}$$

$$k = \frac{y}{x}$$

$$k \times x = \frac{y \times x}{x}$$

$$kx = y$$

Bar Graphs

Bar graphs are used to demonstrate change that is not continuous. These graphs can be used to indicate trends when the data are taken over a long period of time. A meteorologist gathered the precipitation records at right for Hartford, Connecticut, for April 1–15, 1996, and used a bar graph to represent the data.

Precipitation in Hartford, Connecticut April 1–15, 1996

Date	Precipitation (cm)	Date	Precipitation (cm)
April 1	0.5	April 9	0.25
April 2	1.25	April 10	0.0
April 3	0.0	April 11	1.0
April 4	0.0	April 12	0.0
April 5	0.0	April 13	0.25
April 6	0.0	April 14	0.0
April 7	0.0	April 15	6.50
April 8	1.75		

How to Make a Bar Graph

1 Use an appropriate scale and a reasonable starting point for each axis.

2 Label the axes, and plot the data.

3 Choose a title that accurately represents the data.

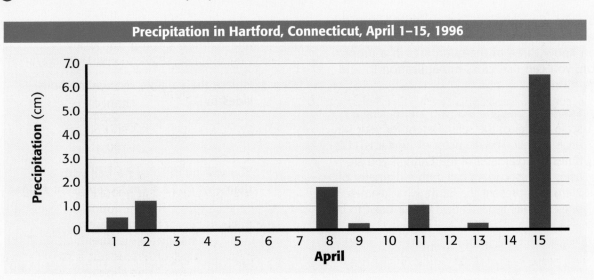

Math Refresher

Science requires an understanding of many math concepts. The following pages will help you review some important math skills.

Averages

An **average,** or **mean,** simplifies a list of numbers into a single number that *approximates* their value.

> **Example:** Find the average of the following set of numbers: 5, 4, 7, and 8.

Step 1: Find the sum.

$$5 + 4 + 7 + 8 = 24$$

Step 2: Divide the sum by the amount of numbers in your set. Because there are four numbers in this example, divide the sum by 4.

$$\frac{24}{4} = 6$$

The average, or mean, is **6.**

Ratios

A **ratio** is a comparison between numbers, and it is usually written as a fraction.

> **Example:** Find the ratio of thermometers to students if you have 36 thermometers and 48 students in your class.

Step 1: Make the ratio.

$$\frac{36 \text{ thermometers}}{48 \text{ students}}$$

Step 2: Reduce the fraction to its simplest form.

$$\frac{36}{48} = \frac{36 \div 12}{48 \div 12} = \frac{3}{4}$$

The ratio of thermometers to students is **3 to 4,** or $\frac{3}{4}$. The ratio may also be written in the form 3:4.

Proportions

A **proportion** is an equation that states that two ratios are equal.

$$\frac{3}{1} = \frac{12}{4}$$

To solve a proportion, first multiply across the equal sign. This is called cross-multiplication. If you know three of the quantities in a proportion, you can use cross-multiplication to find the fourth.

> **Example:** Imagine that you are making a scale model of the solar system for your science project. The diameter of Jupiter is 11.2 times the diameter of the Earth. If you are using a plastic-foam ball with a diameter of 2 cm to represent the Earth, what diameter does the ball representing Jupiter need to be?
>
> $$\frac{11.2}{1} = \frac{x}{2 \text{ cm}}$$

Step 1: Cross-multiply.

$$\frac{11.2}{1} \diagdown \frac{x}{2}$$
$$11.2 \times 2 = x \times 1$$

Step 2: Multiply.

$$22.4 = x \times 1$$

Step 3: Isolate the variable by dividing both sides by 1.

$$x = \frac{22.4}{1}$$
$$x = 22.4 \text{ cm}$$

You will need to use a ball with a diameter of **22.4 cm** to represent Jupiter.

Percentages

A **percentage** is a ratio of a given number to 100.

> **Example:** What is 85 percent of 40?

Step 1: Rewrite the percentage by moving the decimal point two places to the left.

$$.85$$

Step 2: Multiply the decimal by the number you are calculating the percentage of.

$$0.85 \times 40 = 34$$

85 percent of 40 is **34.**

Decimals

To **add** or **subtract decimals,** line up the digits vertically so that the decimal points line up. Then add or subtract the columns from right to left, carrying or borrowing numbers as necessary.

> **Example:** Add the following numbers: 3.1415 and 2.96.

Step 1: Line up the digits vertically so that the decimal points line up.

$$\begin{array}{r} 3.1415 \\ + \ 2.96 \\ \hline \end{array}$$

Step 2: Add the columns from right to left, carrying when necessary.

$$\begin{array}{r} {}^{1\ 1} \\ 3.1415 \\ + \ 2.96 \\ \hline 6.1015 \end{array}$$

The sum is **6.1015.**

Fractions

Numbers tell you how many; **fractions** tell you *how much of a whole.*

> **Example:** Your class has 24 plants. Your teacher instructs you to put 5 in a shady spot. What fraction does this represent?

Step 1: Write a fraction with the total number of parts in the whole as the denominator.

$$\frac{?}{24}$$

Step 2: Write the number of parts of the whole being represented as the numerator.

$$\frac{5}{24}$$

$\frac{5}{24}$ of the plants will be in the shade.

Reducing Fractions

It is usually best to express a fraction in simplest form. This is called *reducing* a fraction.

> **Example:** Reduce the fraction $\frac{30}{45}$ to its simplest form.

Step 1: Find the largest whole number that will divide evenly into both the numerator and denominator. This number is called the greatest common factor (GCF).

factors of the numerator 30: 1, 2, 3, 5, 6, 10, **15,** 30

factors of the denominator 45: 1, 3, 5, 9, **15,** 45

Step 2: Divide both the numerator and the denominator by the GCF, which in this case is 15.

$$\frac{30}{45} = \frac{30 \div 15}{45 \div 15} = \frac{2}{3}$$

$\frac{30}{45}$ reduced to its simplest form is $\frac{2}{3}$.

Adding and Subtracting Fractions

To **add** or **subtract fractions** that have the **same denominator,** simply add or subtract the numerators.

> **Examples:**
>
> $\frac{3}{5} + \frac{1}{5} = ?$ and $\frac{3}{4} - \frac{1}{4} = ?$

Step 1: Add or subtract the numerators.

$$\frac{3}{5} + \frac{1}{5} = \frac{4}{} \text{ and } \frac{3}{4} - \frac{1}{4} = \frac{2}{}$$

Step 2: Write the sum or difference over the denominator.

$$\frac{3}{5} + \frac{1}{5} = \frac{4}{5} \text{ and } \frac{3}{4} - \frac{1}{4} = \frac{2}{4}$$

Step 3: If necessary, reduce the fraction to its simplest form.

$$\frac{4}{5} \text{ cannot be reduced, and } \frac{2}{4} = \frac{1}{2}.$$

To **add** or **subtract fractions** that have **different denominators,** first find the least common denominator (LCD).

> **Examples:**
>
> $\frac{1}{2} + \frac{1}{6} = ?$ and $\frac{3}{4} - \frac{2}{3} = ?$

Step 1: Write the equivalent fractions with a common denominator.

$$\frac{3}{6} + \frac{1}{6} = ? \text{ and } \frac{9}{12} - \frac{8}{12} = ?$$

Step 2: Add or subtract.

$$\frac{3}{6} + \frac{1}{6} = \frac{4}{6} \text{ and } \frac{9}{12} - \frac{8}{12} = \frac{1}{12}$$

Step 3: If necessary, reduce the fraction to its simplest form.

$$\frac{4}{6} = \frac{2}{3}, \text{ and } \frac{1}{12} \text{ cannot be reduced.}$$

Multiplying Fractions

To **multiply fractions,** multiply the numerators and the denominators together, and then reduce the fraction to its simplest form.

> **Example:**
>
> $\frac{5}{9} \times \frac{7}{10} = ?$

Step 1: Multiply the numerators and denominators.

$$\frac{5}{9} \times \frac{7}{10} = \frac{5 \times 7}{9 \times 10} = \frac{35}{90}$$

Step 2: Reduce.

$$\frac{35}{90} = \frac{35 \div 5}{90 \div 5} = \frac{7}{18}$$

Dividing Fractions

To **divide fractions,** first rewrite the divisor (the number you divide *by*) upside down. This is called the reciprocal of the divisor. Then you can multiply and reduce if necessary.

> **Example:**
>
> $\frac{5}{8} \div \frac{3}{2} = ?$

Step 1: Rewrite the divisor as its reciprocal.

$$\frac{3}{2} \longrightarrow \frac{2}{3}$$

Step 2: Multiply.

$$\frac{5}{8} \times \frac{2}{3} = \frac{5 \times 2}{8 \times 3} = \frac{10}{24}$$

Step 3: Reduce.

$$\frac{10}{24} = \frac{10 \div 2}{24 \div 2} = \frac{5}{12}$$

Scientific Notation

Scientific notation is a short way of representing very large and very small numbers without writing all of the place-holding zeros.

> **Example:** Write 653,000,000 in scientific notation.

Step 1: Write the number without the place-holding zeros.

$$653$$

Step 2: Place the decimal point after the first digit.

$$6.53$$

Step 3: Find the exponent by counting the number of places that you moved the decimal point.

$$6.53000000$$

The decimal point was moved eight places to the left. Therefore, the exponent of 10 is positive 8. Remember, if the decimal point had moved to the right, the exponent would be negative.

Step 4: Write the number in scientific notation.

$$6.53 \times 10^8$$

Area

Area is the number of square units needed to cover the surface of an object.

> **Formulas:**
> Area of a square = side × side
> Area of a rectangle = length × width
> Area of a triangle = $\frac{1}{2}$ × base × height
>
> **Examples:** Find the areas.

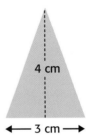

Triangle
Area = $\frac{1}{2}$ × base × height
Area = $\frac{1}{2}$ × 3 cm × 4 cm
Area = **6 cm²**

Rectangle
Area = length × width
Area = 6 cm × 3 cm
Area = **18 cm²**

Square
Area = side × side
Area = 3 cm × 3 cm
Area = **9 cm²**

Volume

Volume is the amount of space something occupies.

> **Formulas:**
> Volume of a cube = side × side × side
>
> Volume of a prism = area of base × height
>
> **Examples:** Find the volume of the solids.

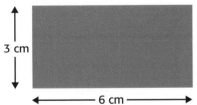

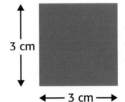

Cube
Volume = side × side × side
Volume = 4 cm × 4 cm × 4 cm
Volume = **64 cm³**

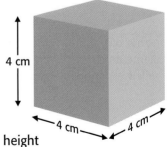

Prism
Volume = area of base × height
Volume = (area of triangle) × height
Volume = $\left(\frac{1}{2} \times 3\text{ cm} \times 4\text{ cm}\right) \times 5\text{ cm}$
Volume = 6 cm² × 5 cm
Volume = **30 cm³**

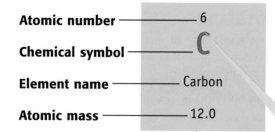

Periodic Table of the Elements

Each square on the table includes an element's name, chemical symbol, atomic number, and atomic mass.

Atomic number — 6

Chemical symbol — C

Element name — Carbon

Atomic mass — 12.0

The background color indicates the type of element. Carbon is a nonmetal.

The color of the chemical symbol indicates the physical state at room temperature. Carbon is a solid.

Background
- Metals
- Metalloids
- Nonmetals

Chemical Symbol
- Solid
- Liquid
- Gas

Period 1

1
H
Hydrogen
1.0

	Group 1	Group 2
Period 2	3 **Li** Lithium 6.9	4 **Be** Beryllium 9.0
Period 3	11 **Na** Sodium 23.0	12 **Mg** Magnesium 24.3

	Group 1	Group 2	Group 3	Group 4	Group 5	Group 6	Group 7	Group 8	Group 9
Period 4	19 **K** Potassium 39.1	20 **Ca** Calcium 40.1	21 **Sc** Scandium 45.0	22 **Ti** Titanium 47.9	23 **V** Vanadium 50.9	24 **Cr** Chromium 52.0	25 **Mn** Manganese 54.9	26 **Fe** Iron 55.8	27 **Co** Cobalt 58.9
Period 5	37 **Rb** Rubidium 85.5	38 **Sr** Strontium 87.6	39 **Y** Yttrium 88.9	40 **Zr** Zirconium 91.2	41 **Nb** Niobium 92.9	42 **Mo** Molybdenum 95.9	43 **Tc** Technetium (97.9)	44 **Ru** Ruthenium 101.1	45 **Rh** Rhodium 102.9
Period 6	55 **Cs** Cesium 132.9	56 **Ba** Barium 137.3	57 **La** Lanthanum 138.9	72 **Hf** Hafnium 178.5	73 **Ta** Tantalum 180.9	74 **W** Tungsten 183.8	75 **Re** Rhenium 186.2	76 **Os** Osmium 190.2	77 **Ir** Iridium 192.2
Period 7	87 **Fr** Francium (223.0)	88 **Ra** Radium (226.0)	89 **Ac** Actinium (227.0)	104 **Rf** Rutherfordium (261.1)	105 **Db** Dubnium (262.1)	106 **Sg** Seaborgium (263.1)	107 **Bh** Bohrium (262.1)	108 **Hs** Hassium (265)	109 **Mt** Meitnerium (266)

A row of elements is called a period.

A column of elements is called a group or family.

Lanthanides	58 **Ce** Cerium 140.1	59 **Pr** Praseodymium 140.9	60 **Nd** Neodymium 144.2	61 **Pm** Promethium (144.9)	62 **Sm** Samarium 150.4
Actinides	90 **Th** Thorium 232.0	91 **Pa** Protactinium 231.0	92 **U** Uranium 238.0	93 **Np** Neptunium (237.0)	94 **Pu** Plutonium 244.1

These elements are placed below the table to allow the table to be narrower.

This zigzag line reminds you where the metals, nonmetals, and metalloids are.

Group 18

2
He
Helium
4.0

Group 13	Group 14	Group 15	Group 16	Group 17
5	6	7	8	9
B	**C**	**N**	**O**	**F**
Boron	Carbon	Nitrogen	Oxygen	Fluorine
10.8	12.0	14.0	16.0	19.0

10
Ne
Neon
20.2

			Group 13	Group 14	Group 15	Group 16	Group 17	Group 18
			13	14	15	16	17	18
			Al	**Si**	**P**	**S**	**Cl**	**Ar**
			Aluminum	Silicon	Phosphorus	Sulfur	Chlorine	Argon
			27.0	28.1	31.0	32.1	35.5	39.9

Group 10	Group 11	Group 12						
28	29	30	31	32	33	34	35	36
Ni	**Cu**	**Zn**	**Ga**	**Ge**	**As**	**Se**	**Br**	**Kr**
Nickel	Copper	Zinc	Gallium	Germanium	Arsenic	Selenium	Bromine	Krypton
58.7	63.5	65.4	69.7	72.6	74.9	79.0	79.9	83.8
46	47	48	49	50	51	52	53	54
Pd	**Ag**	**Cd**	**In**	**Sn**	**Sb**	**Te**	**I**	**Xe**
Palladium	Silver	Cadmium	Indium	Tin	Antimony	Tellurium	Iodine	Xenon
106.4	107.9	112.4	114.8	118.7	121.8	127.6	126.9	131.3
78	79	80	81	82	83	84	85	86
Pt	**Au**	**Hg**	**Tl**	**Pb**	**Bi**	**Po**	**At**	**Rn**
Platinum	Gold	Mercury	Thallium	Lead	Bismuth	Polonium	Astatine	Radon
195.1	197.0	200.6	204.4	207.2	209.0	(209.0)	(210.0)	(222.0)
110	111	112		114		116		118
Uun*	**Uuu***	**Uub***		**Uuq***		**Uuh***		**Uuo***
Ununnilium	Unununium	Ununbium		Ununquadium		Ununhexium		Ununoctium
(271)	(272)	(277)		(285)		(289)		(293)

A number in parenthesis is the mass number of the most stable form of that element.

63	64	65	66	67	68	69	70	71
Eu	**Gd**	**Tb**	**Dy**	**Ho**	**Er**	**Tm**	**Yb**	**Lu**
Europium	Gadolinium	Terbium	Dysprosium	Holmium	Erbium	Thulium	Ytterbium	Lutetium
152.0	157.3	158.9	162.5	164.9	167.3	168.9	173.0	175.0
95	96	97	98	99	100	101	102	103
Am	**Cm**	**Bk**	**Cf**	**Es**	**Fm**	**Md**	**No**	**Lr**
Americium	Curium	Berkelium	Californium	Einsteinium	Fermium	Mendelevium	Nobelium	Lawrencium
(243.1)	(247.1)	(247.1)	(251.1)	(252.1)	(257.1)	(258.1)	(259.1)	(262.1)

*The official names and symbols for the elements greater than 109 will eventually be approved by a committee of scientists.

Physical Science Refresher

Atoms and Elements

Every object in the universe is made up of particles of some kind of matter. **Matter** is anything that takes up space and has mass. All matter is made up of elements. An **element** is a substance that cannot be separated into simpler components by ordinary chemical means. This is because each element consists of only one kind of atom. An **atom** is the smallest unit of an element that has all of the properties of that element.

Atomic Structure

Atoms are made up of small particles called subatomic particles. The three major types of subatomic particles are **electrons, protons,** and **neutrons.** Electrons have a negative electric charge, protons have a positive charge, and neutrons have no electric charge. The protons and neutrons are packed close to one another to form the **nucleus.** The protons give the nucleus a positive charge. Electrons are most likely to be found in regions around the nucleus called **electron clouds.** The negatively charged electrons are attracted to the positively charged nucleus. An atom may have several energy levels in which electrons are located.

Atomic Number

To help in the identification of elements, scientists have assigned an **atomic number** to each kind of atom. The atomic number is the number of protons in the atom. Atoms with the same number of protons are all the same kind of element. In an uncharged, or electrically neutral, atom there are an equal number of protons and electrons. Therefore, the atomic number equals the number of electrons in an uncharged atom. The number of neutrons, however, can vary for a given element. Atoms of the same element that have different numbers of neutrons are called **isotopes.**

Periodic Table of the Elements

In the periodic table, the elements are arranged from left to right in order of increasing atomic number. Each element in the table is in a separate box. An atom of each element has one more electron and one more proton than an atom of the element to its left. Each horizontal row of the table is called a **period.** Changes in chemical properties of elements across a period correspond to changes in the electron arrangements of their atoms. Each vertical column of the table, known as a **group,** lists elements with similar properties. The elements in a group have similar chemical properties because their atoms have the same number of electrons in their outer energy level. For example, the elements helium, neon, argon, krypton, xenon, and radon all have similar properties and are known as the noble gases.

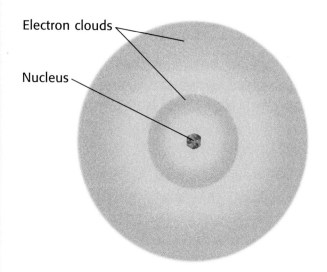

Electron clouds

Nucleus

Molecules and Compounds

When two or more elements are joined chemically, the resulting substance is called a **compound.** A compound is a new substance with properties different from those of the elements that compose it. For example, water, H_2O, is a compound formed when hydrogen (H) and oxygen (O) combine. The smallest complete unit of a compound that has the properties of that compound is called a **molecule.** A chemical formula indicates the elements in a compound. It also indicates the relative number of atoms of each element present. The chemical formula for water is H_2O, which indicates that each water molecule consists of two atoms of hydrogen and one atom of oxygen. The subscript number is used after the symbol for an element to indicate how many atoms of that element are in a single molecule of the compound.

Acids, Bases, and pH

An ion is an atom or group of atoms that has an electric charge because it has lost or gained one or more electrons. When an acid, such as hydrochloric acid, HCl, is mixed with water, it separates into ions. An **acid** is a compound that produces hydrogen ions, H^+, in water. The hydrogen ions then combine with a water molecule to form a hydronium ion, H_3O^+. A **base,** on the other hand, is a substance that produces hydroxide ions, OH^-, in water.

To determine whether a solution is acidic or basic, scientists use pH. The **pH** is a measure of the hydronium ion concentration in a solution. The pH scale ranges from 0 to 14. The middle point, pH = 7, is neutral, neither acidic nor basic. Acids have a pH less than 7; bases have a pH greater than 7. The lower the number is, the more acidic the solution. The higher the number is, the more basic the solution.

Chemical Equations

A chemical reaction occurs when a chemical change takes place. (In a chemical change, new substances with new properties are formed.) A chemical equation is a useful way of describing a chemical reaction by means of chemical formulas. The equation indicates what substances react and what the products are. For example, when carbon and oxygen combine, they can form carbon dioxide. The equation for the reaction is as follows:

$$C + O_2 \rightarrow CO_2.$$

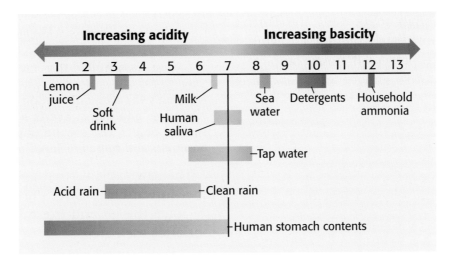

Physical Laws and Equations

Law of Conservation of Energy

The law of conservation of energy states that energy can be neither created nor destroyed.

The total amount of energy in a closed system is always the same. Energy can be changed from one form to another, but all the different forms of energy in a system always add up to the same total amount of energy, no matter how many energy conversions occur.

Law of Universal Gravitation

The law of universal gravitation states that all objects in the universe attract each other by a force called gravity. The size of the force depends on the masses of the objects and the distance between them.

The first part of the law explains why a bowling ball is much harder to lift than a table-tennis ball. Because the bowling ball has a much larger mass than the table-tennis ball, the amount of gravity between the Earth and the bowling ball is greater than the amount of gravity between the Earth and the table-tennis ball.

The second part of the law explains why a satellite can remain in orbit around the Earth. The satellite is carefully placed at a distance great enough to prevent the Earth's gravity from immediately pulling it down but small enough to prevent it from completely escaping the Earth's gravity and wandering off into space.

Newton's Laws of Motion

Newton's first law of motion states that an object at rest remains at rest and an object in motion remains in motion at constant speed and in a straight line unless acted on by an unbalanced force.

The first part of the law explains why a football will remain on a tee until it is kicked off or until a gust of wind blows it off.

The second part of the law explains why a bike's rider will continue moving forward after the bike tire runs into a crack in the sidewalk and the bike comes to an abrupt stop until gravity and the sidewalk stop the rider.

Newton's second law of motion states that the acceleration of an object depends on the mass of the object and the amount of force applied.

The first part of the law explains why the acceleration of a 4 kg bowling ball will be greater than the acceleration of a 6 kg bowling ball if the same force is applied to both.

The second part of the law explains why the acceleration of a bowling ball will be larger if a larger force is applied to it.

The relationship of acceleration (a) to mass (m) and force (F) can be expressed mathematically by the following equation:

$$\text{acceleration} = \frac{force}{mass} \quad \text{or} \quad a = \frac{F}{m}$$

This equation is often rearranged to the form:

$$\text{force} = \text{mass} \times \text{acceleration}$$
$$\text{or}$$
$$F = m \times a$$

Newton's third law of motion states that whenever one object exerts a force on a second object, the second object exerts an equal and opposite force on the first.

This law explains that a runner is able to move forward because of the equal and opposite force the ground exerts on the runner's foot after each step.

Useful Equations

Average speed

$$\text{Average speed} = \frac{\text{total distance}}{\text{total time}}$$

Example: A bicycle messenger traveled a distance of 136 km in 8 hours. What was the messenger's average speed?

$$\frac{136 \text{ km}}{8 \text{ h}} = 17 \text{ km/h}$$

The messenger's average speed was **17 km/h.**

Average acceleration

$$\frac{\text{Average}}{\text{acceleration}} = \frac{\text{final velocity} - \text{starting velocity}}{\text{time it takes to change velocity}}$$

Example: Calculate the average acceleration of an Olympic 100 m dash sprinter who reaches a velocity of 15 m/s south at the finish line. The race was in a straight line and lasted 10 s.

$$\frac{15 \text{ m/s} - 0 \text{ m/s}}{10 \text{ s}} = 1.5 \text{ m/s/s}$$

The sprinter's average acceleration is **1.5 m/s/s south.**

Net force

Forces in the Same Direction

When forces are in the same direction, add the forces together to determine the net force.

Example: Calculate the net force on a stalled car that is being pushed by two people. One person is pushing with a force of 13 N northwest and the other person is pushing with a force of 8 N in the same direction.

$$13 \text{ N} + 8 \text{ N} = 21 \text{ N}$$

The net force is **21 N northwest.**

Forces in Opposite Directions

When forces are in opposite directions, subtract the smaller force from the larger force to determine the net force.

Net force (cont'd)

Example: Calculate the net force on a rope that is being pulled on each end. One person is pulling on one end of the rope with a force of 12 N south. Another person is pulling on the opposite end of the rope with a force of 7 N north.

$$12 \text{ N} - 7 \text{ N} = 5 \text{ N}$$

The net force is **5 N south.**

Density

$$\text{Density} = \frac{\text{mass}}{\text{volume}}$$

Example: Calculate the density of a sponge with a mass of 10 g and a volume of 40 mL.

$$\frac{10 \text{ g}}{40 \text{ mL}} = 0.25 \text{ g/mL}$$

The density of the sponge is **0.25 g/mL.**

Pressure

Pressure is the force exerted over a given area. The SI unit for pressure is the pascal, which is abbreviated Pa.

$$\text{Pressure} = \frac{\text{force}}{\text{area}}$$

Example: Calculate the pressure of the air in a soccer ball if the air exerts a force of 10 N over an area of 0.5 m^2.

$$\text{Pressure} = \frac{10 \text{ N}}{0.5 \text{ m}^2} = 20 \text{ N/m}^2 = 20 \text{ Pa}$$

The pressure of the air inside of the soccer ball is **20 Pa.**

Concentration

$$\text{Concentration} = \frac{\text{mass of solute}}{\text{volume of solvent}}$$

Example: Calculate the concentration of a solution in which 10 g of sugar is dissolved in 125 mL of water.

$$\frac{10 \text{ g of sugar}}{125 \text{ mL of water}} = 0.08 \text{ g/mL}$$

The concentration of this solution is **0.08 g/mL.**

Properties of Common Minerals

Silicate Minerals

Mineral	Color	Luster	Streak	Hardness
Beryl	deep green, pink, white, bluish green, or light yellow	vitreous	none	7.5–8
Chlorite	green	vitreous to pearly	pale green	2–2.5
Garnet	green or red	vitreous	none	6.5–7.5
Hornblende	dark green, brown, or black	vitreous or silky	none	5–6
Muscovite	colorless, gray, or brown	vitreous or pearly	white	2–2.5
Olivine	olive green	vitreous	none	6.5–7
Orthoclase	colorless, white, pink, or other colors	vitreous to pearly	white or none	6
Plagioclase	blue gray to white	vitreous	white	6
Quartz	colorless or white; any color when not pure	vitreous or waxy	white or none	7

Nonsilicate Minerals

Native Elements

Mineral	Color	Luster	Streak	Hardness
Copper	copper-red	metallic	copper-red	2.5–3
Diamond	pale yellow or colorless	vitreous	none	10
Graphite	black to gray	submetallic	black	1–2

Carbonates

Mineral	Color	Luster	Streak	Hardness
Aragonite	colorless, white, or pale yellow	vitreous	white	3.5–4
Calcite	colorless or white to tan	vitreous	white	3

Halides

Mineral	Color	Luster	Streak	Hardness
Fluorite	light green, yellow, purple, bluish green, or other colors	vitreous	none	4
Halite	colorless or gray	vitreous	white	2.5–3

Oxides

Mineral	Color	Luster	Streak	Hardness
Hematite	reddish brown to black	metallic to earthy	red to red-brown	5.6–6.5
Magnetite	iron black	metallic	black	5–6

Sulfates

Mineral	Color	Luster	Streak	Hardness
Anhydrite	colorless, bluish, or violet	vitreous to pearly	white	3–3.5
Gypsum	white, pink, gray, or colorless	vitreous, pearly, or silky	white	1–2.5

Sulfides

Mineral	Color	Luster	Streak	Hardness
Galena	lead gray	metallic	lead gray to black	2.5
Pyrite	brassy yellow	metallic	greenish, brownish, or black	6–6.5

Density (g/cm³)	Cleavage, Fracture, Special Properties	Common Uses
2.6–2.8	1 cleavage direction; irregular fracture; some varieties fluoresce in ultraviolet light	gemstones, ore of the metal beryllium
2.6–3.3	1 cleavage direction; irregular fracture	
4.2	no cleavage; conchoidal to splintery fracture	gemstones, abrasives
3.2	2 cleavage directions; hackly to splintery fracture	
2.7–3	1 cleavage direction; irregular fracture	electrical insulation, wallpaper, fireproofing material, lubricant
3.2–3.3	no cleavage; conchoidal fracture	gemstones, casting
2.6	2 cleavage directions; irregular fracture	porcelain
2.6–2.7	2 cleavage directions; irregular fracture	ceramics
2.6	no cleavage; conchoidal fracture	gemstones, concrete, glass, porcelain, sandpaper, lenses
8.9	no cleavage; hackly fracture	wiring, brass, bronze, coins
3.5	4 cleavage directions; irregular to conchoidal fracture	gemstones, drilling
2.3	1 cleavage direction; irregular fracture	pencils, paints, lubricants, batteries
2.95	2 cleavage directions; irregular fracture; reacts with hydrochloric acid	minor source of barium
2.7	3 cleavage directions; irregular fracture; reacts with weak acid, double refraction	cements, soil conditioner, whitewash, construction materials
3.2	4 cleavage directions; irregular fracture; some varieties fluoresce or double refract	hydrochloric acid, steel, glass, fiberglass, pottery, enamel
2.2	3 cleavage directions; splintery to conchoidal fracture; salty taste	tanning hides, fertilizer, salting icy roads, food preservation
5.25	no cleavage; splintery fracture; magnetic when heated	iron ore for steel, gemstones, pigments
5.2	2 cleavage directions; splintery fracture; magnetic	iron ore
2.89–2.98	3 cleavage directions; conchoidal to splintery fracture	soil conditioner, sulfuric acid
2.2–2.4	3 cleavage directions; conchoidal to splintery fracture	plaster of Paris, wallboard, soil conditioner
7.4–7.6	3 cleavage directions; irregular fracture	batteries, paints
5	no cleavage; conchoidal to splintery fracture	dyes, inks, gemstones

Sky Maps

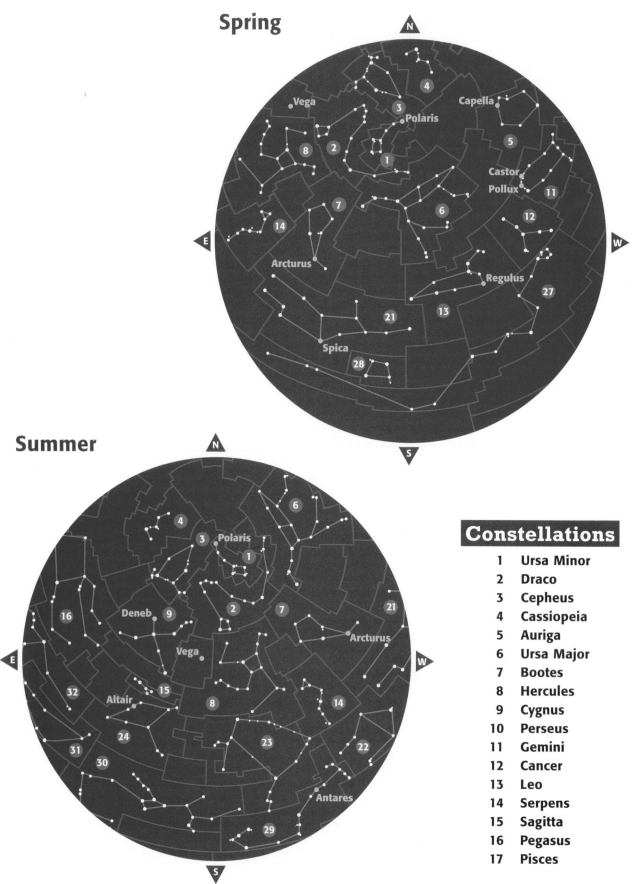

Spring

Summer

Constellations

1	Ursa Minor
2	Draco
3	Cepheus
4	Cassiopeia
5	Auriga
6	Ursa Major
7	Bootes
8	Hercules
9	Cygnus
10	Perseus
11	Gemini
12	Cancer
13	Leo
14	Serpens
15	Sagitta
16	Pegasus
17	Pisces

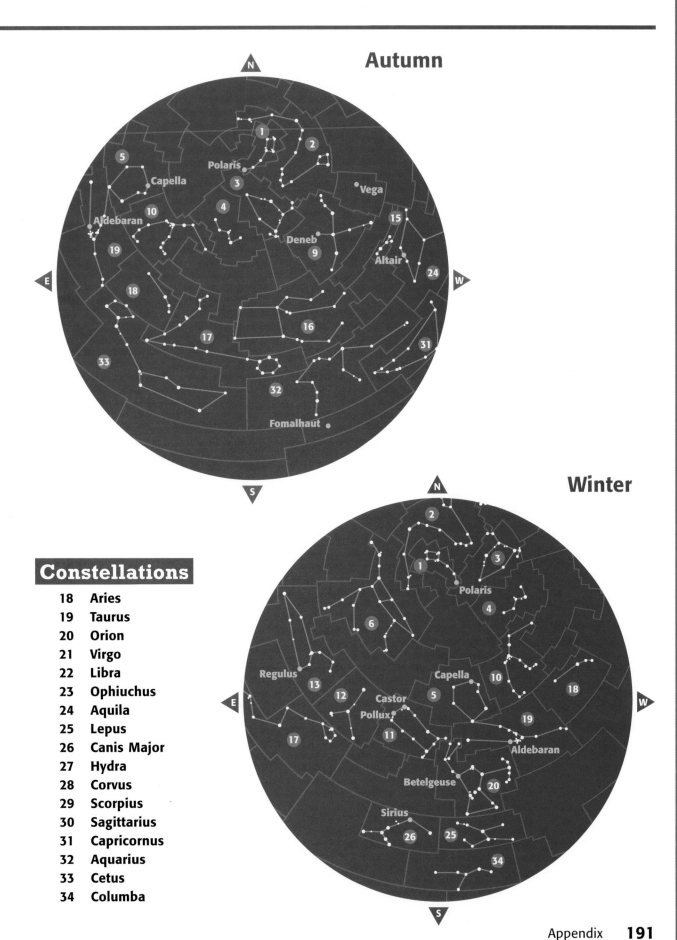

Autumn

Winter

Constellations

18 Aries
19 Taurus
20 Orion
21 Virgo
22 Libra
23 Ophiuchus
24 Aquila
25 Lepus
26 Canis Major
27 Hydra
28 Corvus
29 Scorpius
30 Sagittarius
31 Capricornus
32 Aquarius
33 Cetus
34 Columba

Glossary

A

absolute magnitude the actual brightness of a star (102)

altitude in astronomy, the angle between an object in the sky and the horizon (13)

annular (AN yoo luhr) **eclipse** a solar eclipse during which the outer ring of the sun can be seen around the moon (78)

apparent magnitude how bright a light appears to an observer (102)

artificial satellite any human-made object placed in orbit around a body in space (132)

asteroid a small, rocky body that revolves around the sun (85)

asteroid belt the region of the solar system most asteroids occupy; roughly between the orbits of Mars and Jupiter (85)

astronomical unit (AU) the average distance between the Earth and the sun, or approximately 150,000,000 km (40, 64)

astronomy the study of all physical objects beyond Earth (4)

atmosphere a mixture of gases that surrounds a planet, such as Earth (50)

B

big bang theory the theory that states the universe began with a tremendous explosion (114)

black hole an object with more than three solar masses squeezed into a ball only 10 km across whose gravity is so strong that not even light can escape (109)

C

calendar a system for organizing time; most calendars organize time within a single unit called a year (4)

celestial equator imaginary circle created by extending Earth's equator into space (14)

chromosphere (KROH muh SFIR) a thin region of the sun's atmosphere between the corona and the photosphere; too faint to see unless there is a total solar eclipse (43)

circumpolar stars stars that can be seen at all times of the year and all times of the night (14)

comet a small body of ice, rock, and cosmic dust loosely packed together that gives off gas and dust in the form of a tail as it passes close to the sun (50, 83)

constellation a section of the sky that contains a recognizable star pattern (11)

convective zone a region of the sun where gases circulate in convection currents, bringing the sun's energy to the surface (43)

core the central, spherical part of the Earth below the mantle (49); *also* the center of the sun where the sun's energy is produced (43)

corona the sun's outer atmosphere, which can extend outward a distance equal to 10–12 times the diameter of the sun (43)

cosmic background radiation radiation left over from the big bang that fills all of space (115)

cosmology the study of the origin and future of the universe (114)

crust the thin, outermost layer of the Earth, or the uppermost part of the lithosphere (49)

D

day the time required for the Earth to rotate once on its axis (4)

declination a measure of how far north or south an object is from the celestial equator (14)

density the amount of matter in a given space; mass per unit volume (189)

E

eclipse an event in which the shadow of one celestial body falls on another (78)

ecliptic the apparent path the sun takes across the celestial sphere (14)

electromagnetic spectrum all the wavelengths of electromagnetic radiation (21)

element a pure substance that cannot be separated or broken down into simpler substances by ordinary chemical means (186)

ellipse a closed curve in which the sum of the distances from the edge of the curve to two points inside the ellipse is always the same (40)

elliptical galaxy a spherical or elongated galaxy with a bright center and very little dust and gas (111)

escape velocity the speed and direction a rocket must travel in order to completely break away from a planet's gravitational pull (131)

G

galaxy a large grouping of stars in space (110)

gas giants the large, gaseous planets of the outer solar system (70)

geosynchronous orbit an orbit in which a satellite travels at a speed that matches the rotational speed of the Earth exactly, keeping the satellite positioned above the same spot on Earth at all times (133)

globular cluster a group of older stars that looks like a ball of stars (112)

greenhouse effect the natural heating process of a planet, such as the Earth, by which gases in the atmosphere trap thermal energy (66)

H

horizon the line where the sky and the Earth appear to meet (13)

H-R diagram Hertzsprung-Russell diagram; a graph that shows the relationship between a star's surface temperature and its absolute magnitude (105)

hypothesis a possible explanation or answer to a question (174)

I

irregular galaxy a galaxy that does not fit into any other category; one with an irregular shape (111)

K

Kuiper (KIE per) **Belt** the region of the solar system outside the orbit of Neptune that is occupied by small, icy, cometlike bodies (84)

L

leap year a year in which an extra day is added to the calendar (5)

light-minute a unit of length equal to the distance light travels in space in 1 minute, or 18,000,000 km (64)

light-year a unit of length equal to the distance that light travels through space in 1 year (15, 103)

low Earth orbit an orbit located a few hundred kilometers above the Earth's surface (133)

lunar eclipse an event in which the shadow of the Earth falls on the moon (78)

M

main sequence a diagonal pattern of stars on the H-R diagram (106)

mantle the layer of the Earth between the crust and the core (49)

mass the amount of matter that something is made of; its value does not change with the object's location (34)

meteor a streak of light caused when a meteoroid or comet dust burns up in the Earth's atmosphere before it reaches the ground (86)

meteorite a meteoroid that reaches the Earth's surface without burning up completely (86)

meteoroid a very small, rocky body that revolves around the sun (50, 86)

month roughly the amount of time required for the moon to orbit the Earth once (4)

moon a natural satellite of a planet (75)

N

NASA National Aeronautics and Space Administration; founded to combine all of the separate rocket-development teams in the United States (129)

nebula (NEB yuh luh) a large cloud of dust and gas in interstellar space; the location of star formation (34, 112)

neutron star a star in which all the particles have become neutrons; the collapsed remains of a supernova (109)

nuclear fusion the process by which two or more nuclei with small masses join together, or fuse, to form a larger, more massive nucleus, along with the production of energy (45)

O

observation any use of the senses to gather information (174)

Oort (ort) **cloud** a spherical region of space that surrounds the solar system in which distant comets revolve around the sun (84)

open cluster a group of stars that are usually located along the spiral disk of a galaxy (112)

orbit the elliptical path a body takes as it travels around another body in space; the motion itself (39)

orbital velocity the speed and direction a rocket must have in order to orbit the Earth (131)

P

parallax an apparent shift in the position of an object when viewed from different locations (103)

period of revolution the time it takes for one body to make one complete orbit, or *revolution*, around another body in space (39, 65)

period of rotation the time it takes for an object to rotate once (65)

phases the different appearances of the moon due to varying amounts of sunlight on the side of the moon that faces the Earth; results from the changing relative positions of the moon, Earth, and the sun (77)

photosphere the layer of the sun at which point the gases get thick enough to see; the surface of the sun (43)

planetesimal (PLAN i TES i muhl) the tiny building blocks of the planets that formed as dust particles stuck together and grew in size (36)

plate tectonics the theory that the Earth's lithosphere is divided into tectonic plates that move around on top of the asthenosphere (53)

prograde rotation the counterclockwise spin of a planet or moon as seen from above the planet's north pole (66)

pulsar a spinning neutron star that emits rapid pulses of light (109)

Q

quasar (KWAY ZAHR) a "quasi-stellar" object; a starlike source of light that is extremely far away; one of the most powerful sources of energy in the universe (113)

R

radiation energy transferred as waves or particles (115)

radiative zone a very dense region of the sun in which the atoms are so closely packed that light can take millions of years to pass through (43)

red giant a star that expands and cools once it runs out of hydrogen fuel (107)

reflecting telescope a telescope that uses curved mirrors to gather and focus light (19)

refracting telescope a telescope that uses a set of lenses to gather and focus light (19)

remote sensing gathering information about something without actually being nearby (134)

retrograde orbit the clockwise revolution of a satellite around a planet as seen from above the north pole of the planet (82)

retrograde rotation the clockwise spin of a planet or moon as seen from above the planet's or moon's north pole (66)

revolution the elliptical motion of a body as it orbits another body in space (39, 65)

right ascension a measure of how far east an object is from the point at which the sun appears on the first day of spring (14)

rocket a machine that uses escaping gas to move (128)

rotation the spinning motion of a body on its axis (39, 65)

S

satellite a natural or artificial body that revolves around a planet (75)

scientific method a series of steps that scientists use to answer questions and solve problems (174)

solar eclipse an event in which the shadow of the moon falls on the Earth's surface (78)

solar energy energy from the sun (44)

solar nebula the nebula that formed into the solar system (35)

solar system the system composed of the sun (a star) and the planets and other bodies that travel around the sun (34)

space probe a vehicle that carries scientific instruments to planets or other bodies in space (136)

space shuttle a reusable vehicle that takes off like a rocket and lands like an airplane (143)

space station a long-term orbiting platform from which other vehicles can be launched or scientific research can be carried out (144)

spectrum the rainbow of colors produced when white light passes through a prism or spectrograph (98)

spiral galaxy a galaxy with a bulge in the center and very distinctive spiral arms (110)

sunspot an area on the photosphere of the sun that is cooler than surrounding areas, showing up as a dark spot (47)

supernova the death of a large star by explosion (108)

surface gravity the percentage of your Earth weight you would experience on another planet; the weight you would experience on another planet (65)

T

telescope an instrument that collects electromagnetic radiation from the sky and concentrates it for better observation (18)

temperature a measure of how hot (or cold) something is (35)

terrestrial planets the small, dense, rocky planets of the inner solar system (65)

thrust the force that accelerates a rocket (130)

V

volume the amount of space that something occupies or the amount of space that something contains (183)

W

white dwarf a small, hot star near the end of its life; the leftover center of an old star (106)

Y

year the time required for the Earth to orbit the sun once (4)

Z

zenith an imaginary point in the sky directly above an observer on Earth (13)

Index

A **boldface** number refers to an illustration on that page.

INDEX

Credits

Abbreviations used: (t) top, (c) center, (b) bottom, (l) left, (r) right, (bkgd) background

ILLUSTRATIONS

All work, unless otherwise noted, contributed by Holt, Rinehart & Winston.

Chapter One: Page 5(t), Nenad Jakesevic; 8, Dan McGeehan/Koralick Associates; 11, Stephen Durke/Washington Artists; 12(c), Sidney Jablonski; 13(cl), Stephen Durke/Washington Artists; 14(t), Sidney Jablonski; 15(b), Stephen Durke/Washington Artists; 17, Paul DiMare; 19, Uhl Studios, Inc.

Chapter Two: Page 35(c), Stephen Durke/Washington Artists; 36-37, Paul DiMare; 39(c), Sidney Jablonski; 40(t), Mark Heine; 40(br), Sidney Jablonski; 42(c), Sidney Jablonski; 43(br), Uhl Studios, Inc.; 44, Marty Roper/Planet Rep; 45(c), Marty Roper/Planet Rep; 45(b), Stephen Durke/Washington Artists; 46, Stephen Durke/Washington Artists; 47(b), Sidney Jablonski; 49, Uhl Studios, Inc.; 50(bl), Paul DiMare; 51(tr), Paul DiMare; 53(br), Uhl Studios, Inc.

Chapter Three: Page 64(b), Sidney Jablonski; 65(tr), Sidney Jablonski; 70(tl), Sidney Jablonski; 72(b), Sidney Jablonski; 73(tr), Dan McGeehan/Koralick Associates; 74(cl), Paul DiMare; 76, Stephen Durke/Washington Artists; 77(cl), Sidney Jablonski; 78(c), Paul DiMare; 79(c), Paul DiMare; 84(tl), Stephen Durke/Washington Artists; 84(br), Paul DiMare; 85, Craig Attebery/Jeff Lavaty Artist Agent; 90(br), Sidney Jablonski; 91(cl), Stephen Durke/Washington Artists.

Chapter Four: Page 99(c), Stephen Durke/Washington Artists; 100(tl), Stephen Durke/Washington Artists; 103(c), Sidney Jablonski; 104(tl), Sidney Jablonski; 104(c), Stephen Durke/Washington Artists; 106-107, Stephen Durke/Washington Artists; 115(br), Craig Attebery/Jeff Lavaty Artist Agent; 117(r), Craig Attebery/Jeff Lavaty Artist Agent; 123(cr), Sidney Jablonski.

Chapter Five: Page 129(b), Stephen Durke/Washington Artists; 130(l), John Huxtable/Black Creative; 133(tr), Stephen Durke/Washington Artists; 136, Stephen Durke/Washington Artists; 137, Stephen Durke/Washington Artists; 138, Stephen Durke/Washington Artists; 139(b), Craig Attebery/Jeff Lavaty Artist Agent; 139(tr), Stephen Durke/Washington Artists; 139(br), Stephen Durke/Washington Artists; 141(tl), Paul DiMare; 147(c), Paul DiMare.

Appendix: Page 172(c), Terry Guyer; 174 (b) Mark Mille/Sharon Langley; 184, Kristy Sprott; 185, Kristy Sprott; 190-191, Sidney Jablonski.

PHOTOGRAPHY

Cover and Title Page: David Nunuk/Science Photo Library/ Photo Researchers, Inc.

Sam Dudgeon/HRW Photo: Page viii-1, 156, 157(bc), 158(tr), 158(cl), 158(br), 159(tl), 164, 166, 167.

Table of Contents: iv(tl), Daniel Schaefer/HRW Photo; iv(cl), A. J. Copley/Visuals Unlimited; iv(bl), NASA/TSADO/Tom Stack & Associates; v(tr), George Holton/Photo Researchers, Inc.; v(cr), Stephen Durke/Washington Artists; v(b), Sam Dudgeon/HRW Photo; vi(tl), NASA; vi(bl), NASA; vii(tl), Anglo-Australian Telescope Board; vii(cl), X-Ray Astronomy Group, Leicester University/Science Photo Library/Photo Resesarchers, Inc.; vii(bl), John Sanford/Astrostock.

Chapter One: pp. 2-3 Roger Ressmeyer/CORBIS; 3 HRW Photo; 4, George Holton/Photo Researchers, Inc.; 6(tl), J. McKim Mallville/University of Colorado; 6(cl), Telegraph Colour Library/FPG; 7(tr), Tha British Library Picture Library; 7(br), David L. Brown/Tom Stack & Associates; 9(tr), The Bridgeman Art Library; 9(bl), Scala/Art Resource; 10, Roger Ressmeyer/Corbis; 13(br), Peter Van Steen/HRW Photo; 13(bkgd), Johnny Johnson/Index Stock; 14(bl), A.J. Copley/Visuals Unlimited; 16(tl), Jim Cummings/FPG International/PNI; 16(cl), Mike Yamashita/Woodfin Camp/PNI; 16(c, br), NASA; 17(tr), Jerry Lodriguss/Photo Researchers, Inc.; 17(cr), Tony & Daphne Hallas/Science Photo Library/Photo Researchers, Inc.; 18(bl-bkgd), David Nunuk/Science Photo Library/Photo Researchers, Inc.; 18(br-bkgd), Jerry Lodriguss; 18(bl, br), Peter Van Steen/HRW Photo; 20(tl), Simon Fraser/Science Photo Library/Photo Researchers, Inc.; 20(b), NASA; 20(inset), Roger Ressmeyer/Corbis Images; 21(keyboard), Chuck O'Rear/Woodfin Camp & Associates, Inc.; 21(sunburn), Andy Christiansen/HRW Photo; 21(x-ray), David M. Dennis/Tom Stack & Associates; 21(head), Michael Scott/Stone; 22(all NASA except bl), David Parker/Science Photo Library/Photo Researchers, Inc.; 23(tr), Larry Mulvehill/Photo Researchers, Inc.; 23(cr), Harvard-Smithsonian Center for Astrophysics; 25 Sam Dudgeon/HRW Photo; 26(c), George Holton/Photo Researchers, Inc.; 27(cr), Daniel Schaefer/HRW Photo; 28, Jerry Lodriguss/Photo Researchers, Inc.; 30, NASA; 31, Benjamin Shearn/FPG.

Chapter Two: pp. 32-33 David Malin/Anglo-Australian Observatory; 32 Roger Ressmeyer/CORBIS; 33 HRW Photo; 34, David Malin/Anglo-Australian Observatory/Royal Observatory, Edinburgh; 38(tl), Royal Observatory, Edinberg/AATB/Science Photo Library/Photo Researchers, Inc; 38(insets),

NASA/Liaison Agency; 41(br), Michael Freeman/Bruce Coleman; 47, John Bova/Photo Researchers, Inc; 48, Earth Imaging/Stone; 51(bl), SuperStock; 52(bl), Breck P. Kent/Animals Animals/Earth Scenes; 52(br), John Reader/Science Photo Library/Photo Researchers, Inc; 54 Courtesy NASA; 55 Sam Dudgeon/HRW Photo; 58, NASA/TSADO/Tom Stack& Associates; 59, John T. Whatmough/JTW Incorporated; 60(bl), NSO/NASA; 61, Dean Congerngs/National Geographic Society Image Collection.

Chapter Three: pp. 62-63 Lynette Cook/Science Photo Library/Photo Researchers, Inc.; 63 HRW Photo; 64(l), Hulton Getty/Liaison Agency; 64(tr), NASA; 65, NASA/Mark S. Robinson; 66(tl), NASA; 66(bl), Mark Marten/NASA/Science Source/Photo Researchers, Inc.; 67(tr), Frans Lanting/Minden Pictures; 67(br), 68(c) NASA; 68(tl), World Perspective/Stone; 68-69(b), NASA; 69(cr), NASA; 70, NASA/Peter Arnold, Inc.; 71(all), 72(tl), 73, 74(tl), 75(l, br), NASA; 77(all), John Bova/Photo Researchers, Inc.; 78(bl), Fred Espenak; 79(tr), Jerry Lodriguss/Photo Researchers, Inc.; 80(all), 81(tr), NASA; 81(br), USGS/Science Photo Library/Photo Researchers, Inc.; 82, World Perspectives/Stone; 83(cl), Bob Yen/Liaison Agency; 83(br), Bill & Sally Fletcher/Tom Stack & Associates; 85(tr), NASA/Science Photo Library/Photo Researchers, Inc.; 86(bc), Breck P. Kent/Animals Animals/Earth Scenes; 86(bl), E.R. Degginger/Bruce Coleman Inc.; 86(br), Ken Nichols/Institute of Meteorites; 86(cl), Dennis Wilson/Science Photo Library/Photo Researhers, Inc.; 87, NASA; 88, Victoria Smith/HRW Photo; 90, 92(bl), NASA; 92(tr), Ken Nichols/Institute of Meteorites.

Chapter Four: pp. 96-97 Jean-Charles/Cuillandre/Canada-France-Hawaii Telescope/Science Photo Library/Photo Researchers; 96 Courtesy NASA; 97 HRW Photo; 98(tc), Phil Degginger/Color-Pic, Inc.; 98(bl), John Sanford/Astrostock; 98(tr), E. R. Degginger/Color-Pic, Inc.; 100(cr), Allan Morton/Science Photo Library/Photo Researchers, Inc.; 101, Magrath Photography/Science Photo Library/Photo Researchers, Inc.; 102, Andre Gallant/Image Bank; 105(c), Astrophysics Library, Princeton University; 108(br), Dr. Christopher Burrows, ESA/STScl/NASA; 108(cl, bl), Anglo-Australian Telescope Board; 109, David Hardy/Science Photo Library/Photo Researchers Inc.; 110, Bill & Sally Fletcher/Tom Stack & Associates; 111(bl), Dennis Di Cicco/Peter Arnold, Inc.; 111(tr), David Malin/Anglo-Australian Observatory; 112(tl), I M House/Stone; 112(br), Bill & Sally Fletcher/Tom Stack & Associates; 112(bl), Jerry Lodriguss/Photo Researchers, Inc.; 113, NASA/CXC/Smithsonian Astrophysical Observatory; 115(tr), Pictures Unlimited, Inc; 118 Sam Dudgeon/HRW Photo; 119, John Sanford/Astrostock; 120(c), John Sanford/Astrostock; 121, I M House/Stone; 122(bl), NASA; 122(tr), David Nunuk/Science Photo Library/Photo Researchers Inc; 124(all), NASA; 125(tl), The Open University.

Chapter Five: pp. 126-127, Smithsonian Institution/Lockheed Corporation/Courtesy of Ft. Worth Museum of Science and History; 127, HRW Photo; 128(tr), Gustav Dore/Hulton Getty/Liaison Agency; 128(bl), NASA; 129(tr), Hulton Getty Images/Liaison Agency; 132(cr), Brian Parker/Tom Stack & Associates; 132(k), NASA; 133(br), Hesler, Chester, Jentoff-Nilsen/ NASA Goddard Lab of Atmospheres & Nielsen, U. of Hawaii; 134, Aerial Images, Inc. and SOVINFORMSPUTNIK; 135(tr, cr), EROS Data Center/USGS; 136(tr), NASA; 136(bkgr), Jim Ballard/Stone; 136(br), TSADO/JPL/Tom Stack & Associates; 137(bkgd), Jim Ballard/Stone; 137 (bkgd), NASA/Liaison Agency; 137 (bkgd), Jim Ballard/Stone; 138(c), NASA; 138(bl), JPL/NASA/Liaison Agency; 138(bkgd), 139(bkgd), Jim Ballard/Stone; 140(tl, bl), JPL/NASA; 142, SuperStock; 143(tr, b), 144, NASA; 145(tr), NASA/Science Photo Library/Photo Researchers, Inc.; 145(bl), 146 NASA; 148 NASA/Stone; 149 Sam Dudgeon/HRW Photo; 150(c), Hesler, Chester, Jentoff-Nilsen/ NASA Goddard Lab of Atmospheres & Nielsen, U. of Hawaii; 151(c), 152(bl), NASA; 152(cr), Zvi Har'El/Jules Vern; 153, Dr. Gene Feldman, NASA GSFC/Photo Researchers, Inc. .

LabBook/Appendix: "LabBook Header", "L", Corbis Images; "a", Letraset Phototone; "b", and "B", HRW; "o", and "k", images ©2001 PhotoDisc/HRW; Page 157(tr), John Langford/HRW Photo; 157(cl), Michelle Bridwell/HRW Photo; 157(br), Image ©2001 PhotoDisc, Inc./HRW; 158(bl), Stephanie Morris/HRW Photo; 159(tr), Jana Birchum/HRW Photo; 159 (b), Peter Van Steen/HRW Photo; 161, 162, 163, Peter Van Steen/HRW Photo; 168, Jeff Hunter/The Image Bank; 173(tr), Peter Van Steen/HRW Photo.

Feature Borders: Unless otherwise noted below, all images copyright ©2001 PhotoDisc/HRW. "Across the Sciences" 154, all images by HRW; "Careers" 125, sand bkgd and Saturn, Corbis Images; DNA, Morgan Cain & Associates; scuba gear, ©1997 Radlund & Associates for Artville; "Eye on the Environment" 31, clouds and sea in bkgd, HRW Photo; bkgd grass, red eyed frog, Corbis Images; hawks, pelican, Animals Animals/Earth Scenes; rat, Visuals Unlimited/John Grelach; endangered flower, Dan Suzio/Photo Researchers, Inc.; "Scientific Debate" 61, 94, Sam Dudgeon/HRW Photo; "Science Fiction" 95, 155, saucers, Ian Christopher/Greg Geisler; book, HRW; bkgd, Stock Illustration Source; "Science Technology and Society" 30, 60, robot, Greg Geisler; "Weird Science" 124, mite, David Burder/Tony Stone; atom balls, J/B Woolsey Associates; walking stick, turtle, EclectiCollection.

Self-Check Answers

Chapter 1—Observing the Sky

Page 9: Ptolemy and Tycho Brahe thought that the universe was Earth-centered. Copernicus and Galileo thought the universe was sun-centered.

Page 12: No, the object is within the boundaries of the constellation.

Chapter 2—Formation of the Solar System

Page 35: The balance between pressure and gravity keeps a nebula from collapsing.

Page 37: The giant gas planets were massive enough for their gravity to attract hydrogen and helium.

Page 48: The Earth has enough mass that gravitational pressure crushed and melted rocks during its formation. The force of gravity pulled this material toward the center, forming a sphere. Asteroids are not massive enough for their interiors to be crushed or melted.

Chapter 3—A Family of Planets

Page 81: The surface of Titan is much colder than the surface of the Earth.

Chapter 4—The Universe Beyond

Page 102: The two stars would have the same apparent magnitude.

Chapter 5—Exploring Space

Page 133: It requires much less fuel to reach LEO.